Advanced / Pets

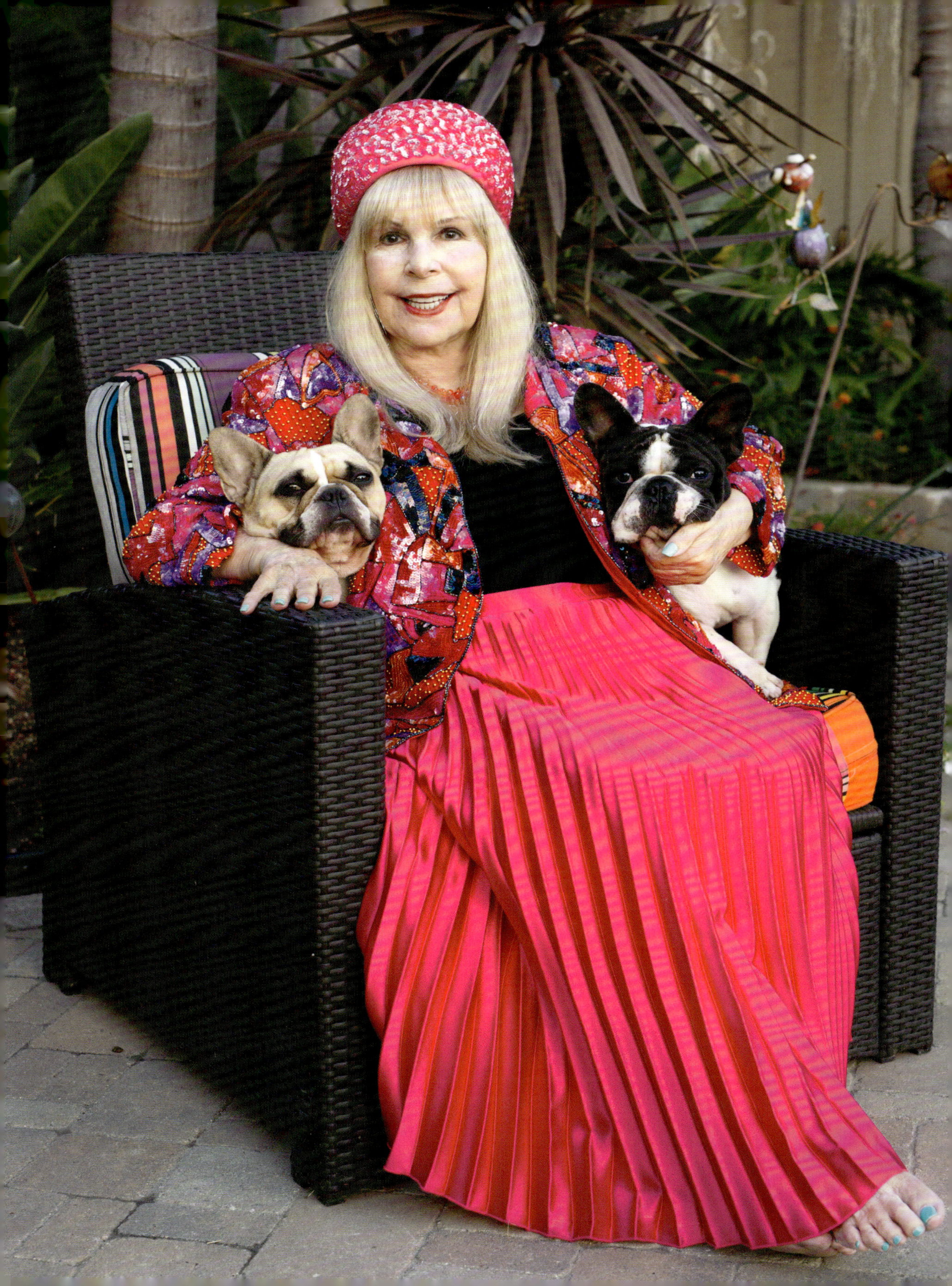

Advanced Pets

Ari Seth Cohen

pH powerHouse Books | Brooklyn, NY

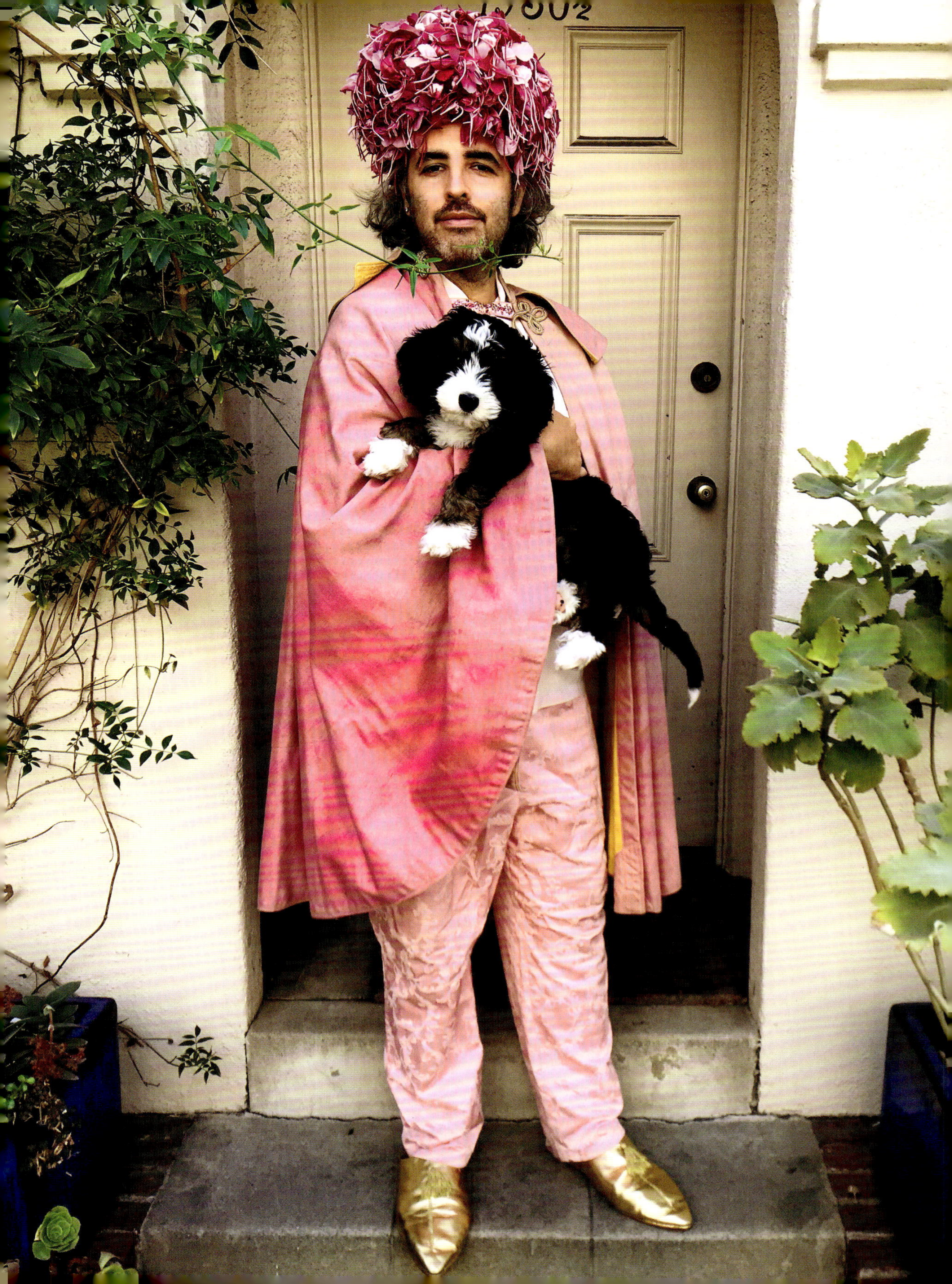

Introduction

I've always been an old soul. Growing up, my eccentricity delighted some of my family members, but kids my own age were less than impressed. I often felt alienated and alone. Then we got our first dog, a sheltie named Rusty. The moment I laid eyes on this adorable and gentle spirit, I instantly felt loved and accepted unconditionally. I could be myself around him, and he quickly became my best friend. From then on, I knew my life would be filled with dogs.

A few years later, my mom heard about a Chow-Lab rescue in need of a home. Two Step danced his way into our lives. He would enter the room on his two hind legs, waltzing majestically, tongue out, tail wagging, ready to play. He was wise, loyal, and loving to all. When I was finally old enough to take care of my own dog, we rescued Shadow, my first true soulmate in dog form. She was a beautiful Chow mix with brilliant, fluffy black fur and the sweetest eyes you could imagine. She was shaking nervously when we first brought her home, so, that night, I invited her to sleep in my bed. As she rolled over, I noticed a huge laceration on her belly. We rushed her to the vet. Over the next few weeks we nursed her back to health. From then on, Shadow never left my side. School days were spent in anticipation of the final bell, when I could rush home and see my sweet girl. She became my everything.

My mom kept the house full of dogs while I was away at college. There was Roxy, the adorable and fiercely protective bulldog, and the giant, goofy Crosby with his intimidating bark and gentle spirit. I loved all of my mom's precious pooches, but nothing could compare to the special bond I had with my childhood pups. After college, I moved to New York to start my career, and it wasn't until my early thirties that I finally felt ready to adopt a dog of my own. I was searching for the kind of love I'd had with Two Step and Shadow and often told my husband, Eric, who is even more dog-obsessed than me, how much these magnificent mutts meant to me. One day he came across a gorgeous Chow mix at a local shelter. Her black and gold coloring reminded me of Two Step and her fluffy, shiny coat of Shadow. Her name was Fancy. We rushed uptown to meet her and instantly fell in love. The vet at the shelter informed us that Fancy had a history of cancer and that it was likely to return. It was too late—we were all in. Fancy was a queen among dogs, strutting around the East Village with pride in her majestic fur coat. She possessed a quiet elegance, and even though she required very little emotionally, her calming and sweet demeanor made our little family feel complete.

Five years into our love affair, we were devastated to learn that Fancy's cancer had returned and was incurable. It was heartbreaking to watch her decline. We devoted ourselves to ensuring that her final days were filled with love and comfort, and eventually made the excruciating decision to let her go. I mourned for several months and cried rivers of tears. My baby girl was gone, but at least I could take comfort in knowing that she was finally free of pain. After some time, I settled into a dogless life, vowing that I would never allow myself to love another dog like that again. The loss was too much to bear.

Much to my chagrin, a year later my dog-crazy husband announced that he had found his dream puppy, a ten-week-old Bernedoodle with a mad look in his eyes. I didn't feel emotionally ready for the journey, but a part of me longed for the kind of love I had shared with Fancy. We brought Vincent "Vinnie" von Doodle home in October of 2020. I soon realized that not all puppies are sweet and cuddly. Vinnie would lunge at us his with his razor sharp puppy fangs and shredded anything he could get his paws on. On walks he'd jump up and try to bite me after a few minutes. Our neighbor Raphael went to hug him one day and ended up with a puppy-sized hole in the butt of his jeans. Vinnie squirmed every time I tried to hold him. He was stubborn, relentless, and definitely not the type of dog I'd been hoping for. Eric was totally in love and kept trying to reassure me that it would get better, but I was filled with resentment and disappointment. I couldn't imagine ever loving this bratadoodle.

As a caretaker, I took my job as trainer very seriously. After a year and a half of crazy zoomies and constant, rascally, uncontrollable energy, my hard work started to pay off. Vinnie was glued to me. This is what I had always wanted from a dog, but I just couldn't love him. Maybe it was Fancy's memory keeping me from forming a new bond, or maybe it was just too soon.

Vinnie started to soften and so did I. Now, at three years old, he is my best friend. His intelligence is astounding, his beauty even more so. He is silly and sweet and dreamy. He sleeps cuddled up next to me and never wants to leave my side. I love this little guy. He's helped me realize that no matter how hard it can get, I will never want to live a life without dogs. They are pure goodness, even when they are naughty. Life would be boring without all of the joy and frustration, laughter and tears, and love and loss that dogs bring—and I can't stand boring!

I have always found a kinship with other animal lovers. For the past few years, I have been documenting some of my favorite fashion icons and muses with their beloved pets. My work has always been about love—the love we receive from honoring our self-expression and the love between friends, family, and partners.

The bond between animals and humans is equally sacred, and it is one of the purest expressions of love that we can experience in our lifetime. I hope these photos and stories encourage us to cherish these unique relationships and to respect the majesty of our animal friends.

I've searched for genuine connection my entire life, and I've found it time and time again with my furry friends. I will forever be grateful for the dogs who have come into my life—the ones that protected me, saved me, and provided me with boundless love. I hope that I have done the same for them.

Ari Seth Cohen

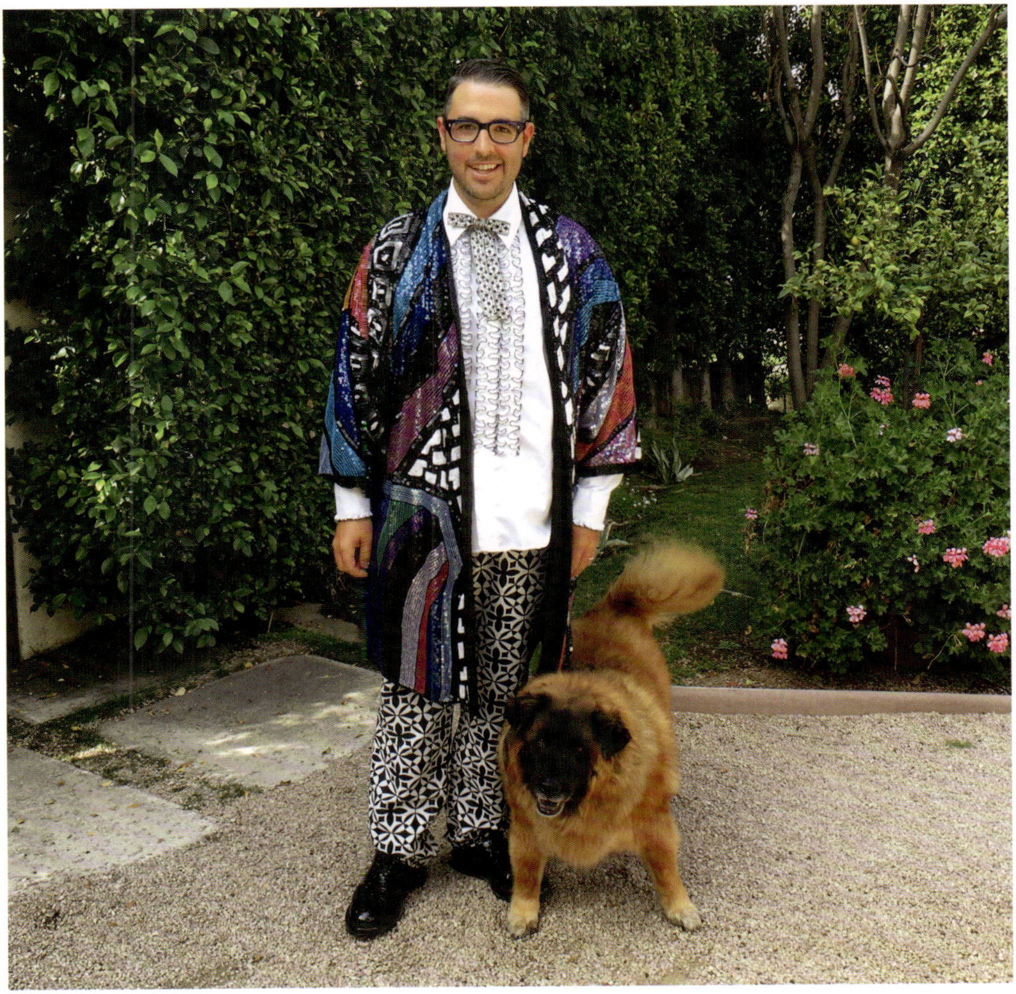

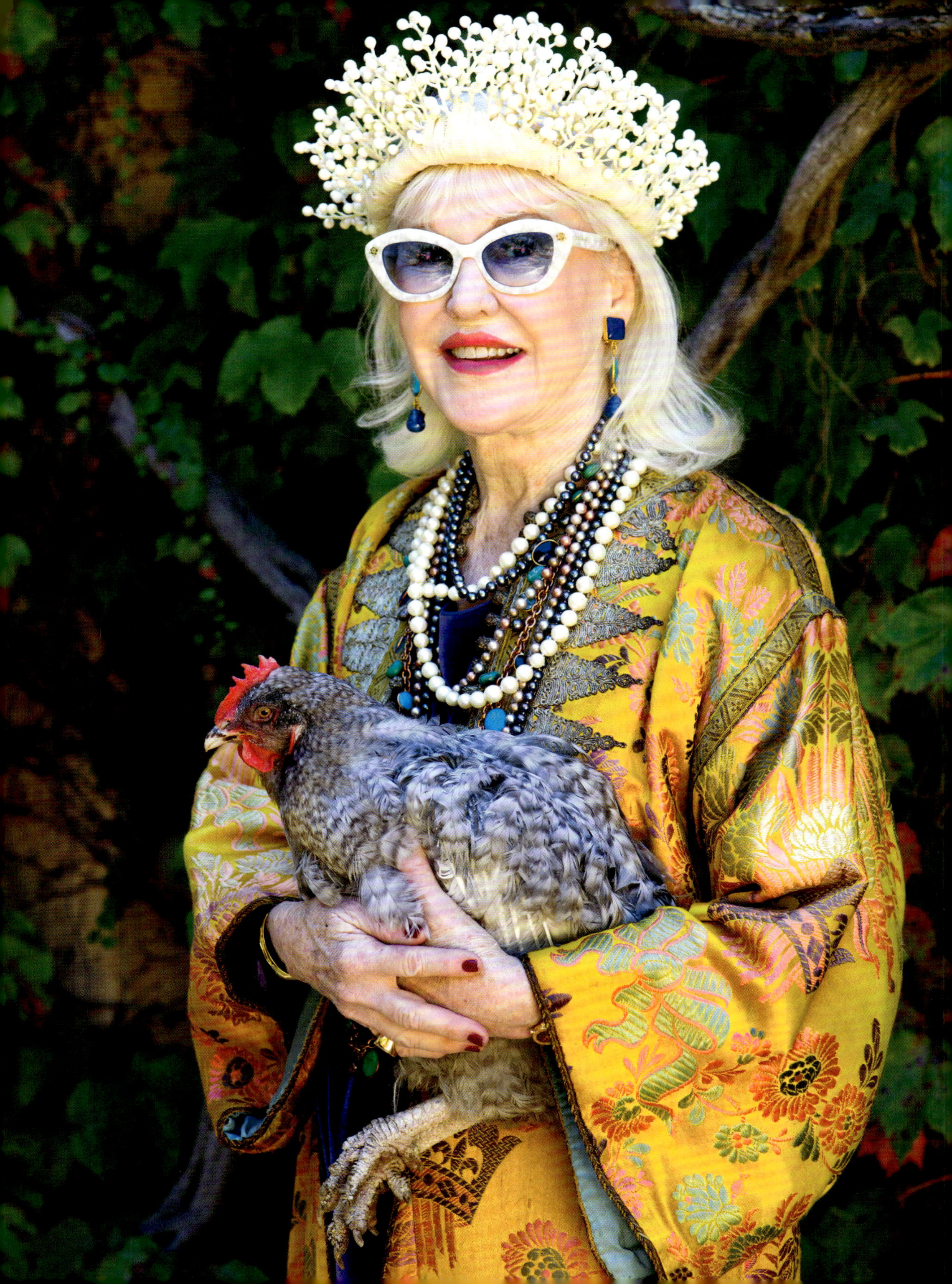

Penelope and Friends

Ever since I was a tiny child, I have loved animals of all kinds. I had a pet possum when I was little who got along just fine with our dogs. It was divine. I also love chickens—they are so much fun. I even love the animals who don't like people. I have a sign in the bathroom that says, "What I love about people are their dogs." I'm hoping I can always stay in my house so I can continue to have a ton of animals around.

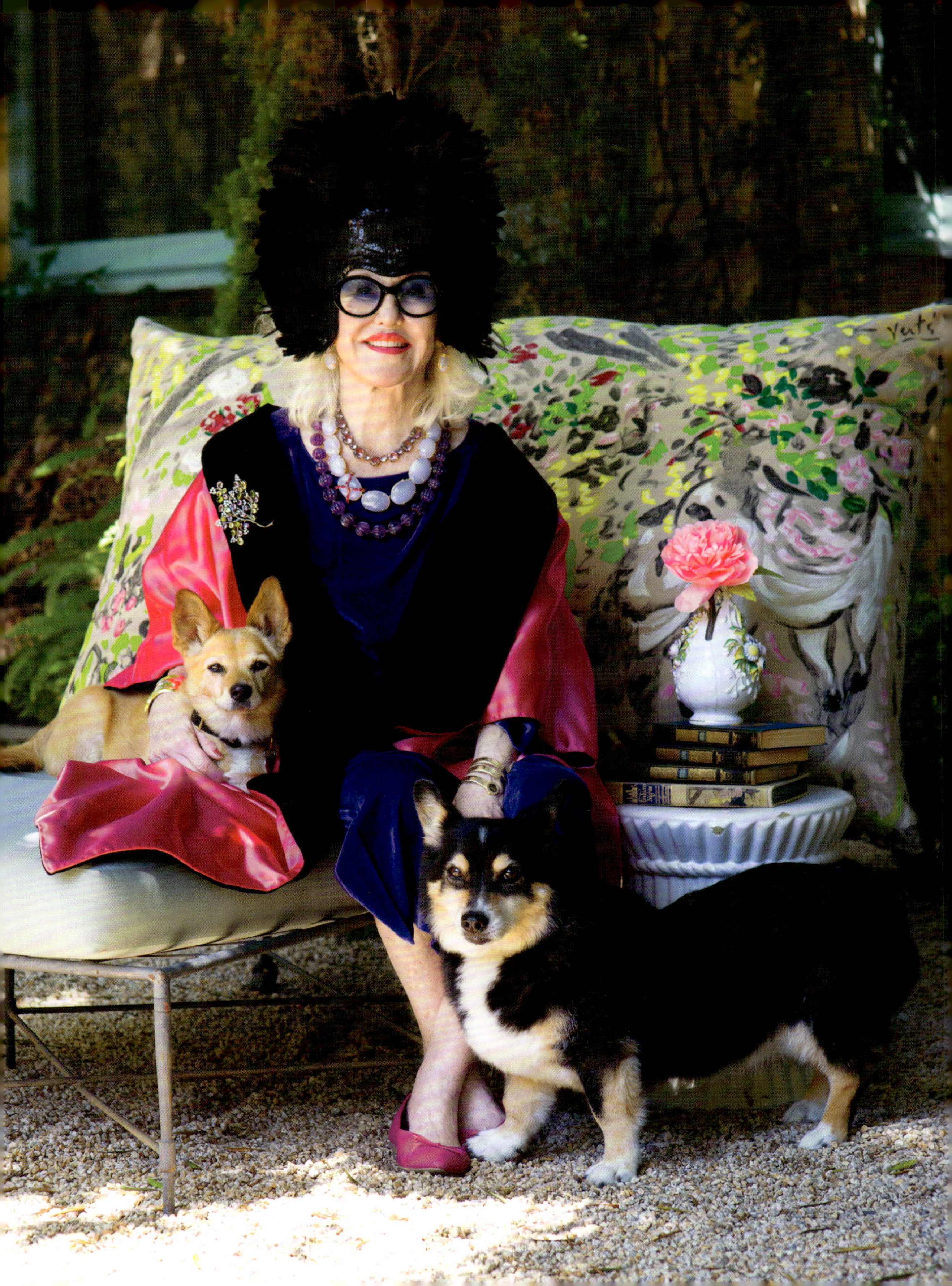

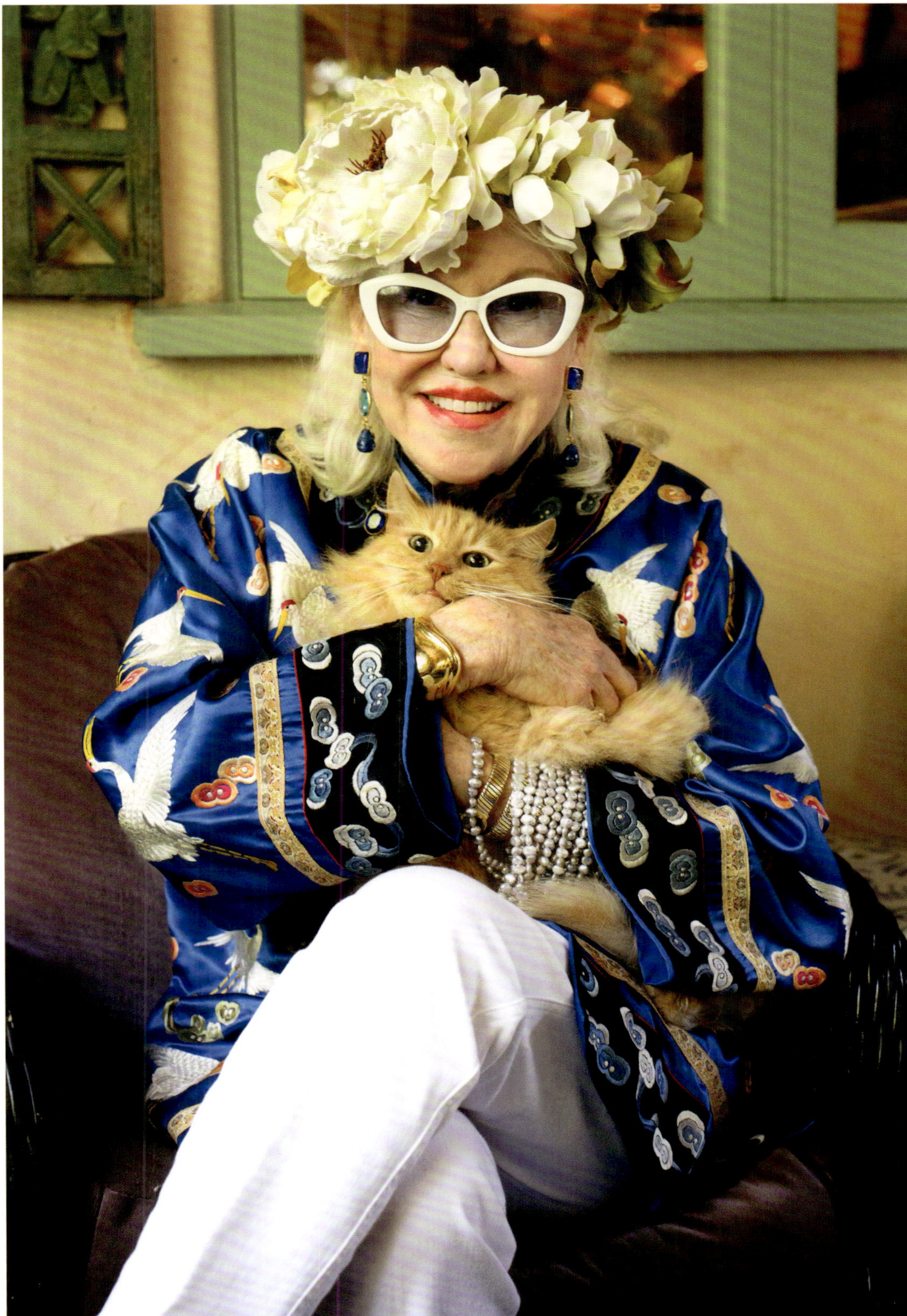

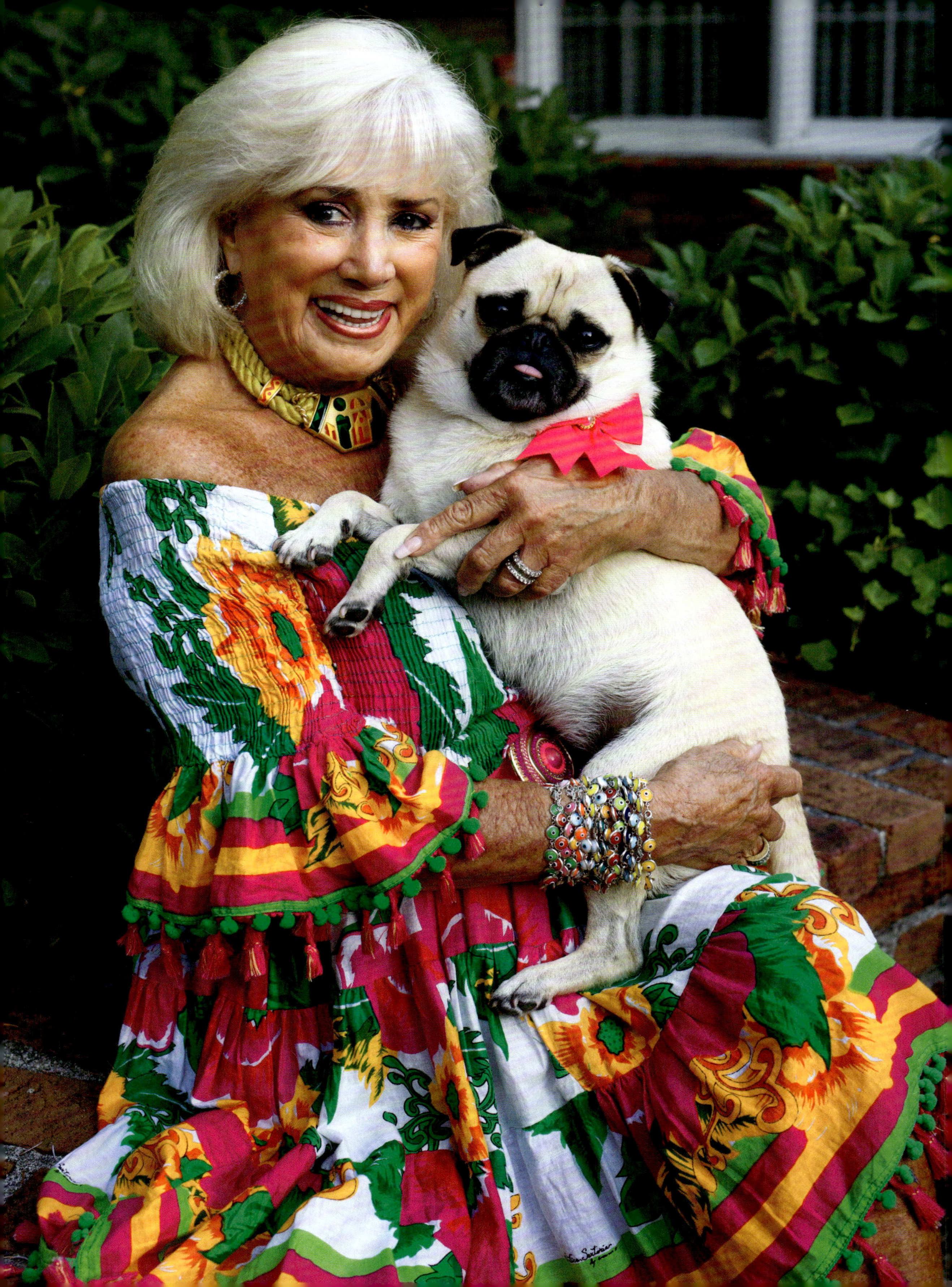

Jackie and Betty

Betty has been the greatest addition to our family. I didn't grow up with dogs, so this is a new experience for me, and probably one of the best experiences anyone can have: the love of a fabulous little pug. First of all, she's perfect; secondly she's beautiful; and thirdly, she's a princess, so she fits right in with all the other princesses in my life. She's very special, not just to me, but to the general public.

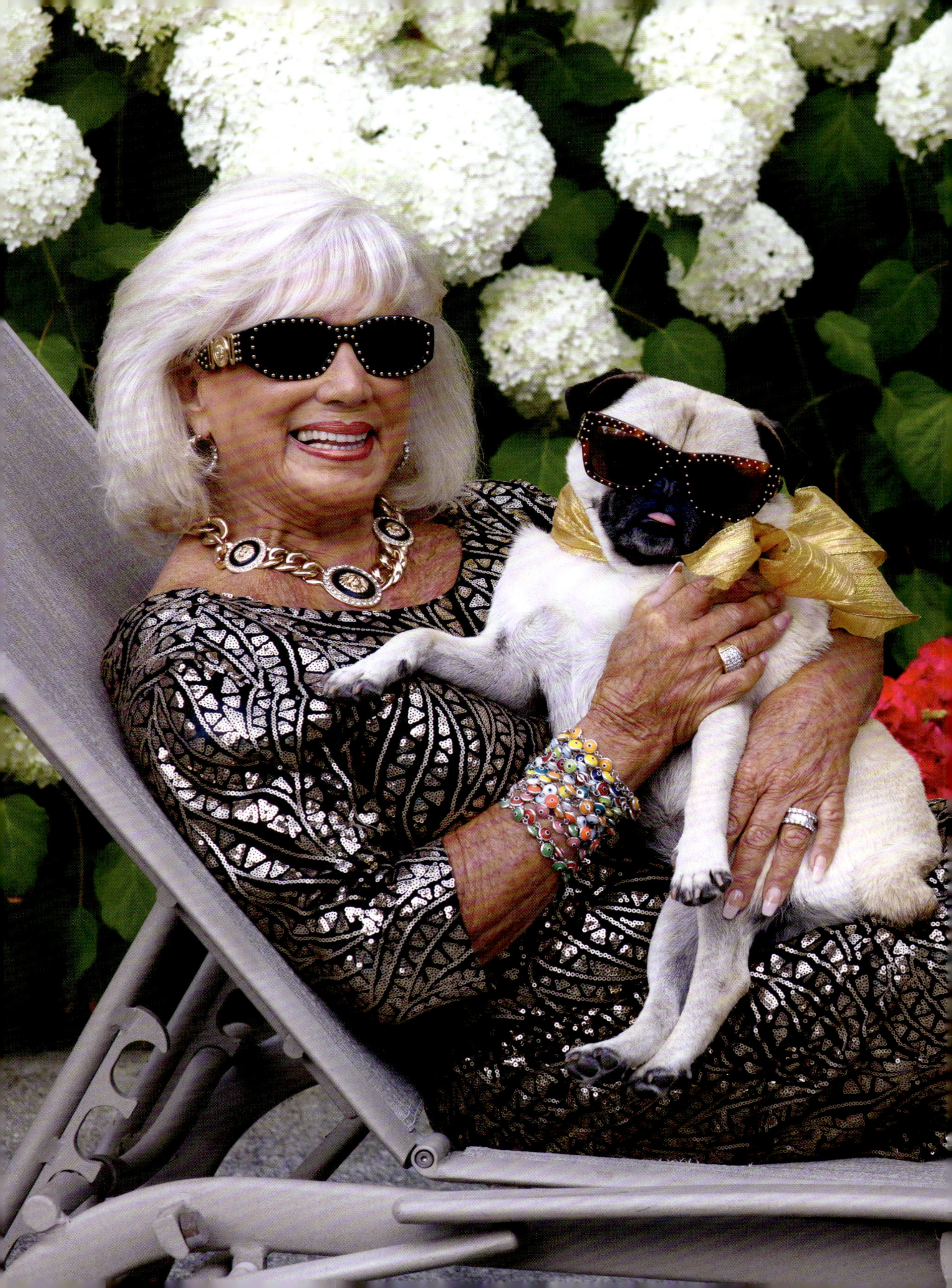

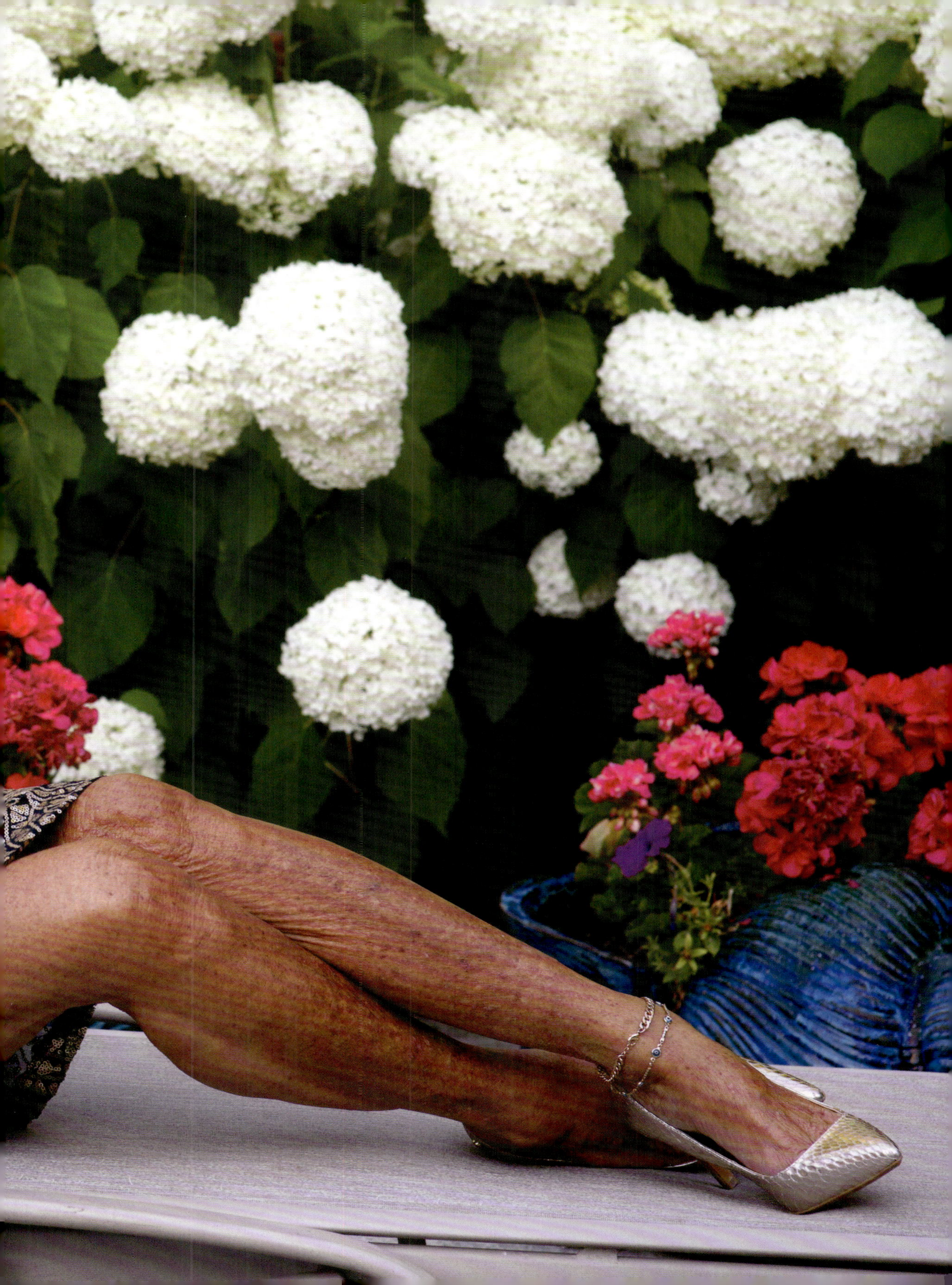

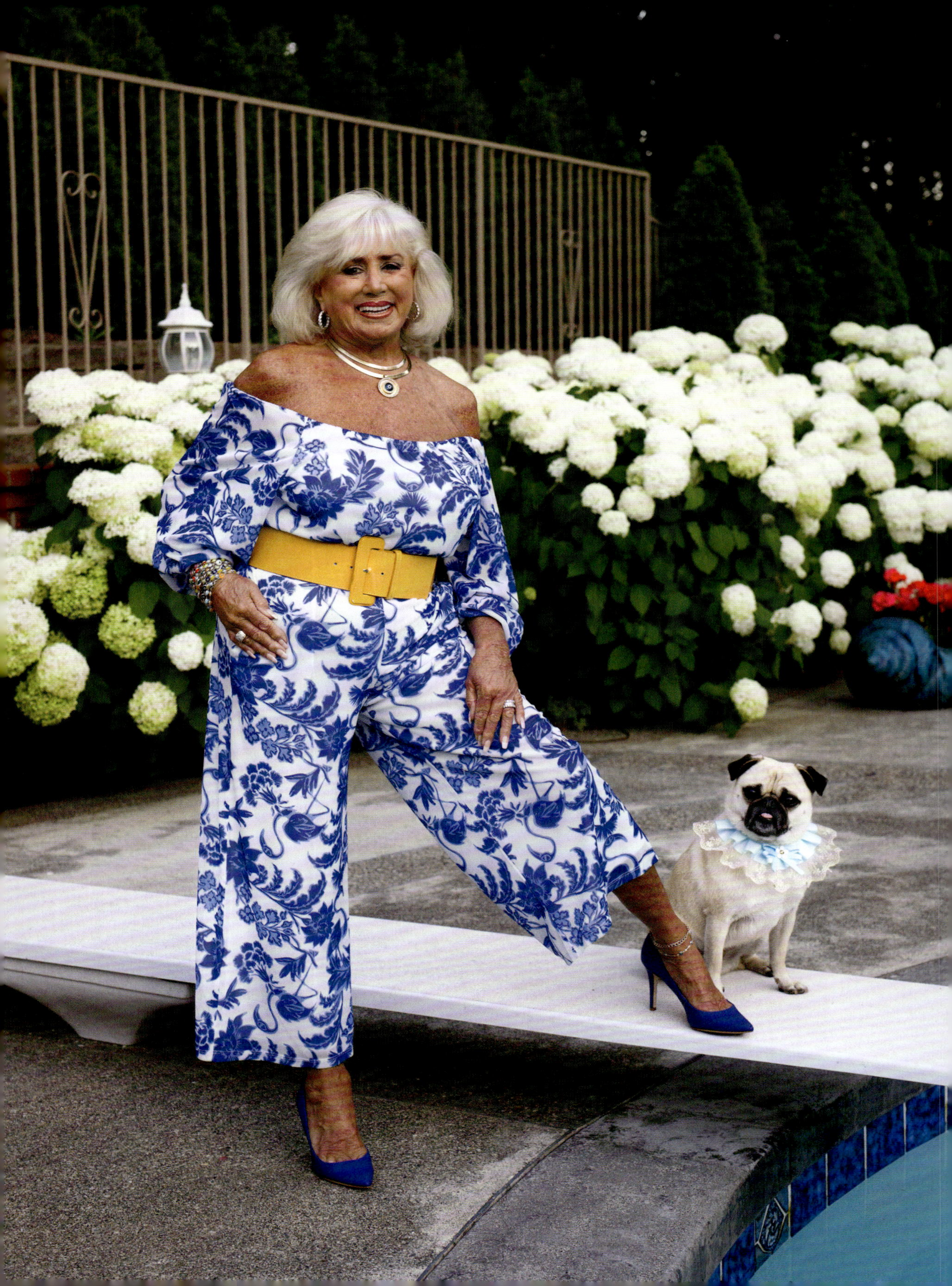

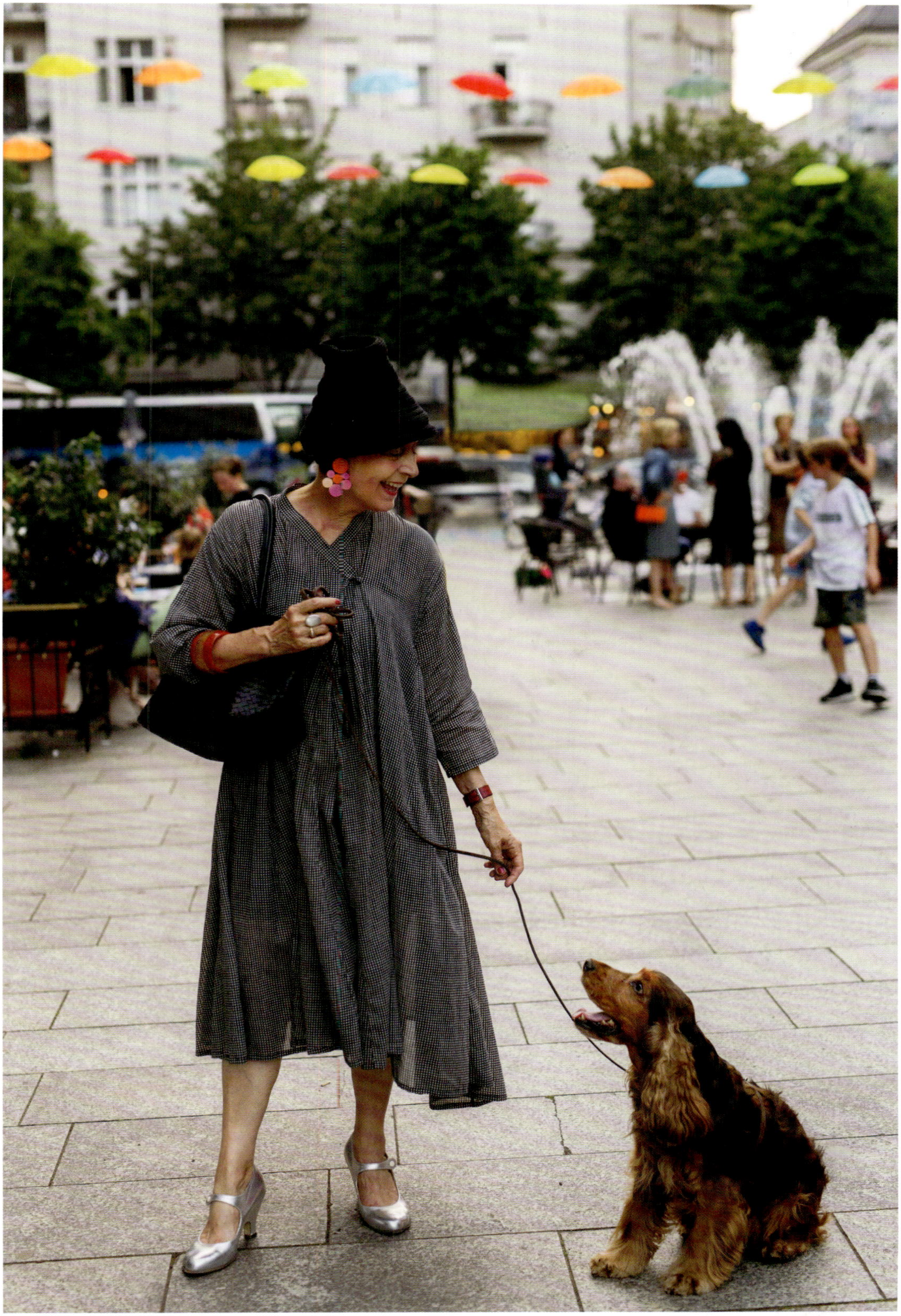

Dolores and Daisy

I have always thought the saying "dogs are a man's best friend" was quite corny. That was until my husband Allan got very sick and our dog Daisy stayed by his side night and day. She was so still and quiet it felt as though she was in a trance helping to guide him to another place. After his passing, she slept on his side of the bed and laid in his closet for months. She became a keen watchdog and would hardly let anyone near me. I'm never afraid, living alone in this big house, knowing that my fourteen-pound dog will protect me. Now, Daisy really is my best friend.

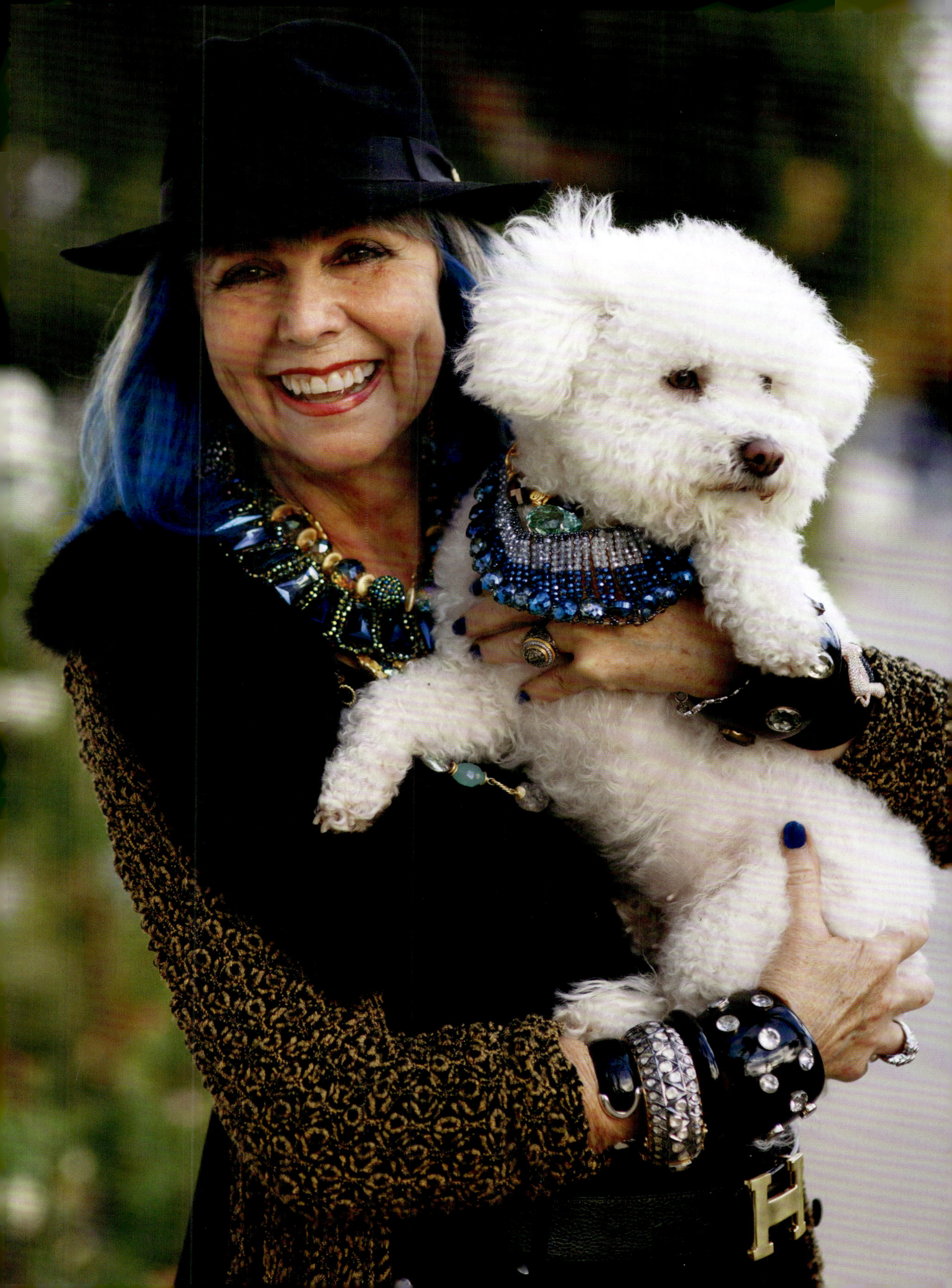

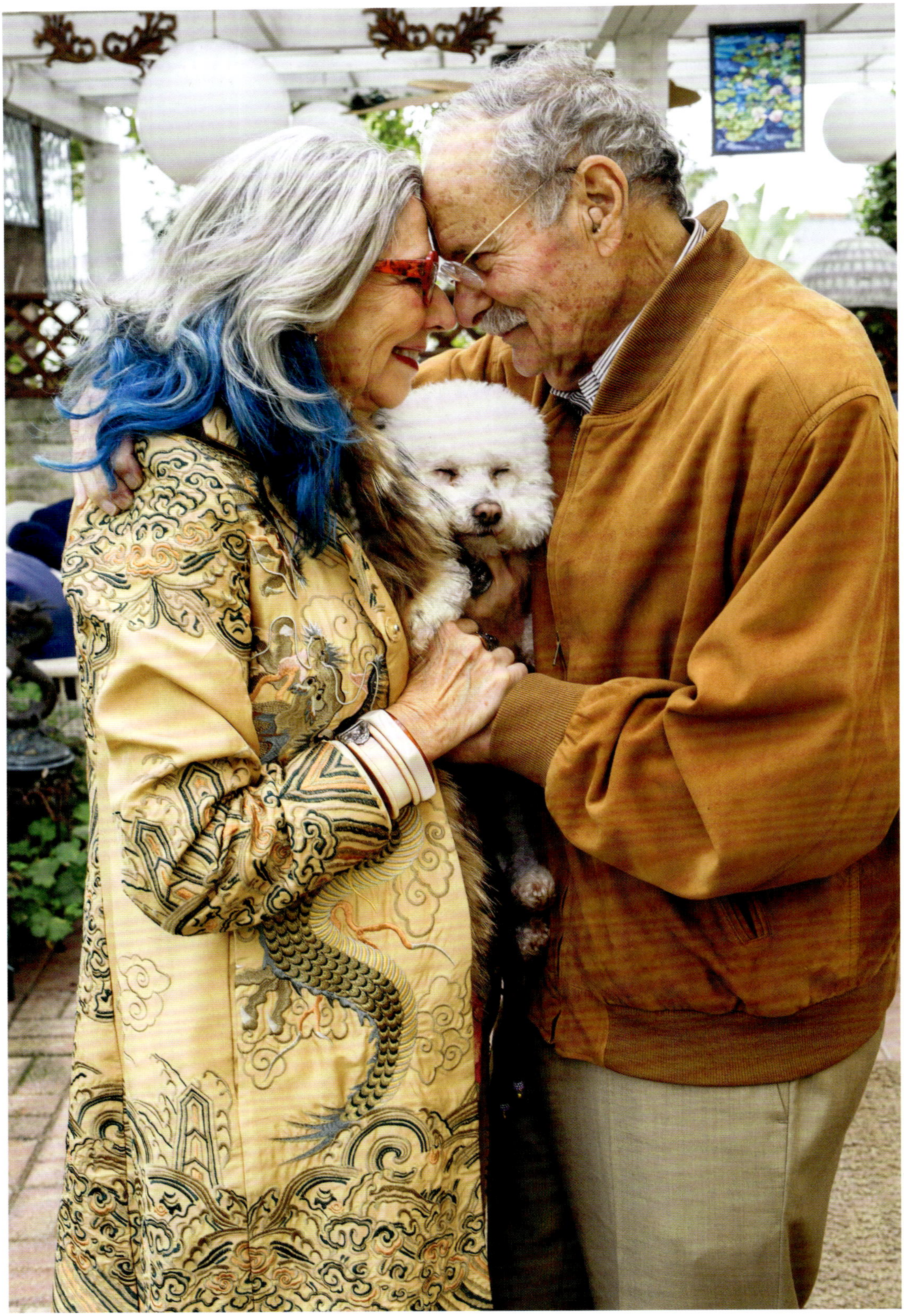

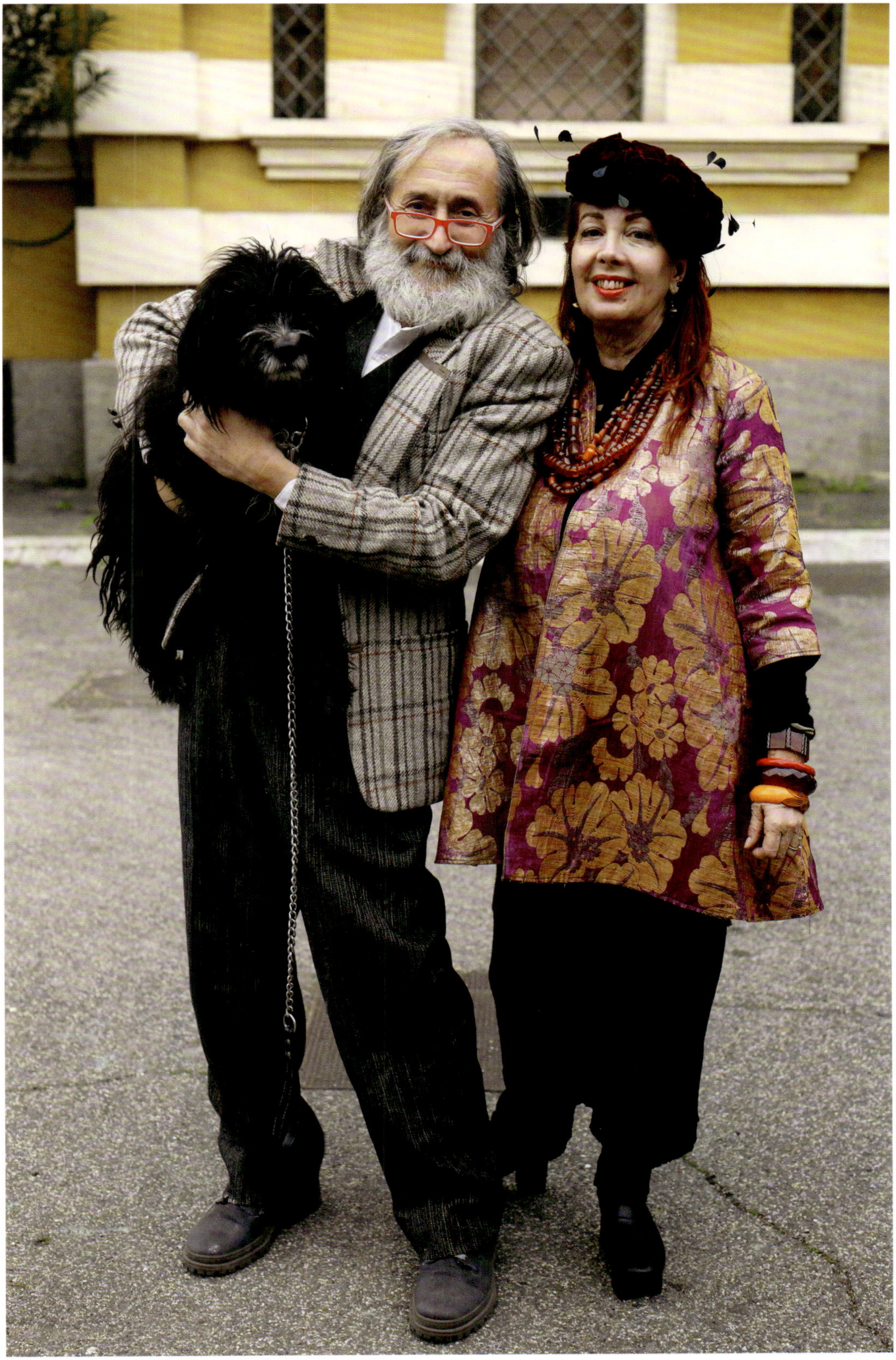

Arlinda and Otis

If Otis were human, he'd be the president of the nonjudgmental club. From witnessing bad hair days to morning breath, fashion choices to impromptu dance moves—he is the best and most accepting friend a nana could have.

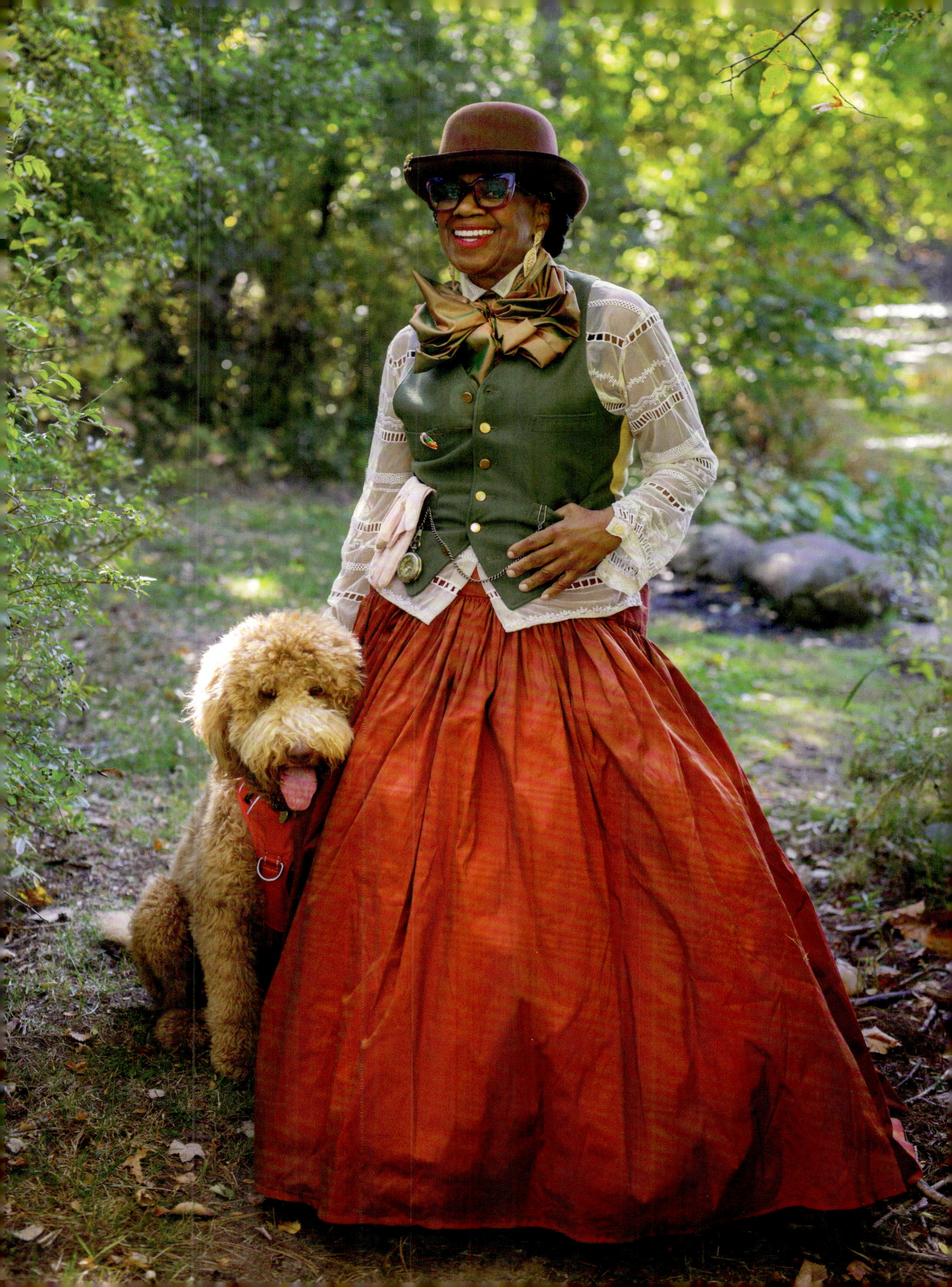

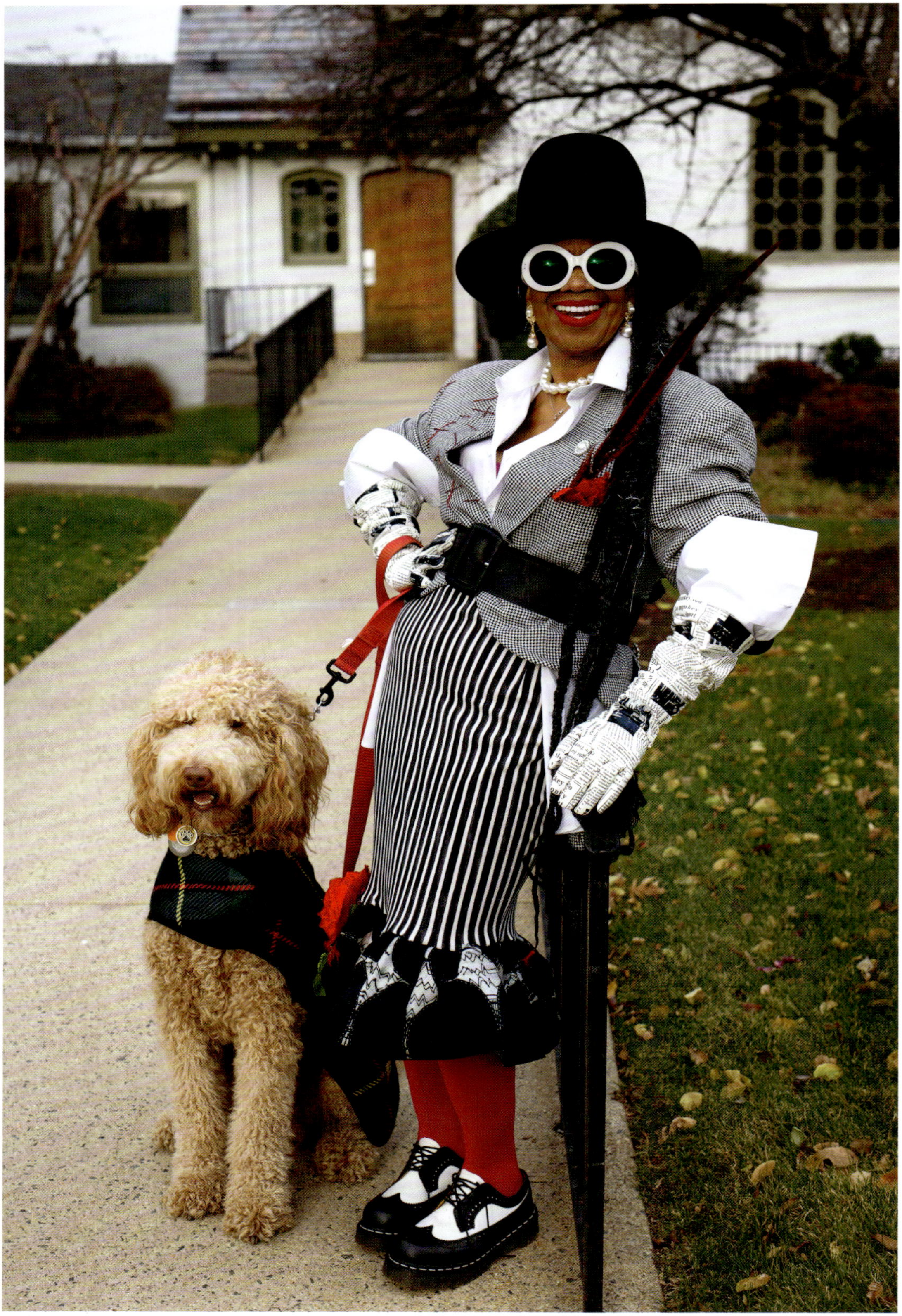

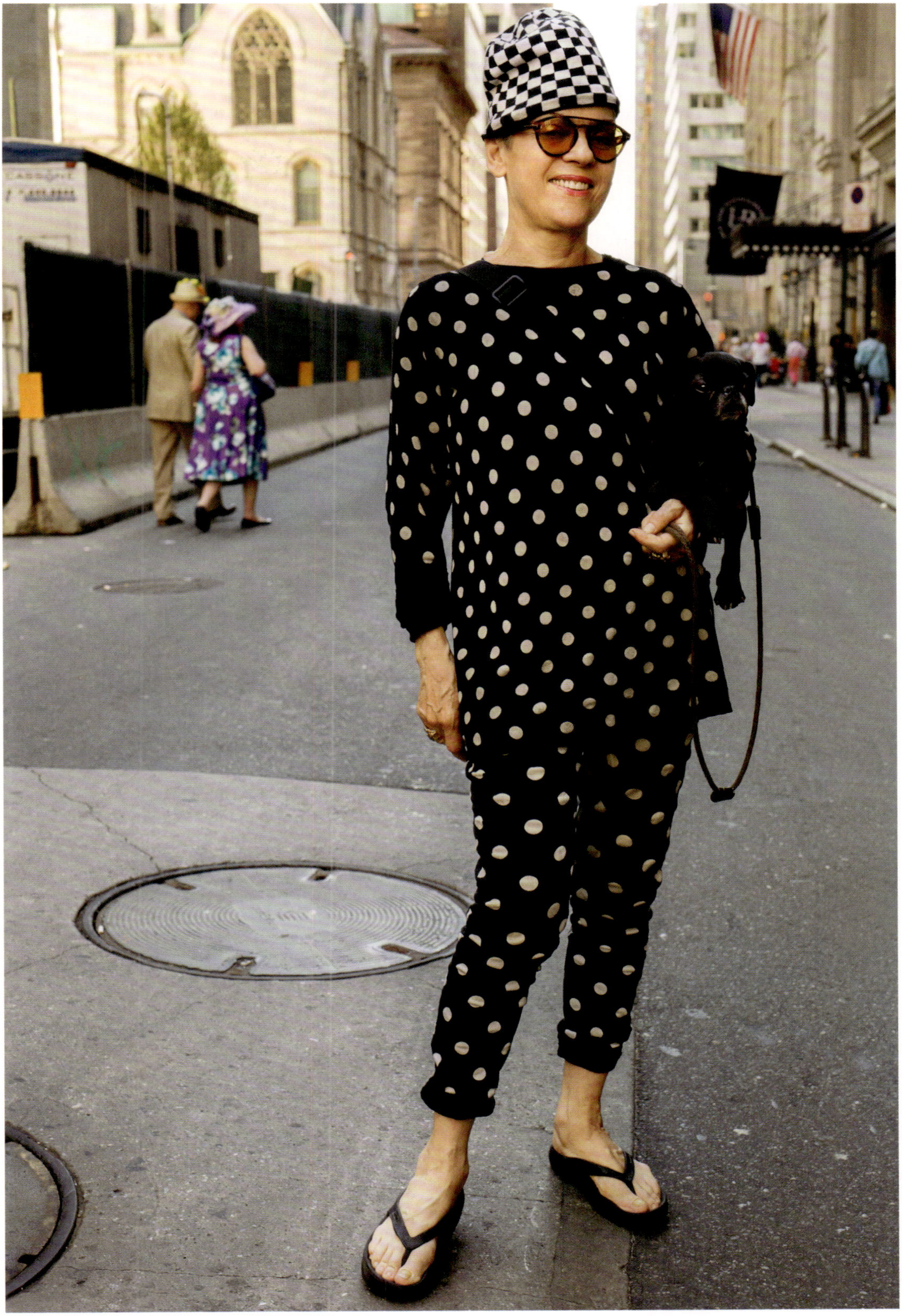

Sandra and Lucy

This beautiful seven-year-old bovine's name is Lucy Daisy. She is wise beyond her age, and, although I have taught her many things, Lucy has taught me something far more valuable about holding on, letting go, and finding your own way in the world.

After a traumatic birth during which her mother died, Lucy joined my animal-assisted therapy program, helping humans learn about connection and trust while we bottle-fed her and cared for her needs. After four years, I knew this orphaned cow had grown up and needed to be with others of her kind, but her introduction into the large herd was difficult. She did not know how to interact well with cows and was immediately ostracized.

It was heartbreaking to watch her standing for months on the fringes of the herd, but Lucy persisted and slowly carved out a place for herself. Now she is thriving, appropriately asserting herself, and recently birthed a calf. What a joy it has been to see her demonstrate such resilience. We humans could benefit from her story: we are all stronger than we think we are.

From Lucy, I have learned about resilience, the marvelous gift and resource that all living things have been granted. We simply need to tap into this rather than allowing ourselves to become victims.

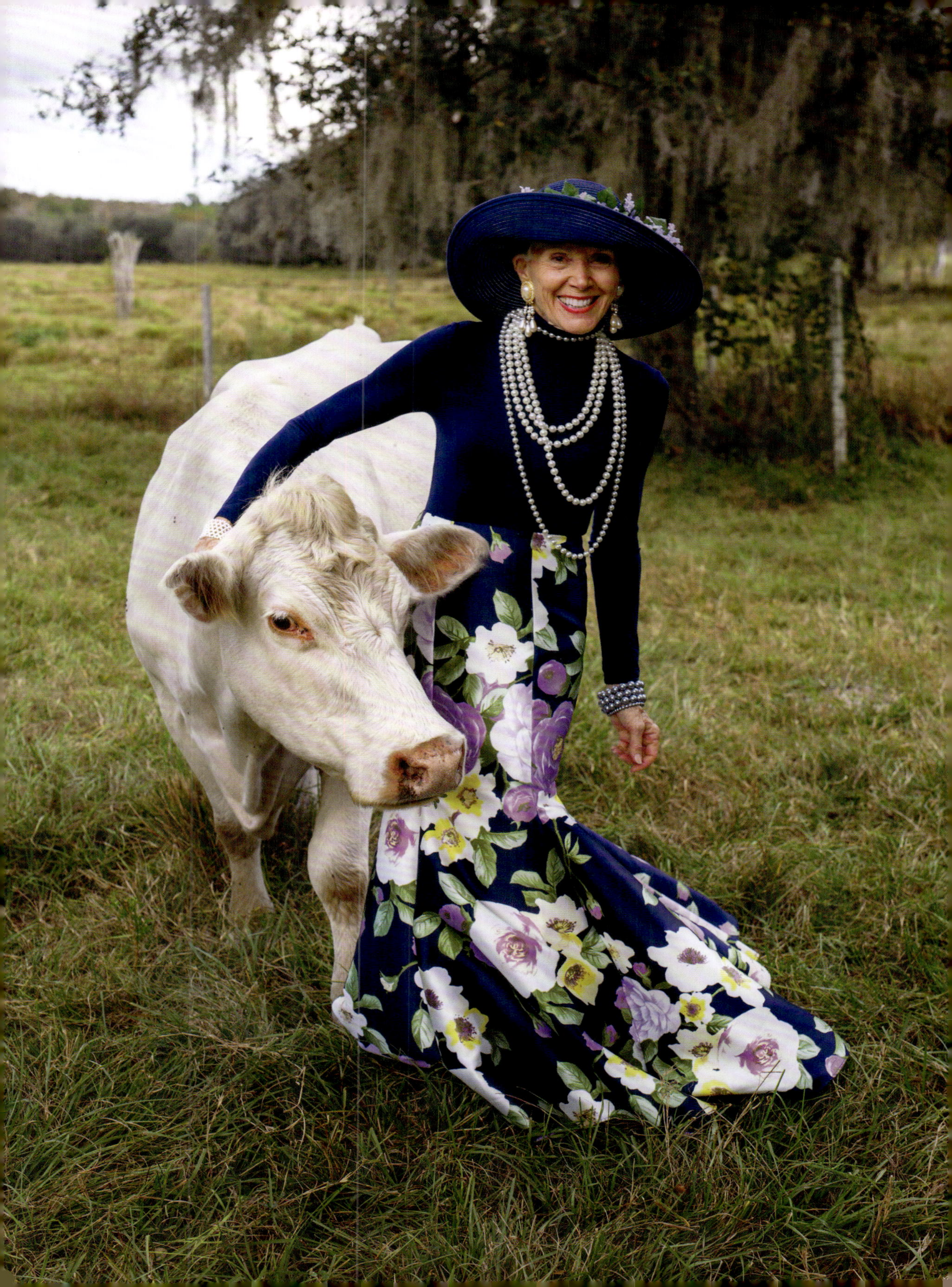

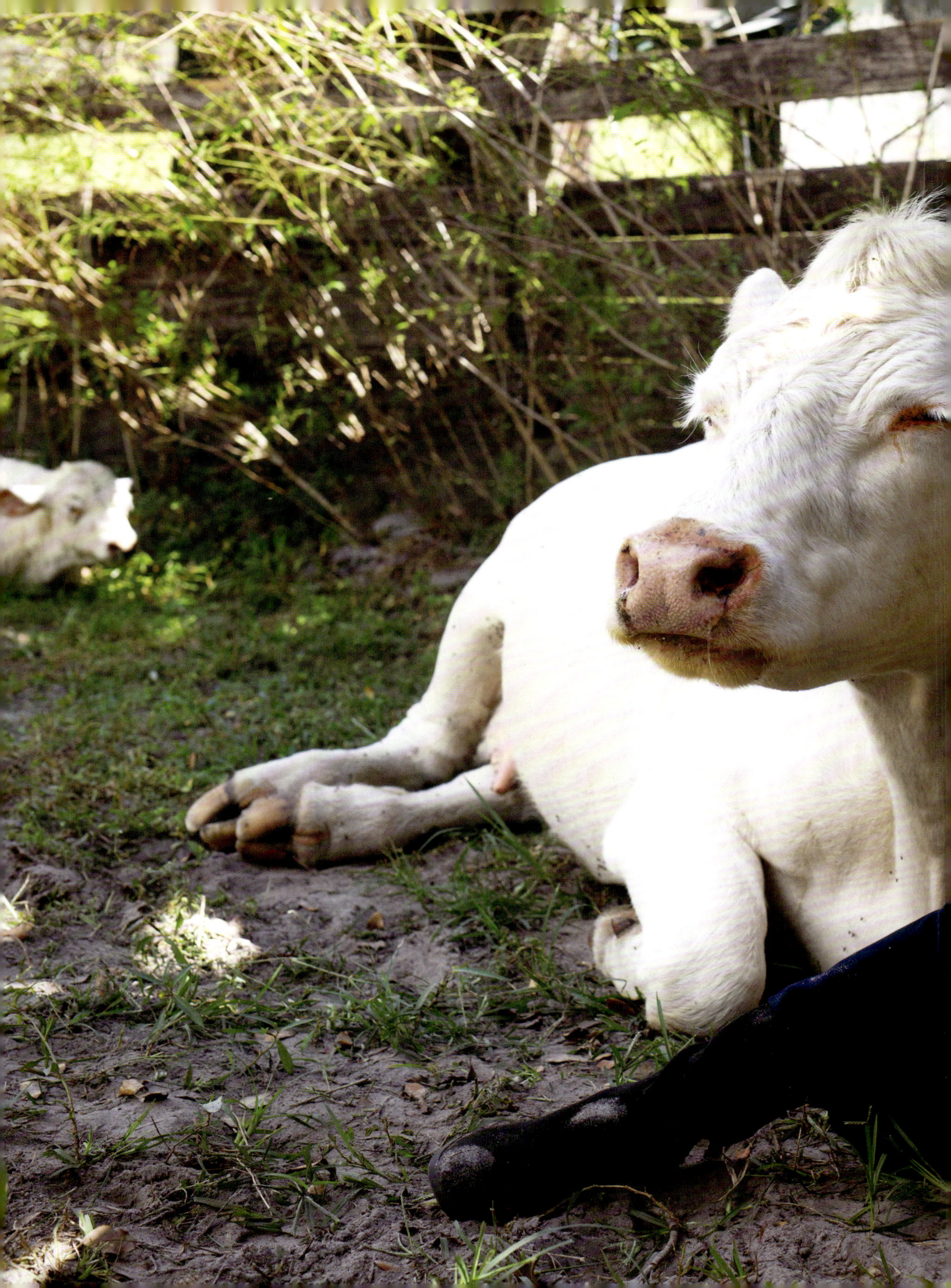

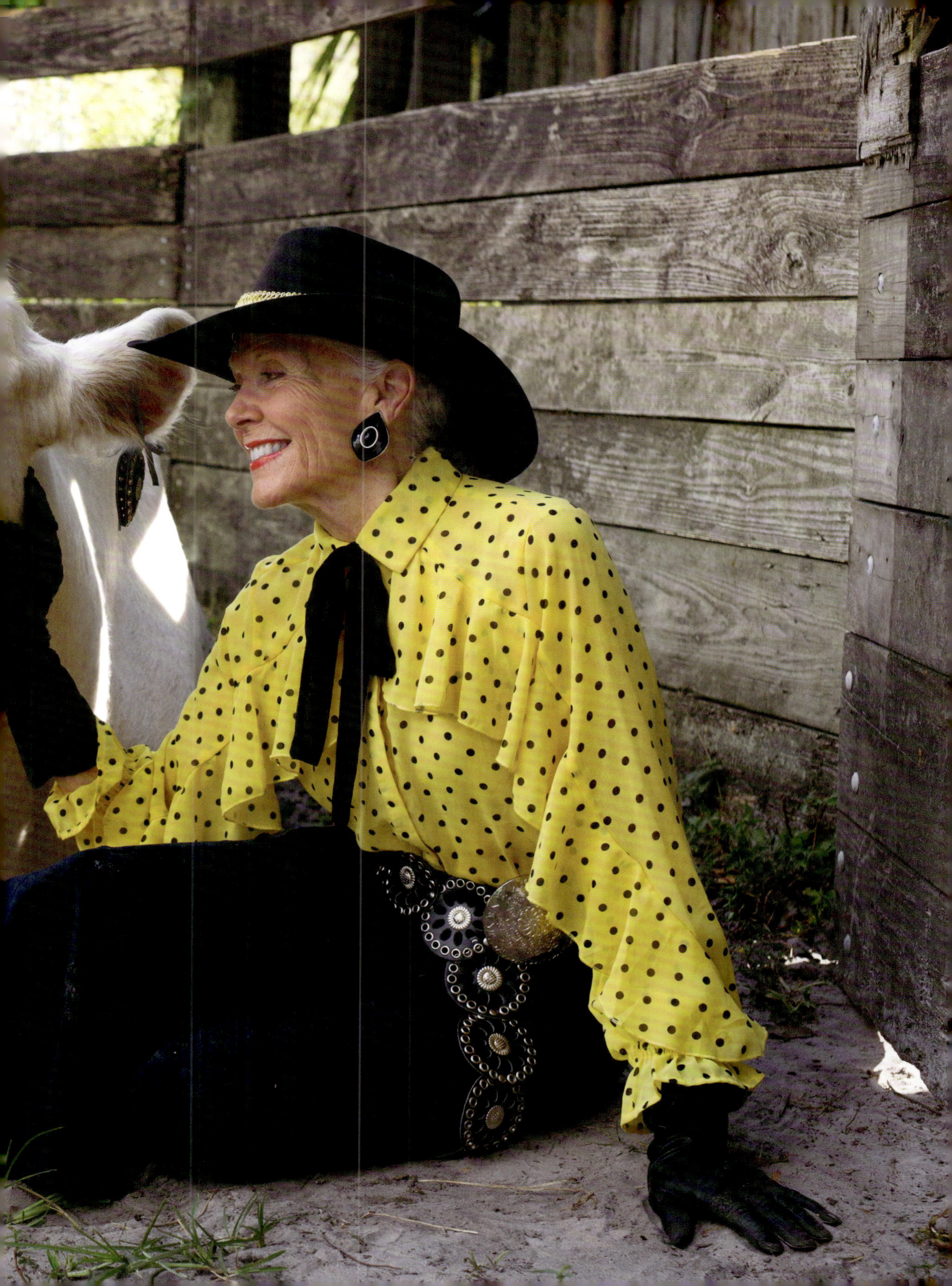

Sue, Pepsi, and Mel

My dog Pepsi is the kindest soul. She accompanies me to work every day and holds the title Director of Wellness. Her calmness helps remind me to slow down and enjoy life's simple pleasures.

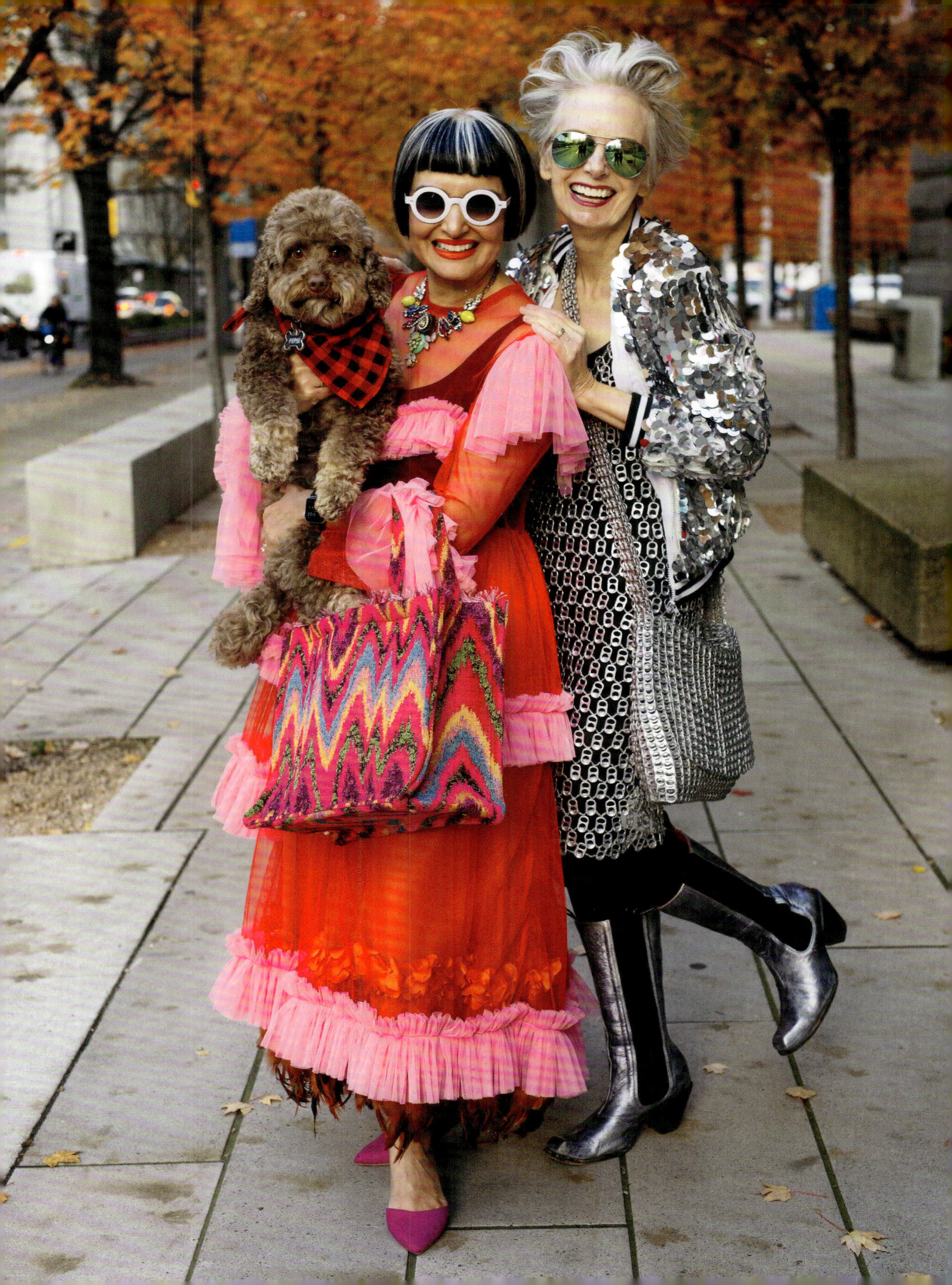

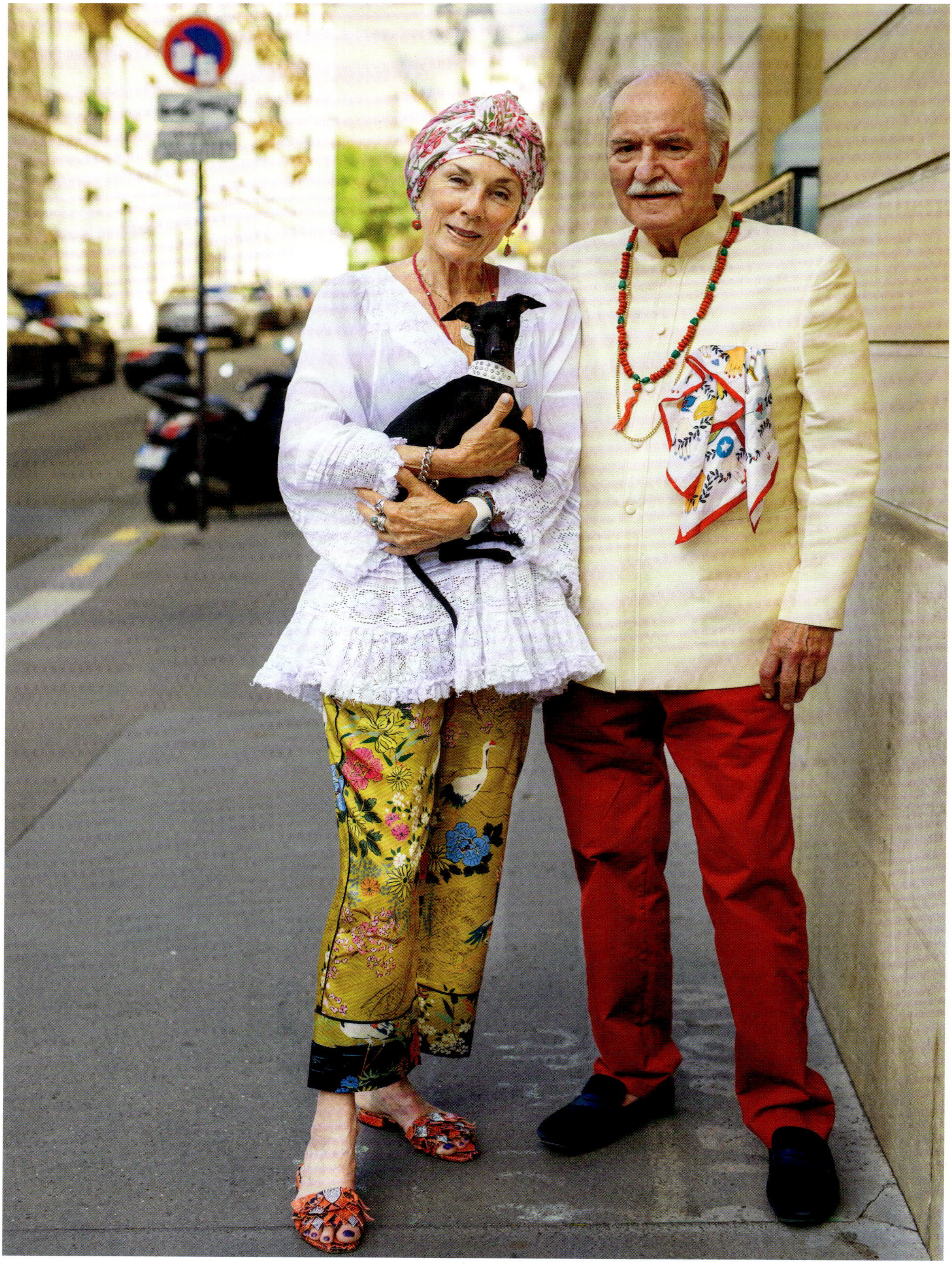

Jennie, Oskar, and Shau Ming

I was born in the Chinese Year of the Dog. I have owned many of these wonderful four-footed creatures, each and every one a special character. I grew up in Africa and dogs were always a part of our life there. I traveled from Europe to Asia for over twenty years with mother and daughter white poodles. Once, in Paris, I began a love story with a small Italian greyhound. I have always loved the companionship of my dogs, their warm bodies sleeping next to me. Having been a foreigner in so many countries, my dogs have always been a great help in meeting new people.

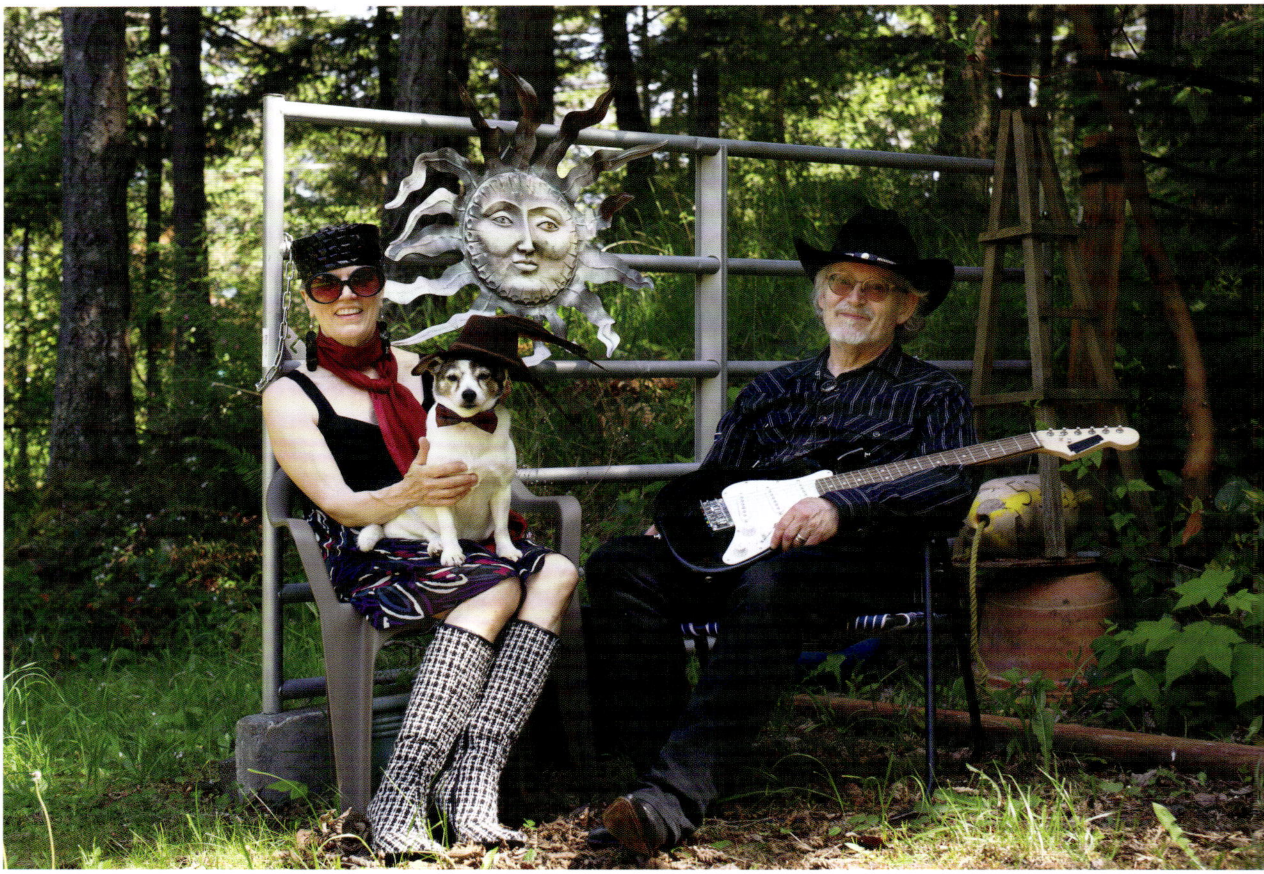

Leslie, Paul, and Bert

Bert was originally my younger sister's dog. She died suddenly from an infection alone, if not for Bert. We are pretty sure he sat by her side the entire time.

Paul and I had had a long-standing no pets policy, but when we went down to my sister's house after she passed away, Bert came running and jumped into my arms. It was as though he was saying, "I really need a person and I pick you." So we brought him home and he's just been the love of our lives. I am training him to be a diabetic alert service dog to help me. He's just the smartest, sweetest, funniest little kid. We have a level of communication that goes beyond what I thought people and animals could achieve. Our friend likes to say that Bert is a higher being in a dog suit.

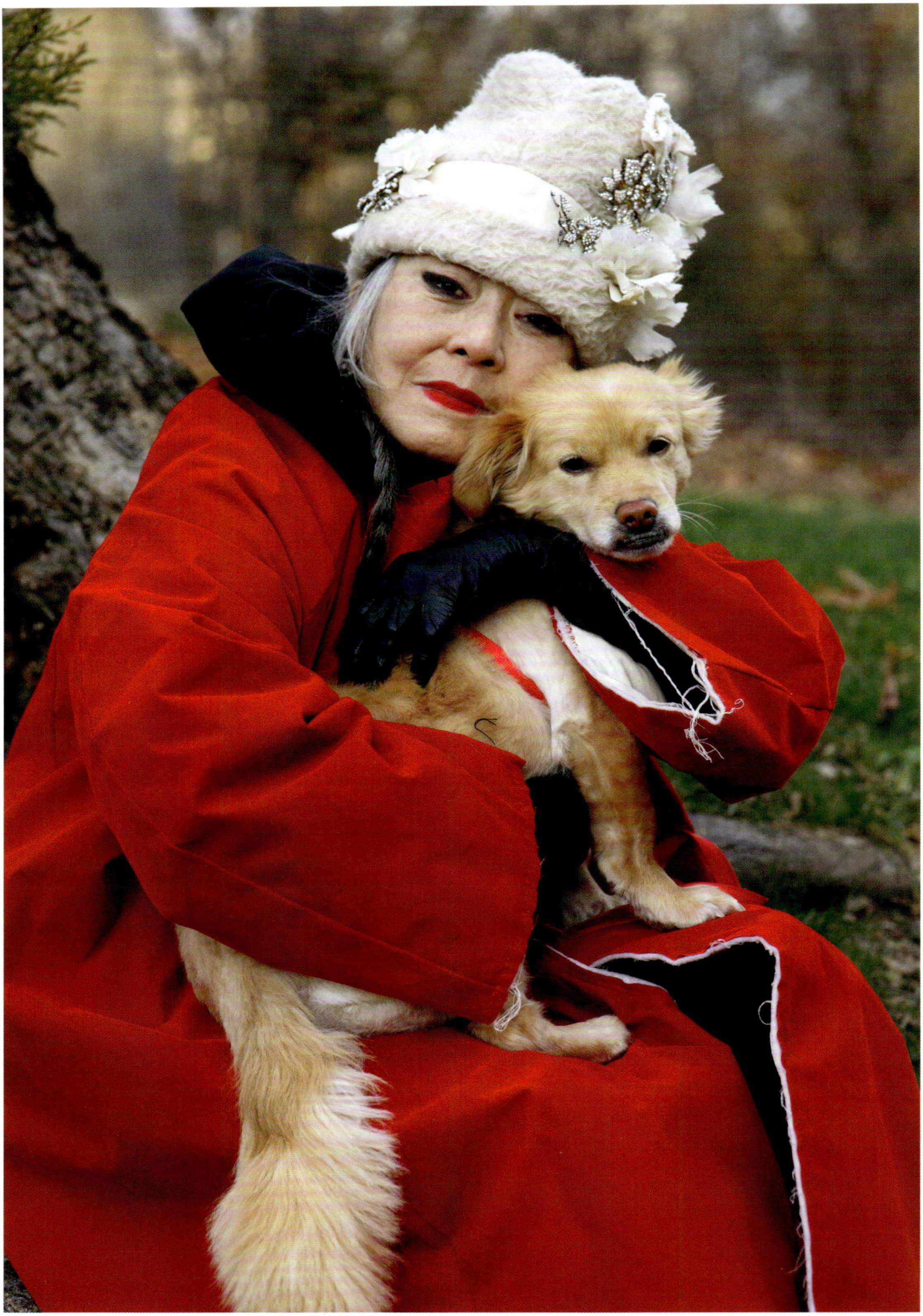

Gemma and Comet

I wanted a puppy to keep me company after moving to the Hudson Valley from Manhattan. I searched for more than a year until I finally came across Comet who had the sweetest little face. When I picked him up it was love at first sight! He knew I was his new mom immediately. He is a really good boy and has lot of patience. Every time we get in the car, he sits in the driver's seat and insists on driving.

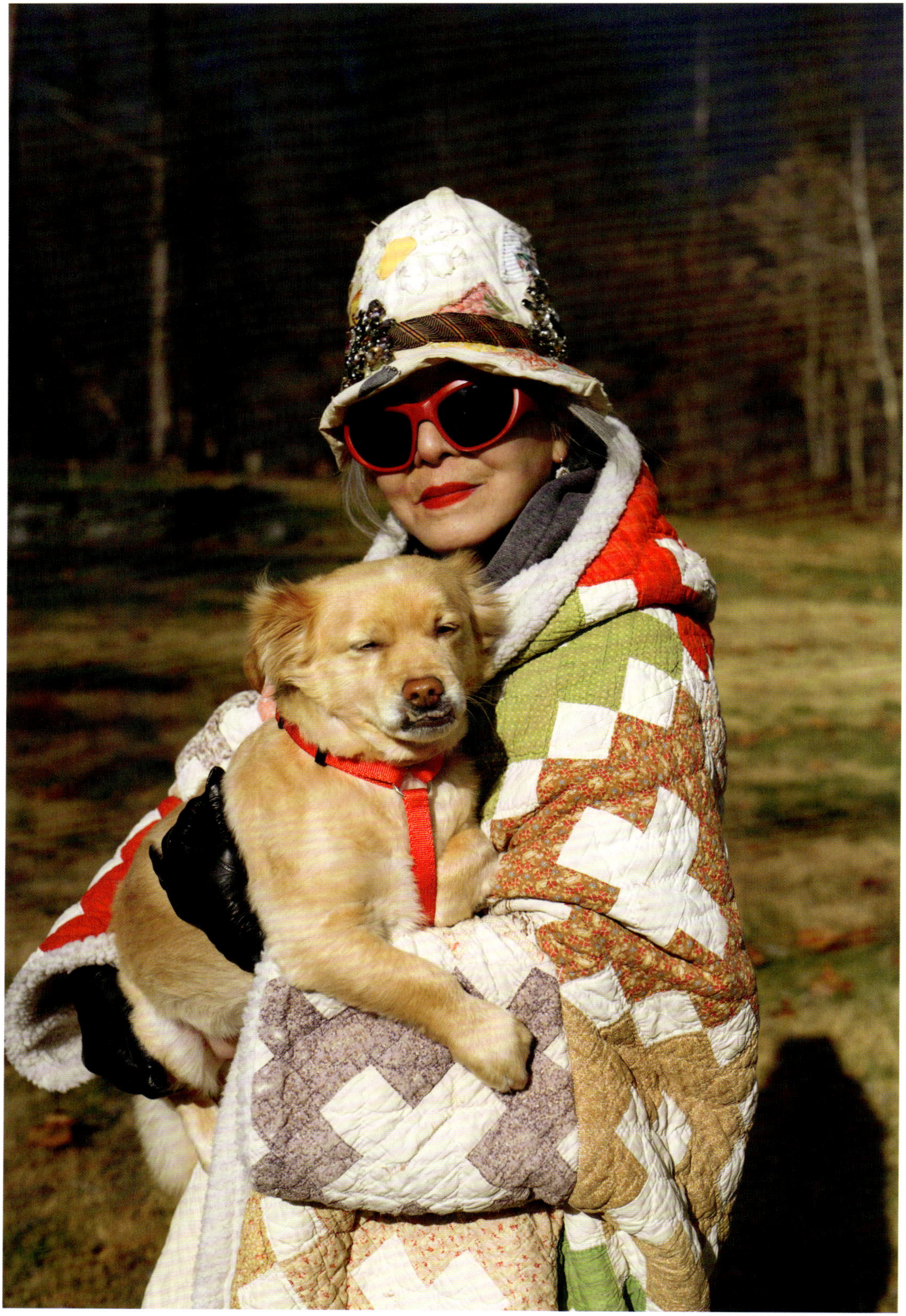

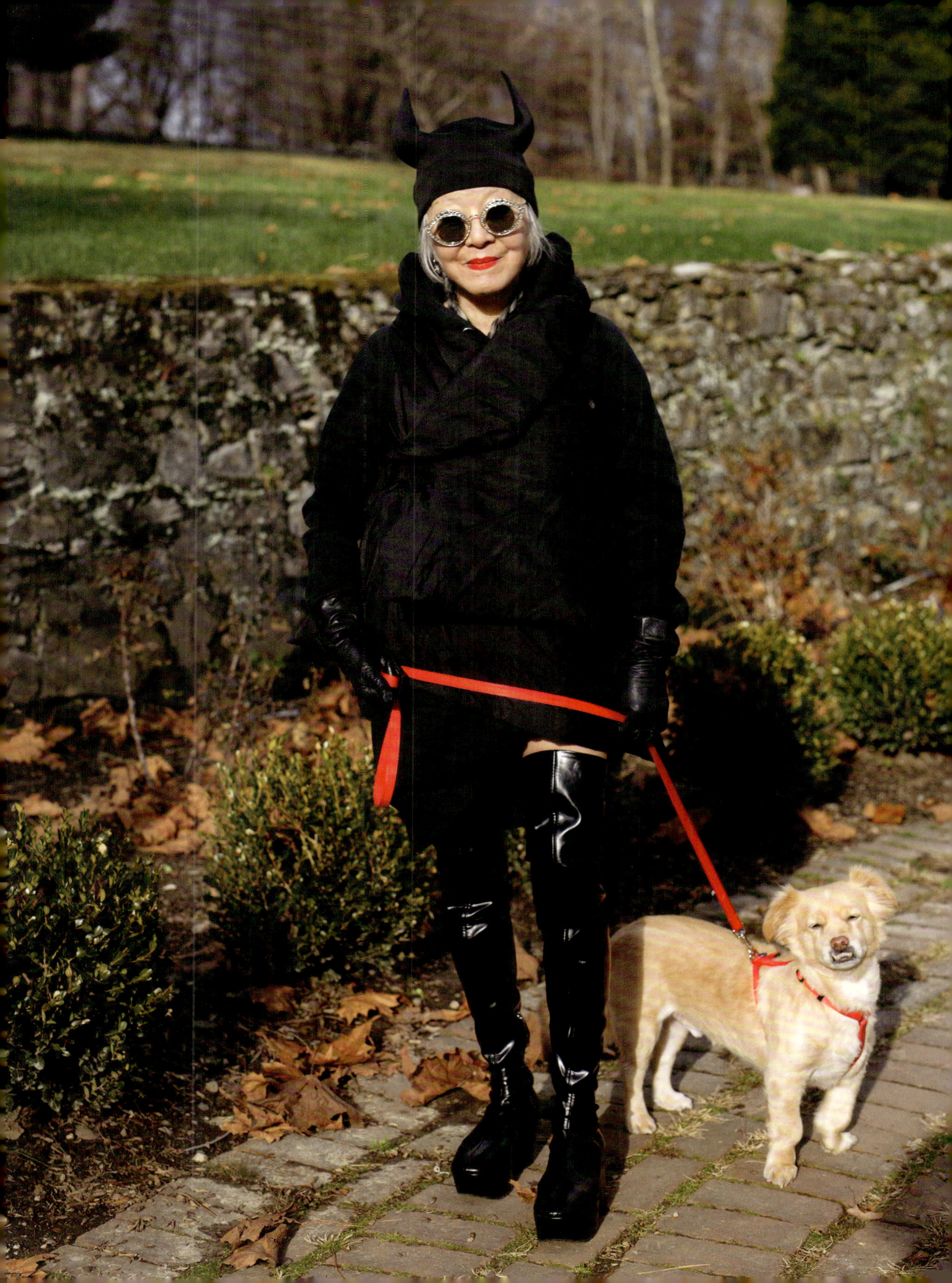

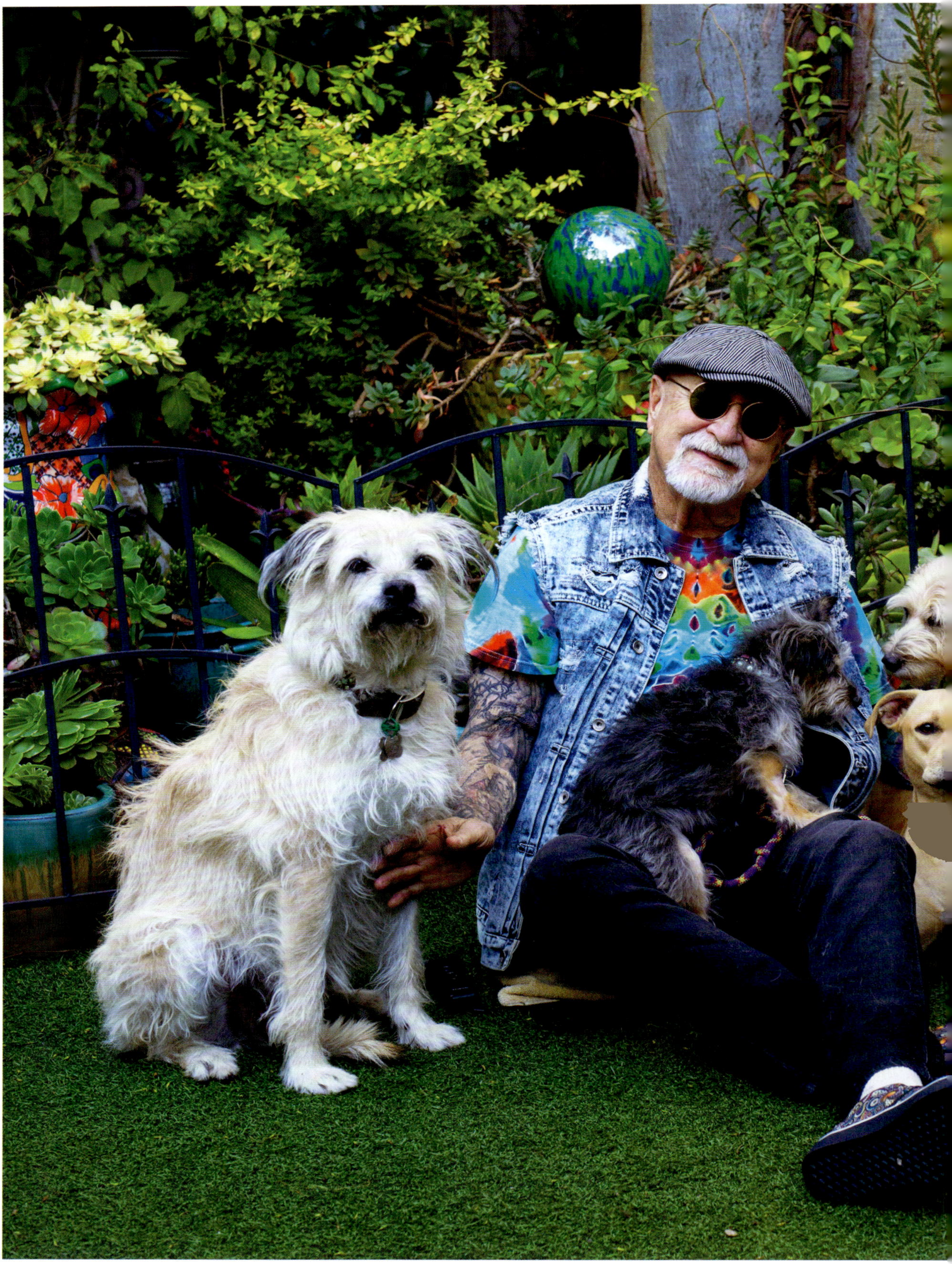

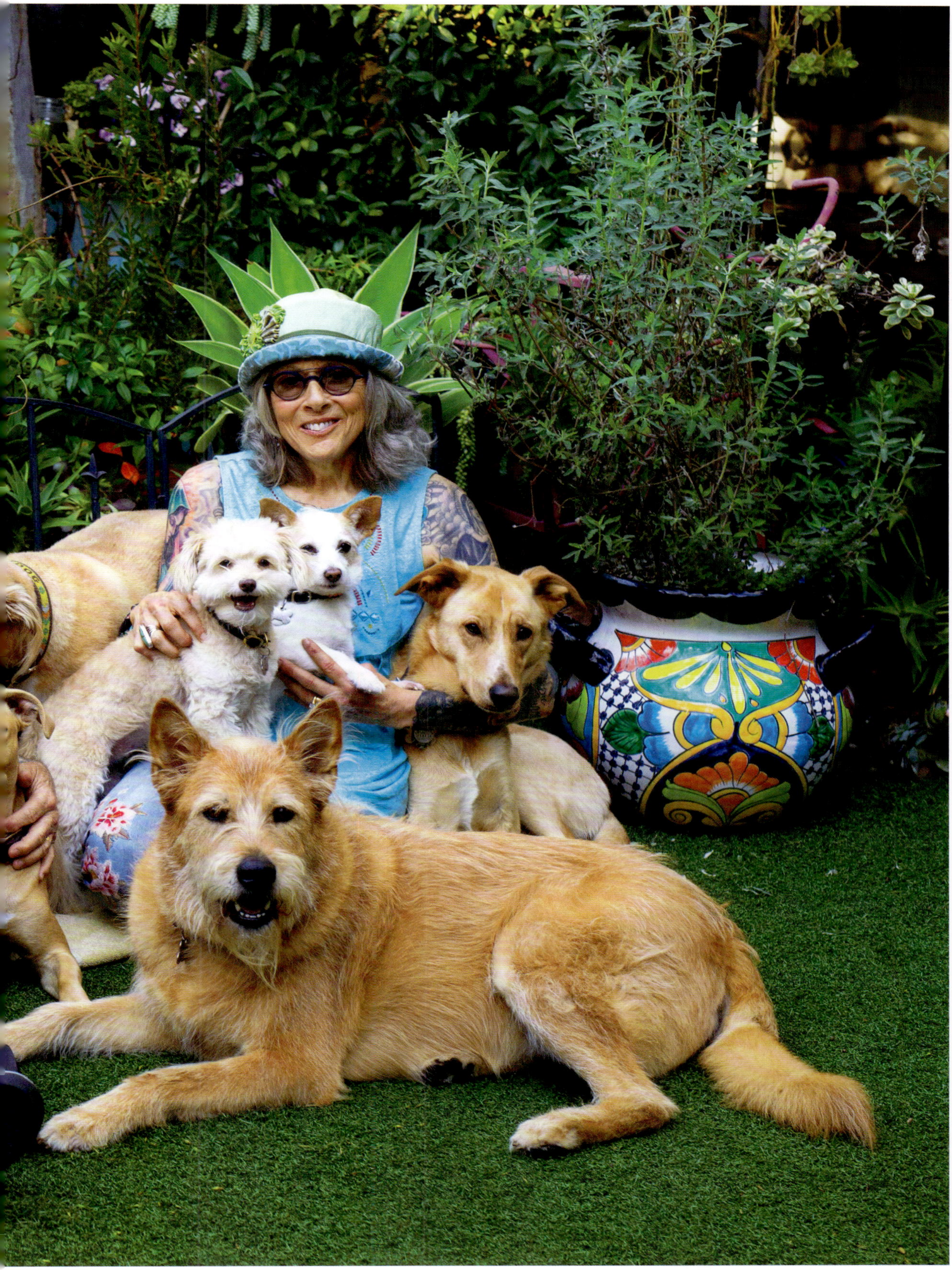

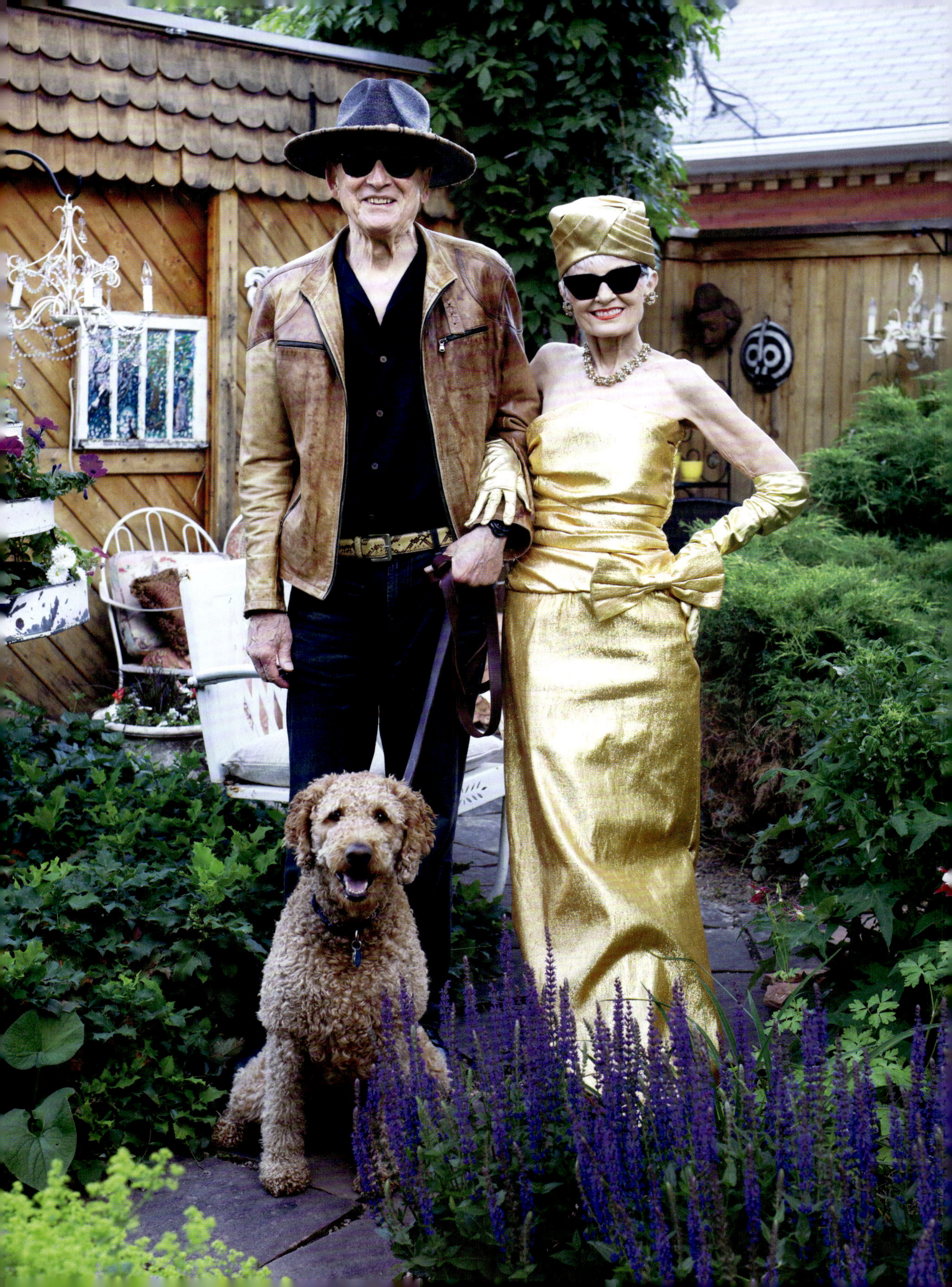

Jeff, Judith, and Tulo

Jeff: I've had a lot of dogs almost all my life. The last one died at ten and a half years old and I decided that was enough dogs for me. It was too painful. Tulo is a great dog; she's easy and sweet. After an eleven-year hiatus it was perfect timing to have her in my life. My son travels a lot so I'm Tulo's grandpa, which means I have a lot of responsibility but not FULL responsibility.

Judith: The last time that I had a dog was years ago, when our beloved sheltie had to be put down two weeks after my husband Nelson's fatal cancer diagnosis. At the age of eighty, spending time with the gentle and playful Tulo is comforting, joyful, and healing.

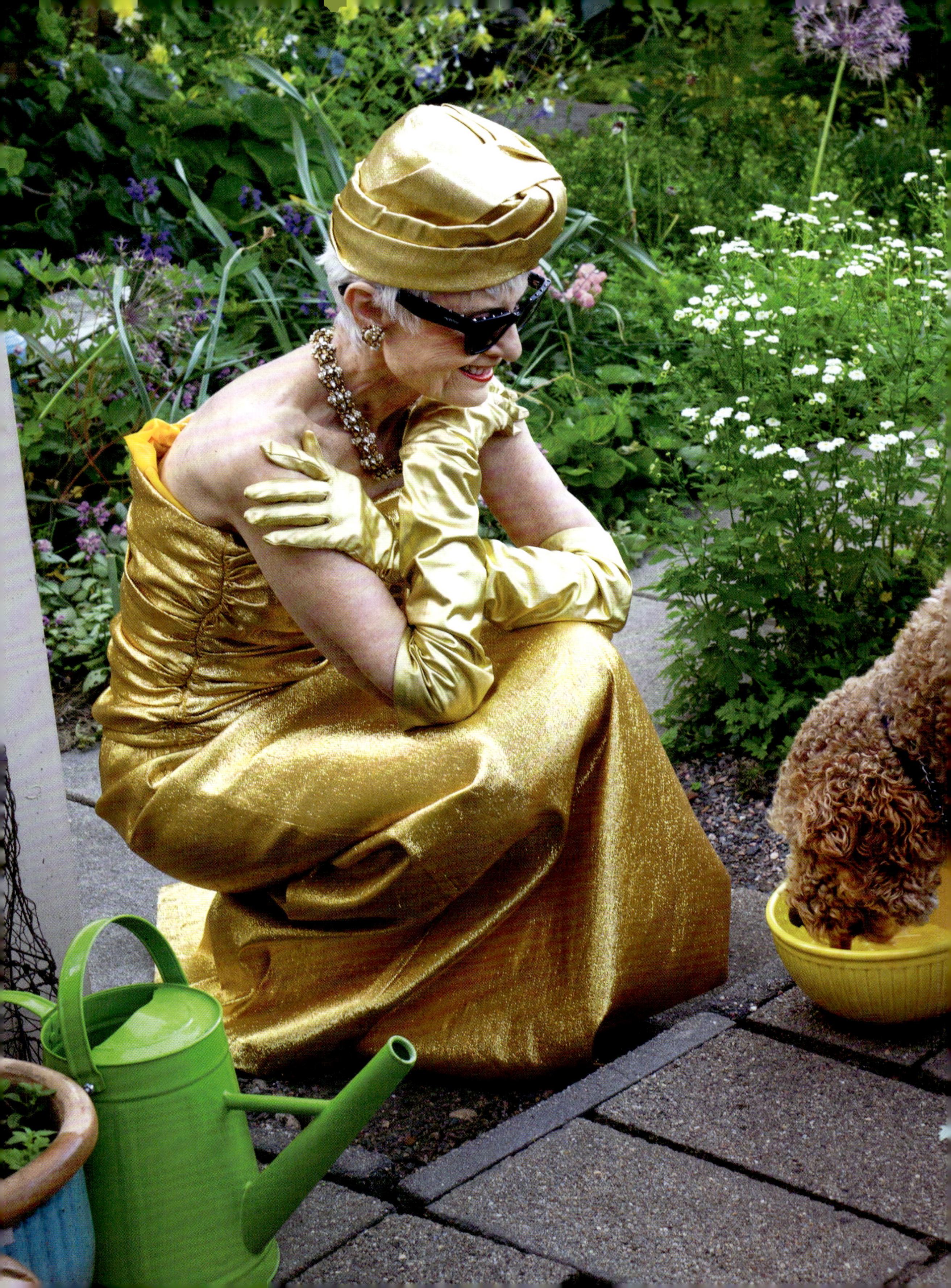

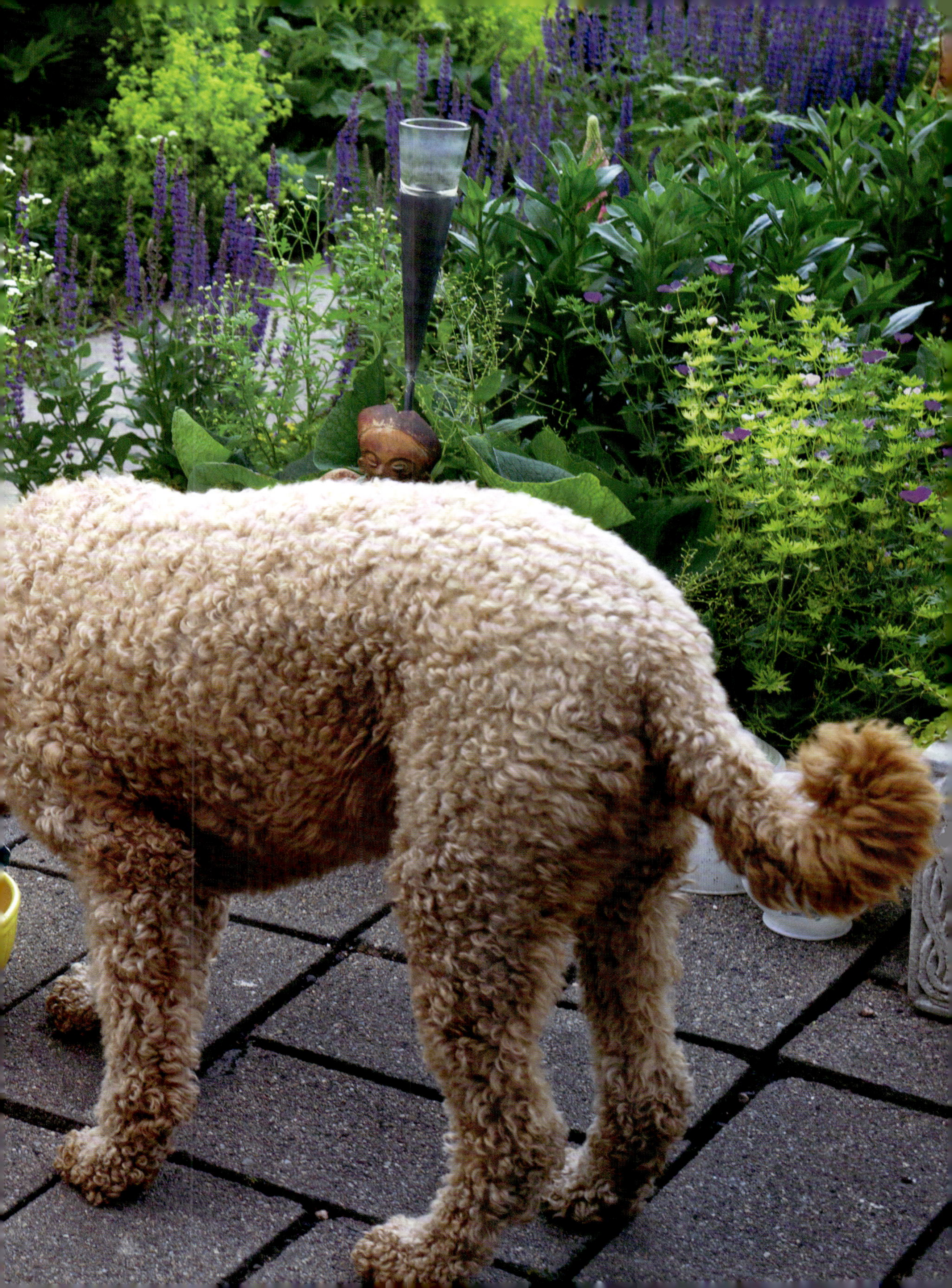

Deborah and Louie

In June 2020, my two cocker spaniels, Cordelia and Willie, died within a week of each other and it was devastating. Six weeks later, somebody asked me if I could take Louie because they knew that I adopted old cocker spaniels. Louie means the world to me. He keeps me grounded. He's my reason to get up in the morning.

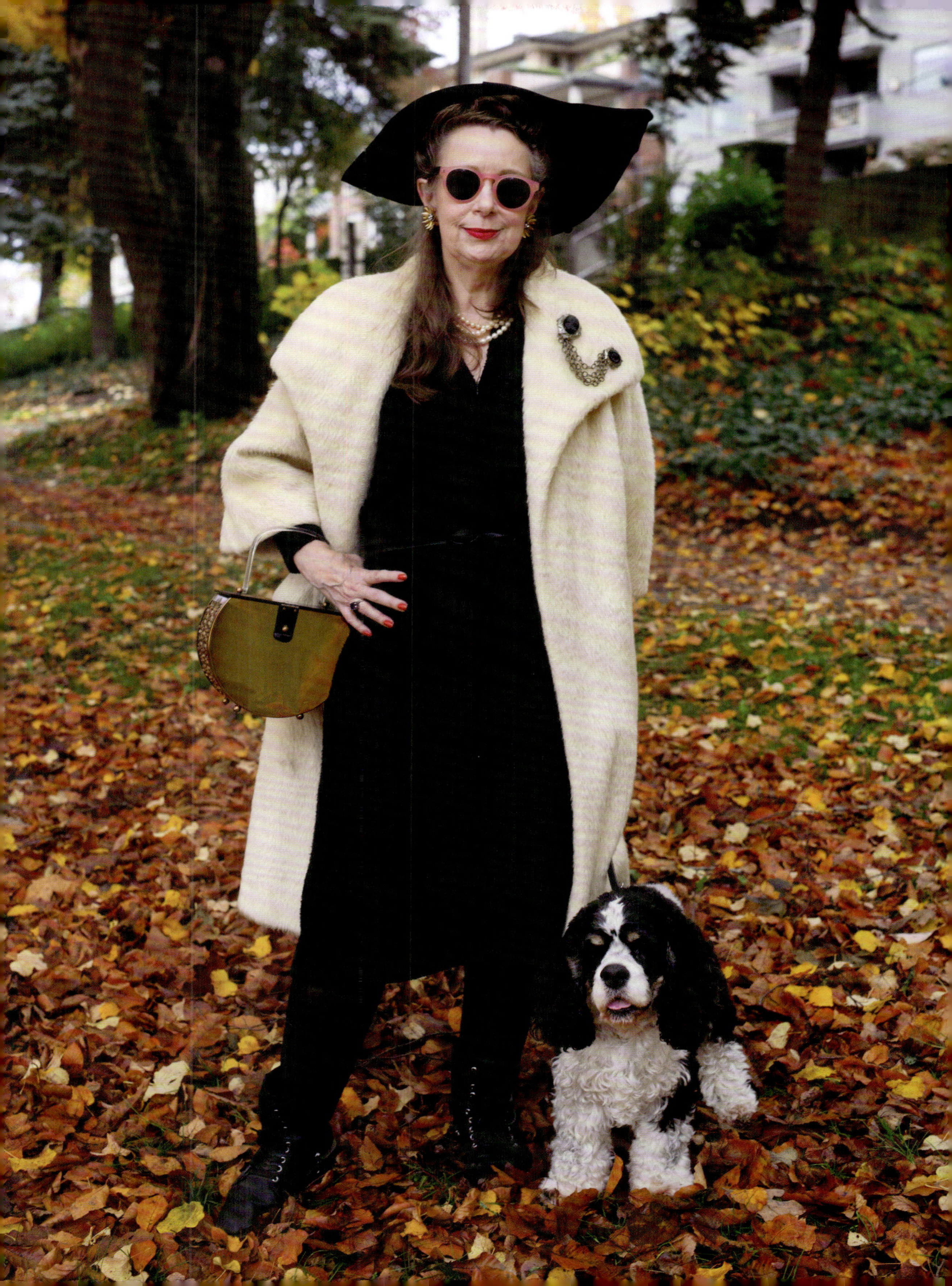

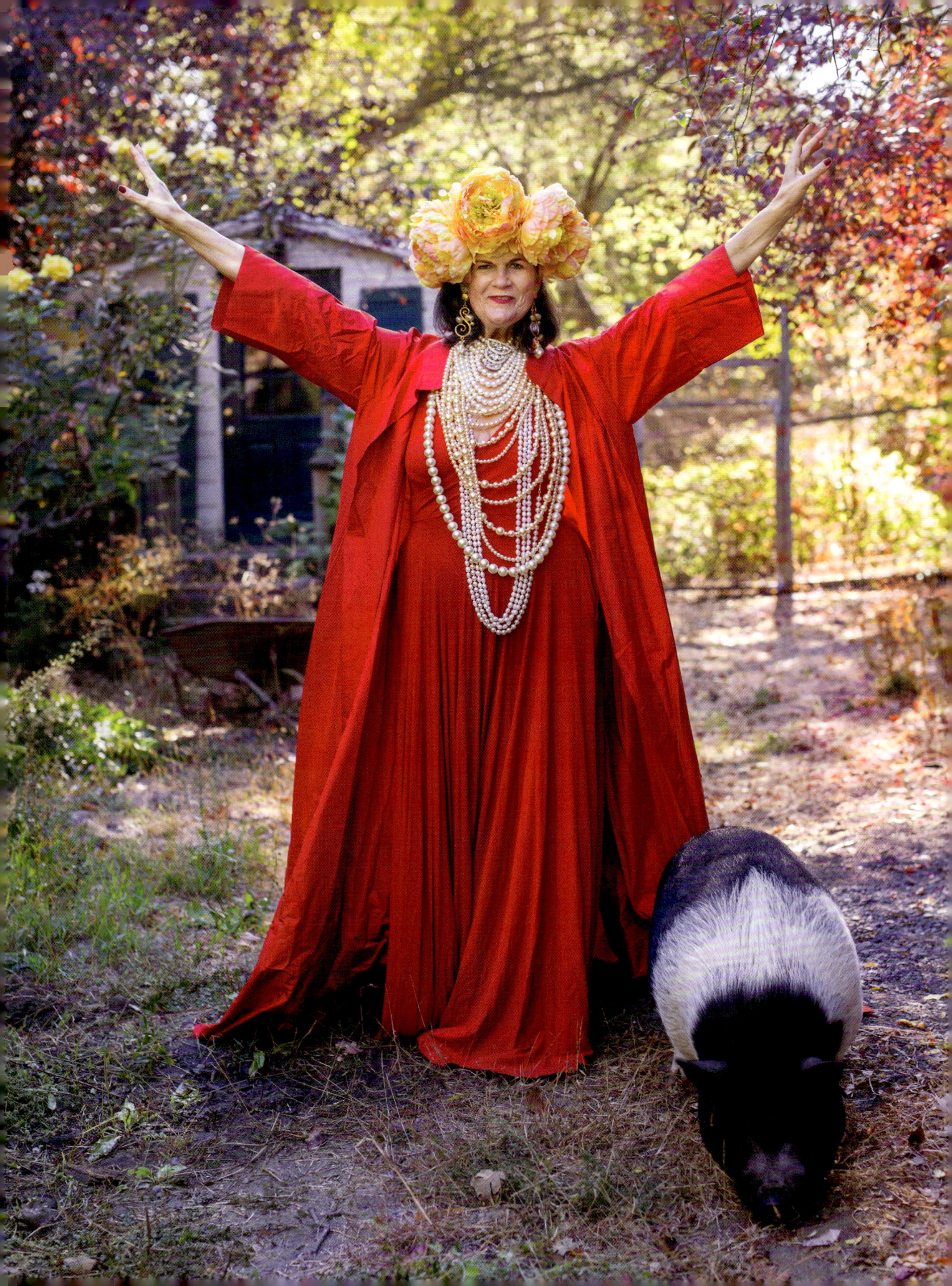

Elizabeth, Bansky, and Ruby

Banksy arrived in my kitchen on Valentine's Day, a gift from my son. I had always wanted a pig so I was ecstatic about the surprise. Banksy has become a living part of our home, as he is a teacup pig and learned to live inside with us. Pigs are very smart animals. He learned his name instantly. He learned the doggy door in two days! Plus he puts himself to bed every night by 8 p.m. I am always astounded by how he manages to get his blanket over his body just so perfectly. He slept on the floor by my side of the bed, but eventually moved to the living room after he no longer fit. He adores his Johnny Was blankets and numerous pillows. Every night he takes his spot at our dinner table between the cat and the dog to wait his turn for a bite. I bet you are thinking he is spoiled? Just a wee bit. I should have had a small farm. I do regret not having a cow and a donkey and a few sheep to go along with the other beasties. I heard my calling and missed it.

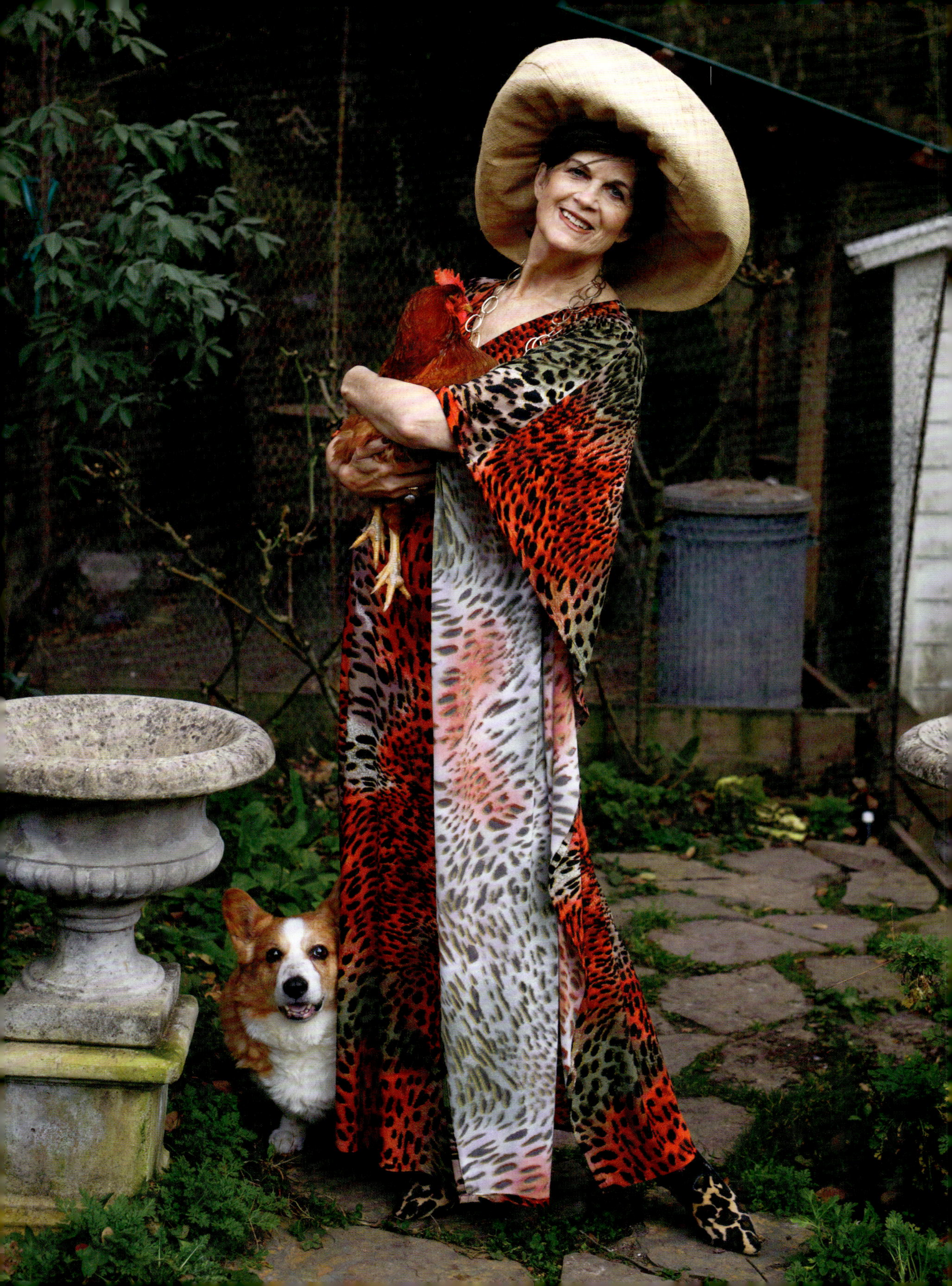

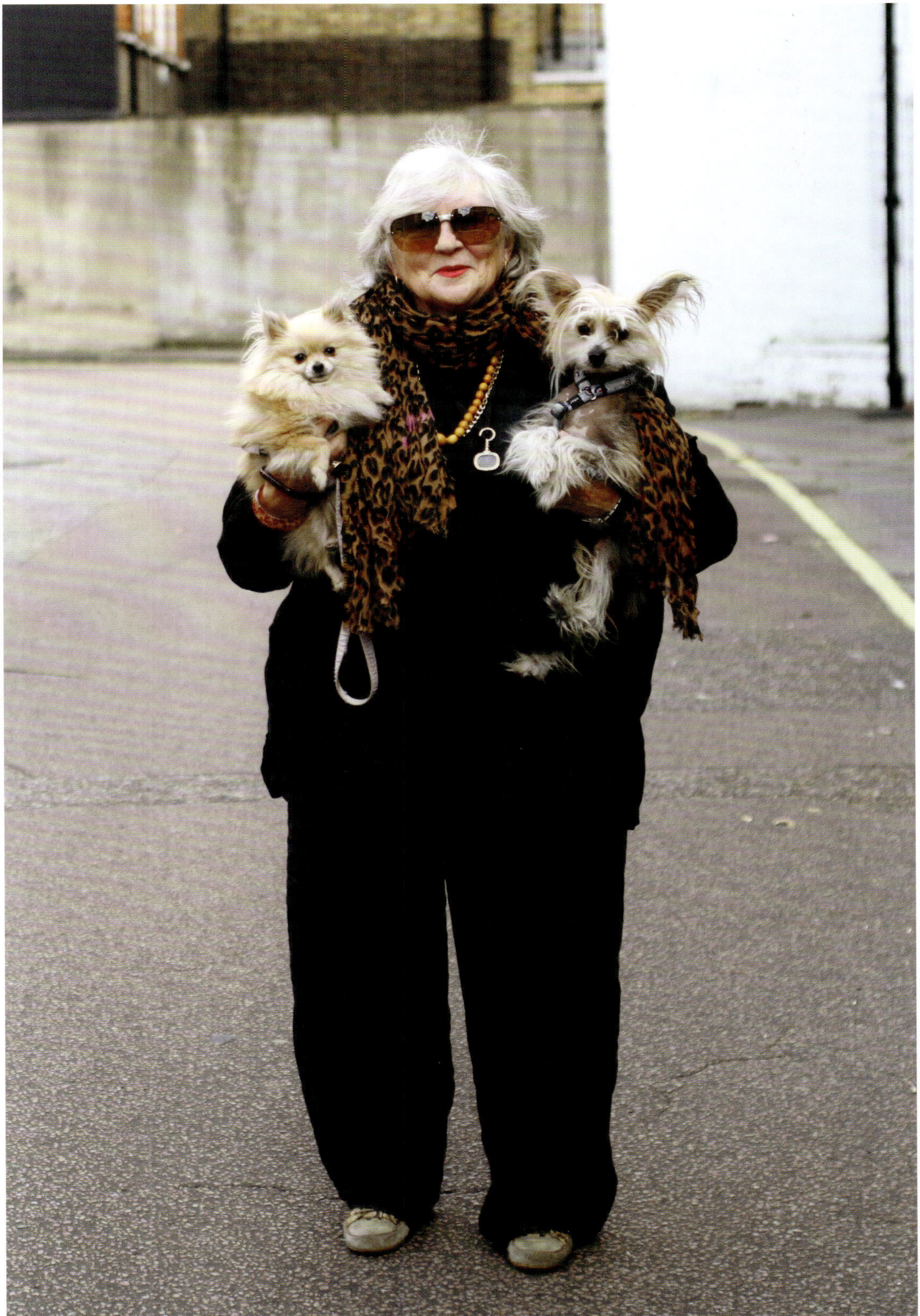

Sylvia and Quincy

I'd always wanted a dog, but my mother was very pristine. She was pretty much the Black June Cleaver. When I got married, I had the pleasure of picking out our little Quincy. He's such a joy. He's mild mannered and different from what I imagined a pitbull to be. Quincy is always there when you are down and need affection. He is compassionate, lovable, and adores cuddling.

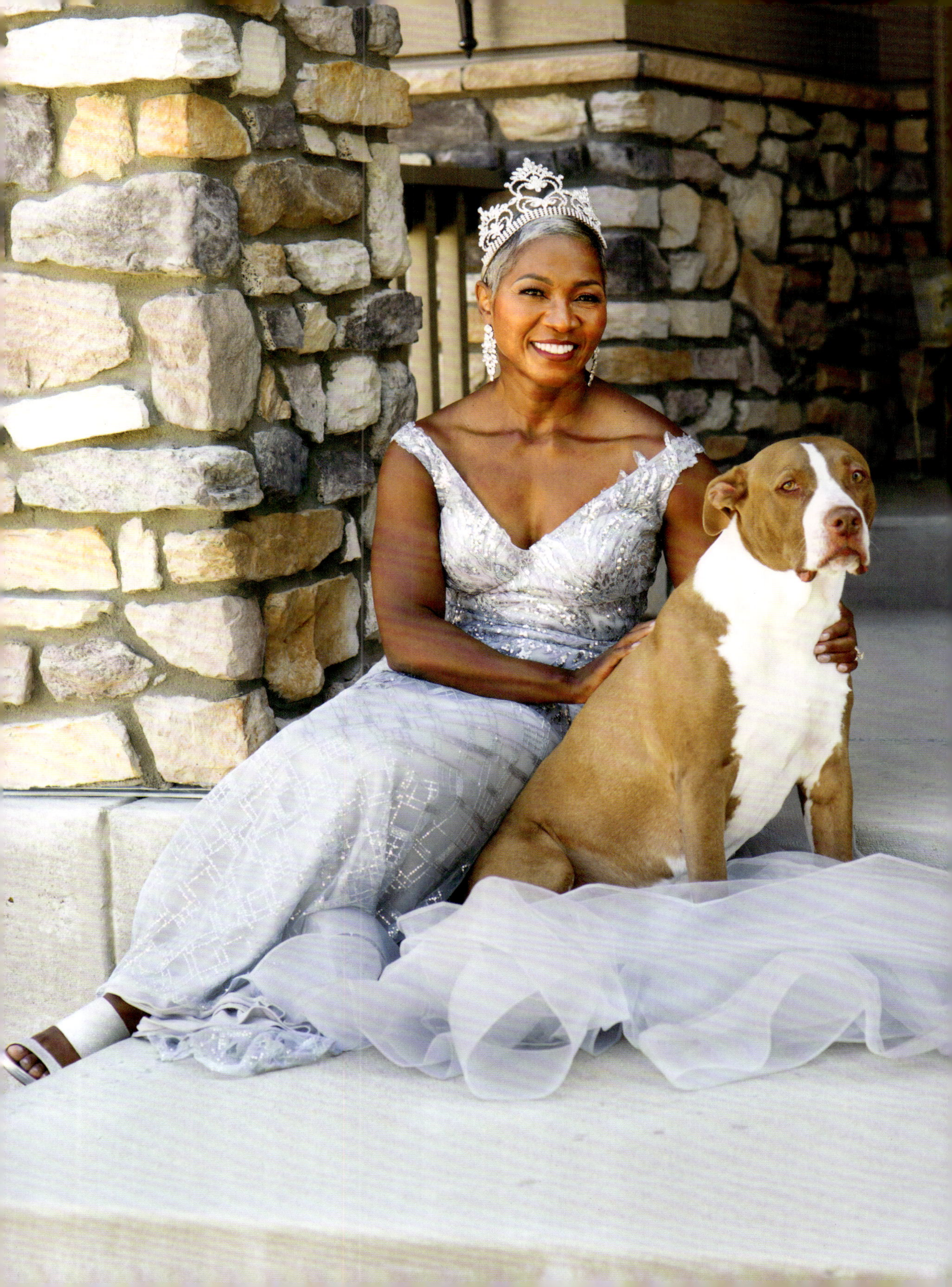

“For me, true love is Winky. He is the love of my life and my best friend and I’m just besotted.”

Linda and Winks

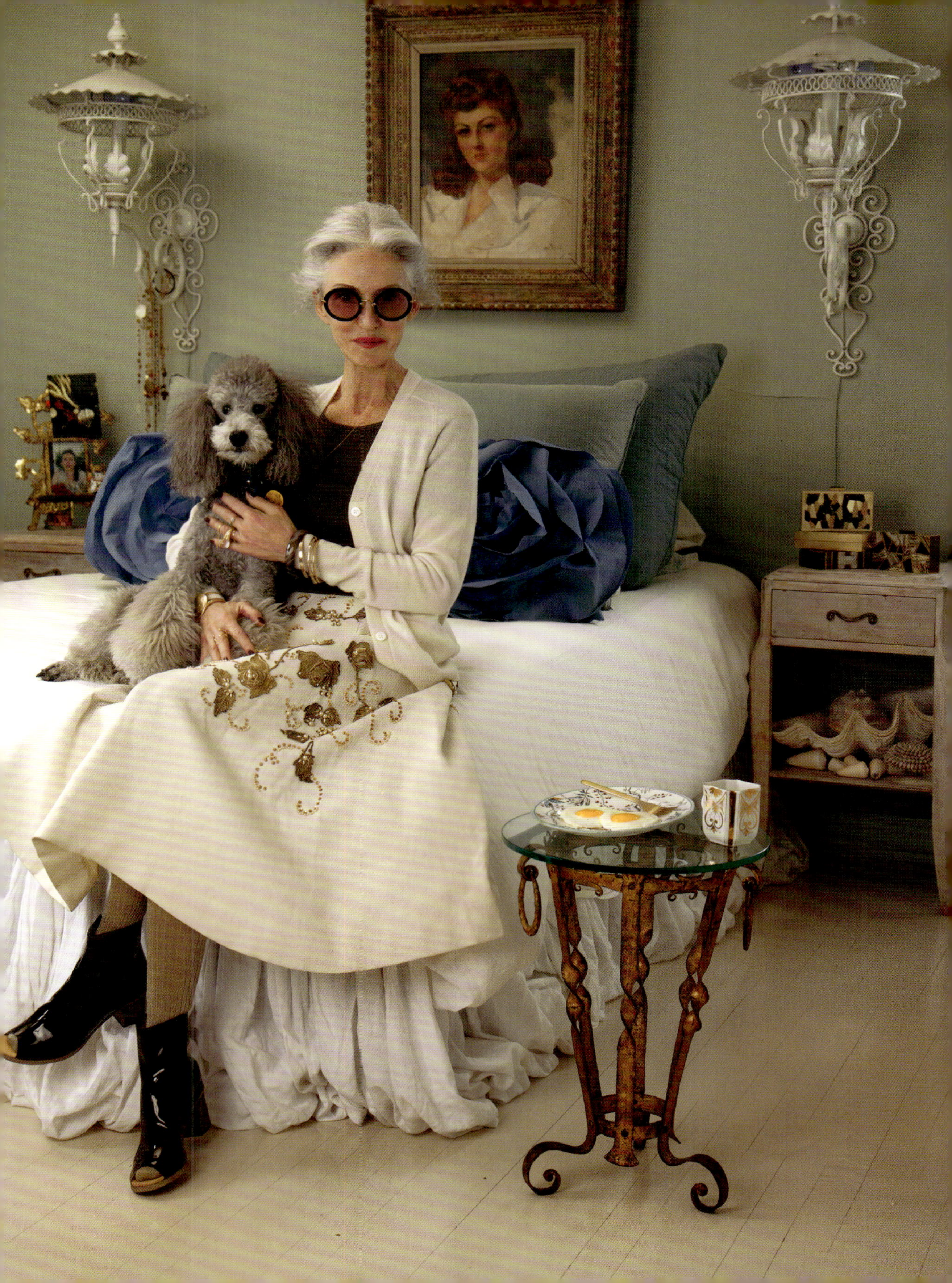

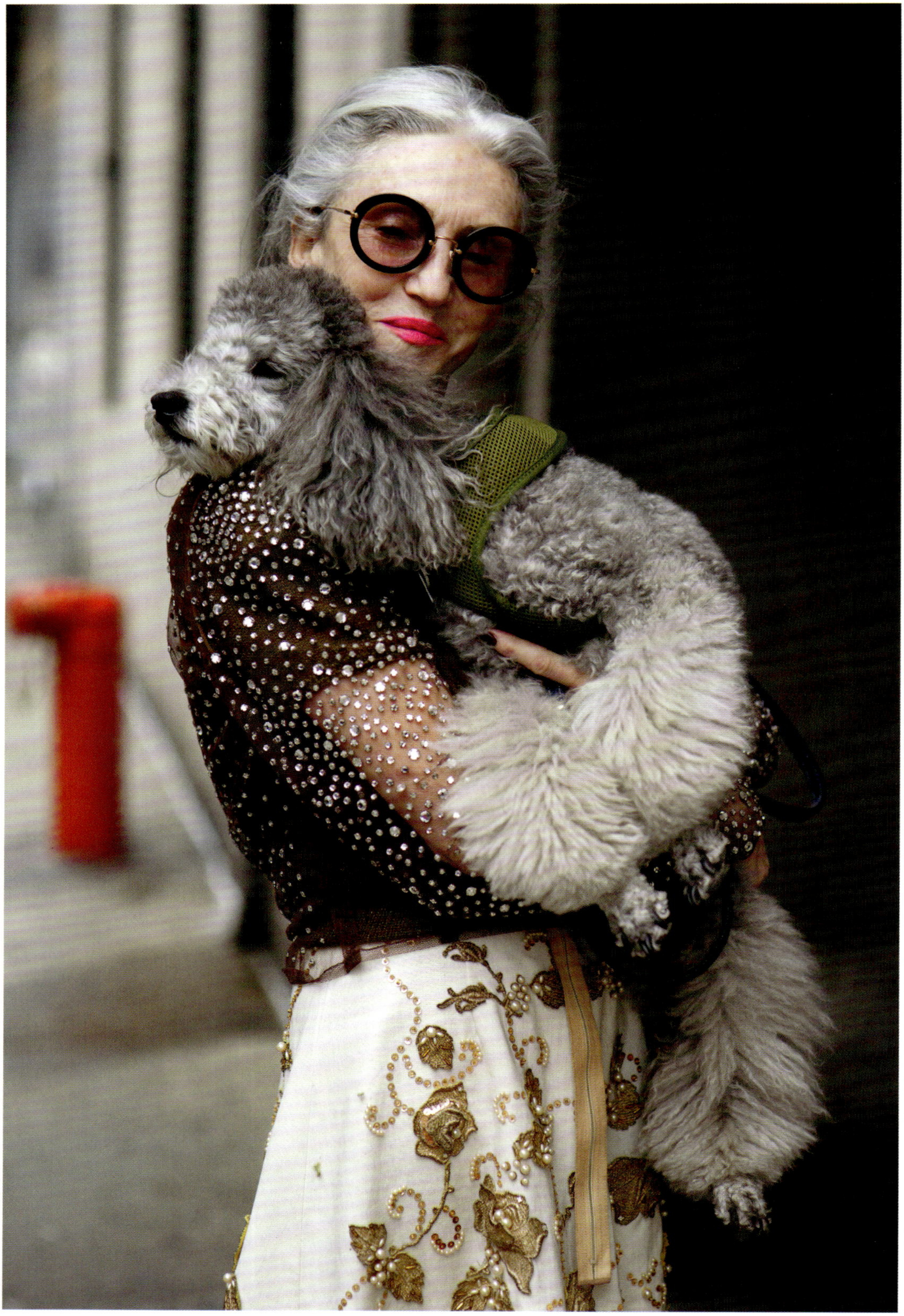

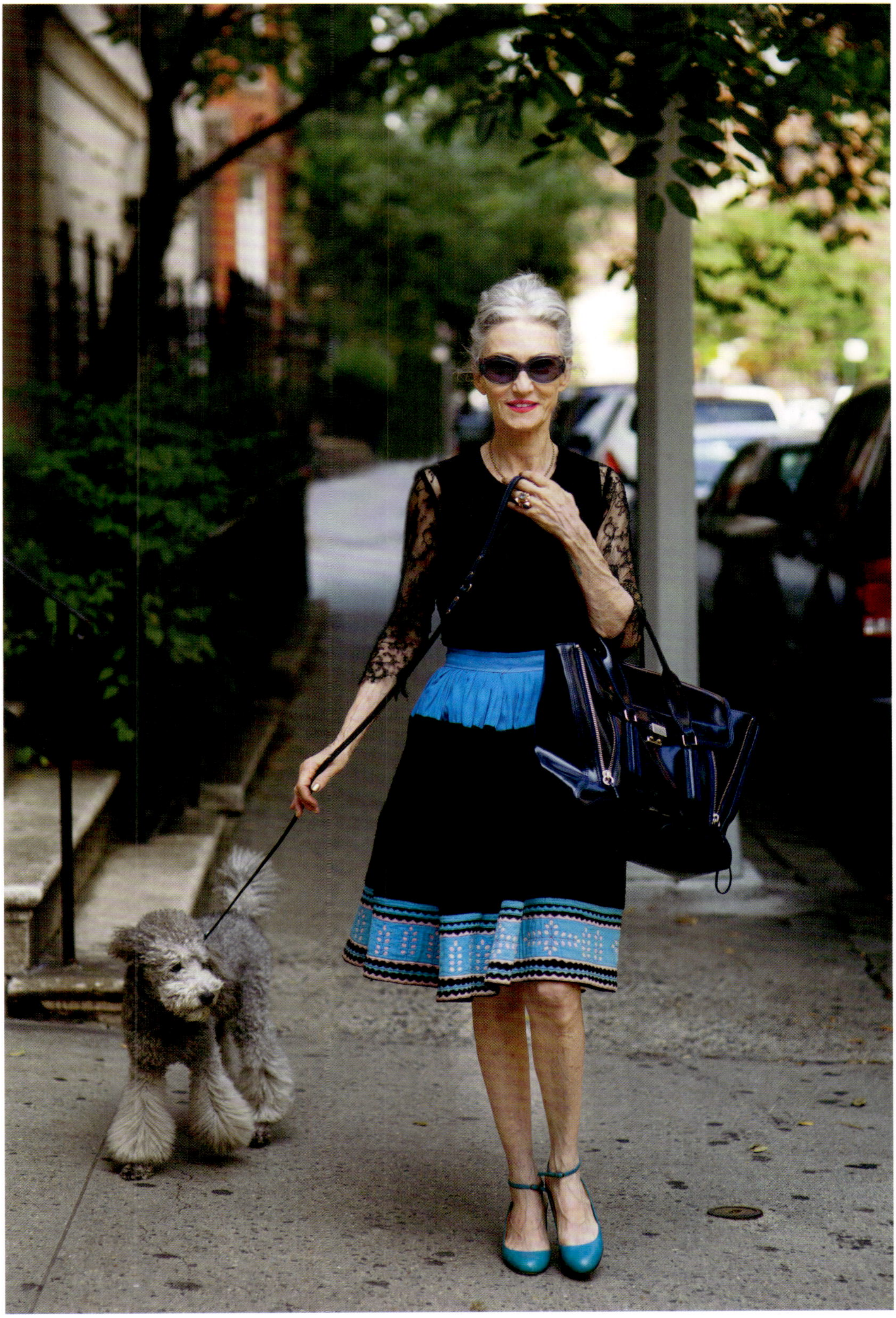

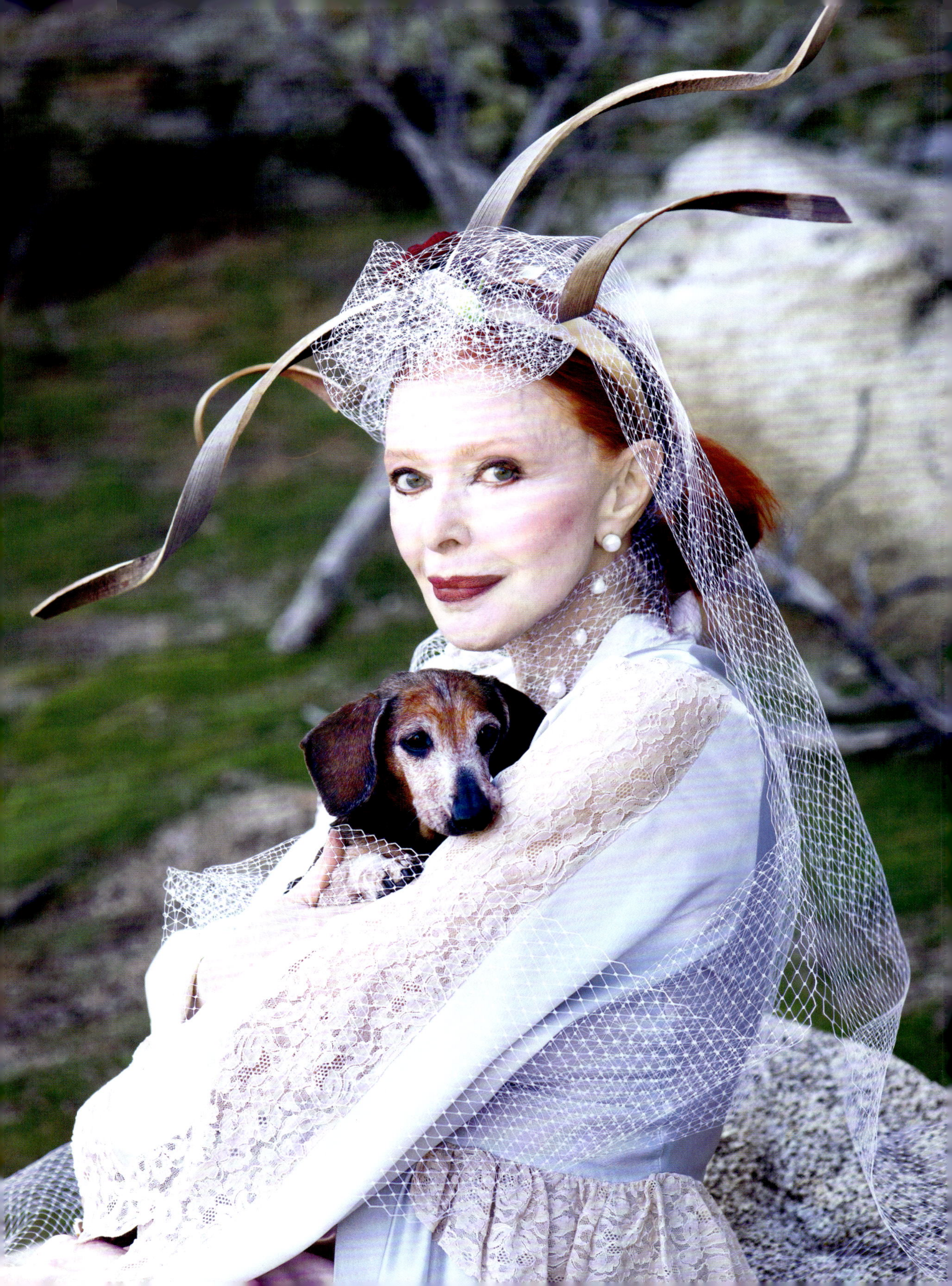

Valerie and Lucy

Every dog owner eventually comes to think of their dog as special. Our Lucy became a very special dog (after a prolonged training in bathroom etiquette), exchanging love with us for twenty-one years. Loving her was as easy as it was to love the six other dachshunds that preceded her. You have to own one (or be owned by one) to understand this stubborn and quirky breed and their seduction. I hope to see her again if we both end up in heaven.

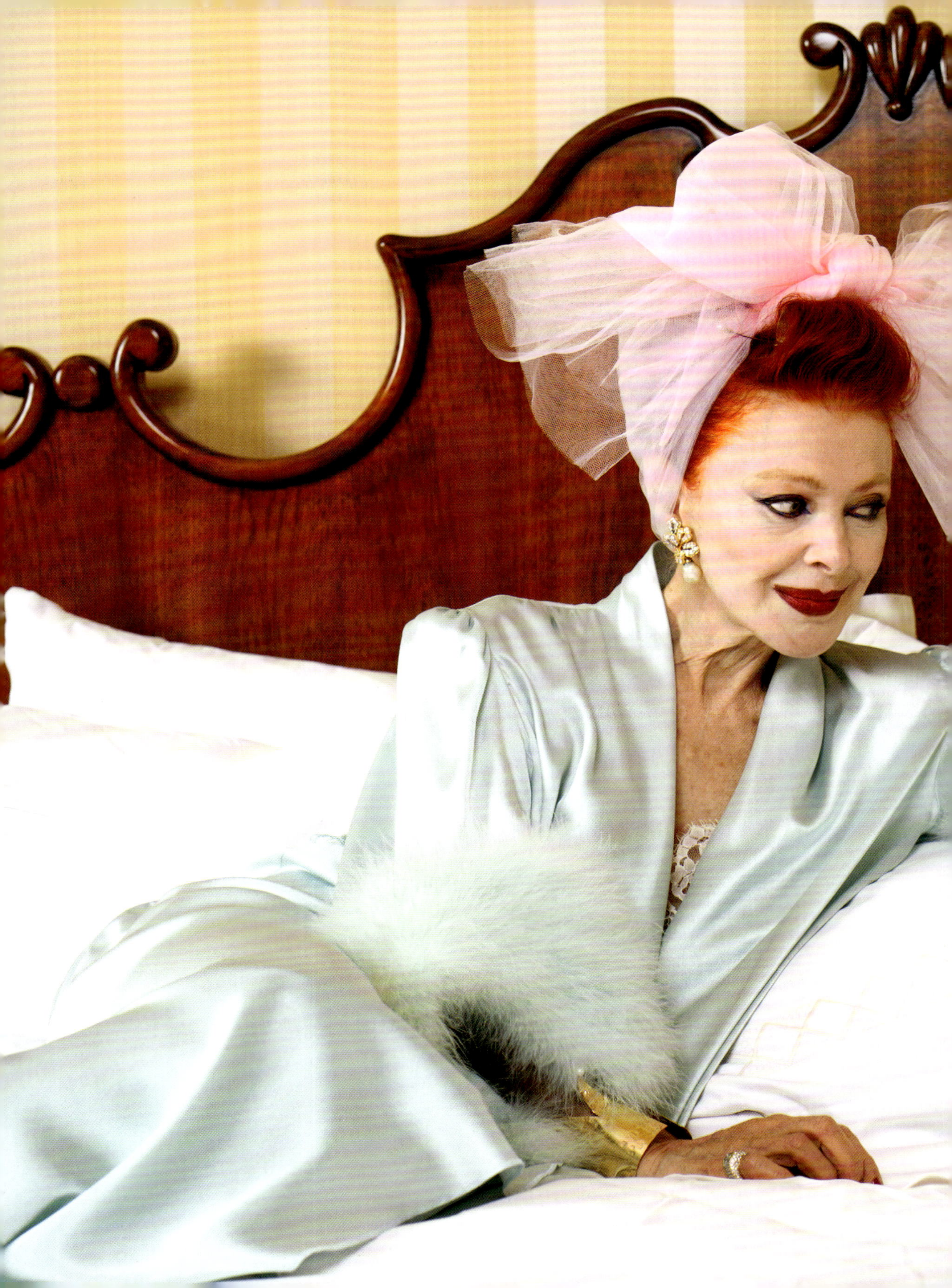

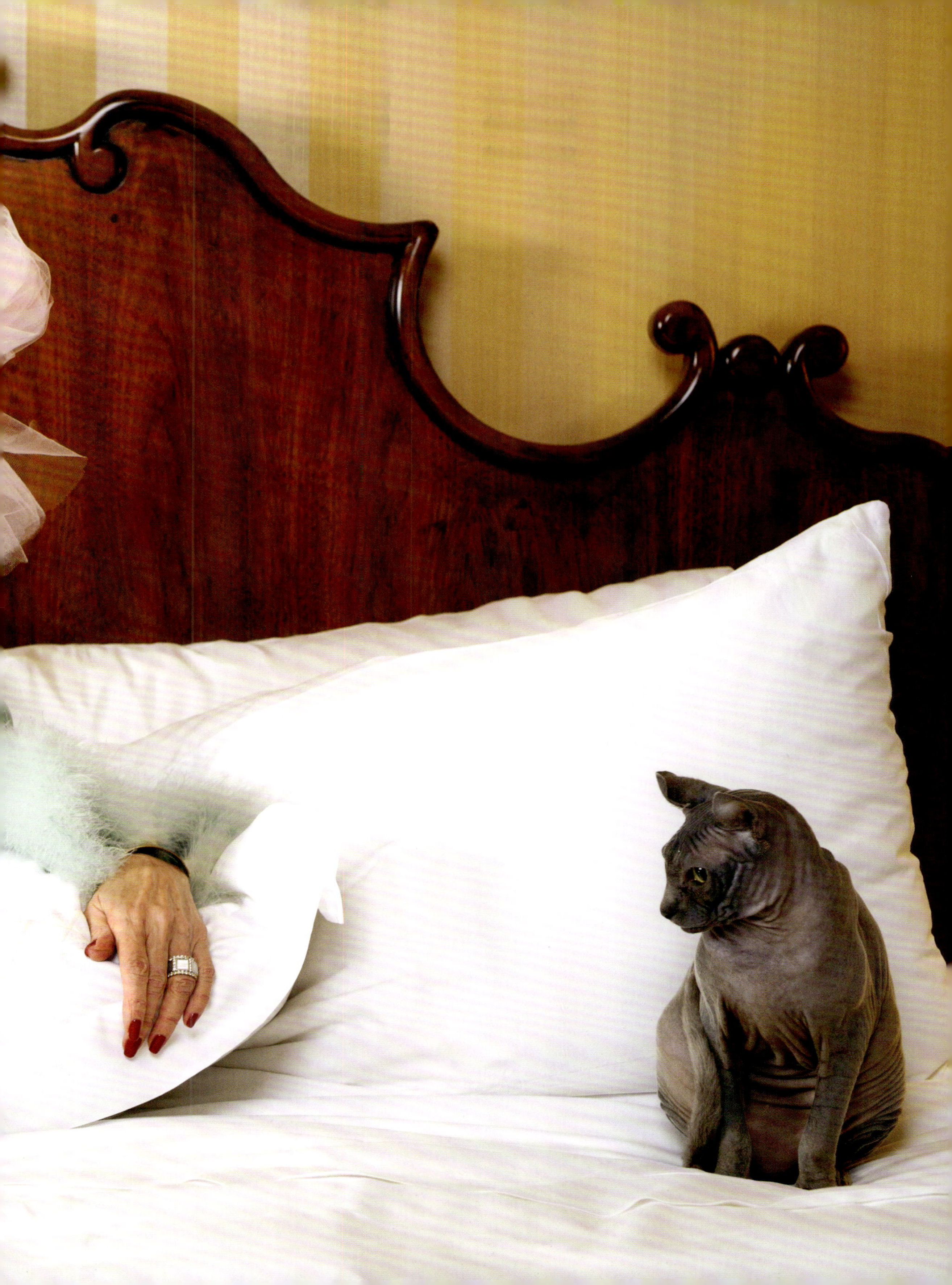

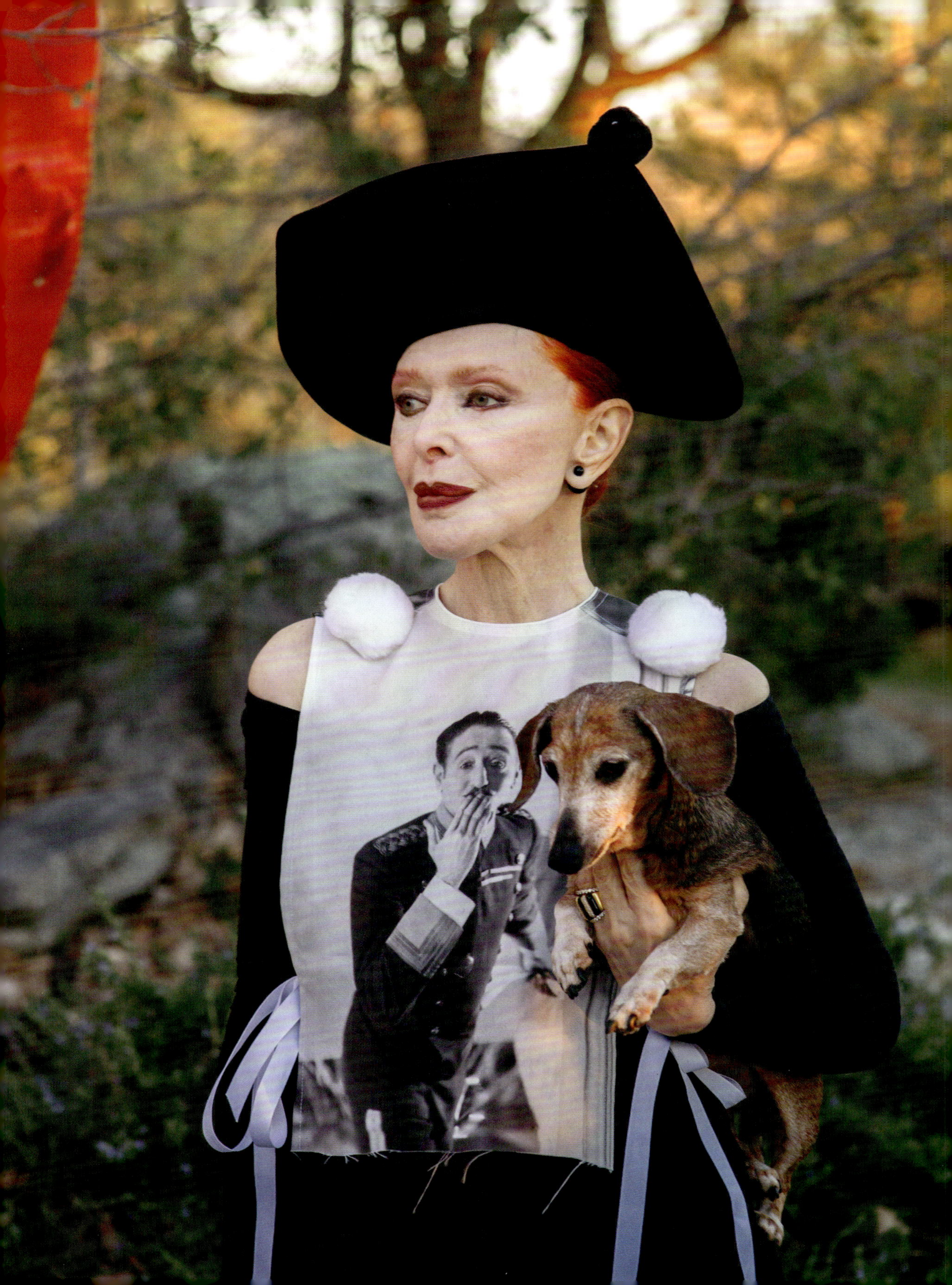

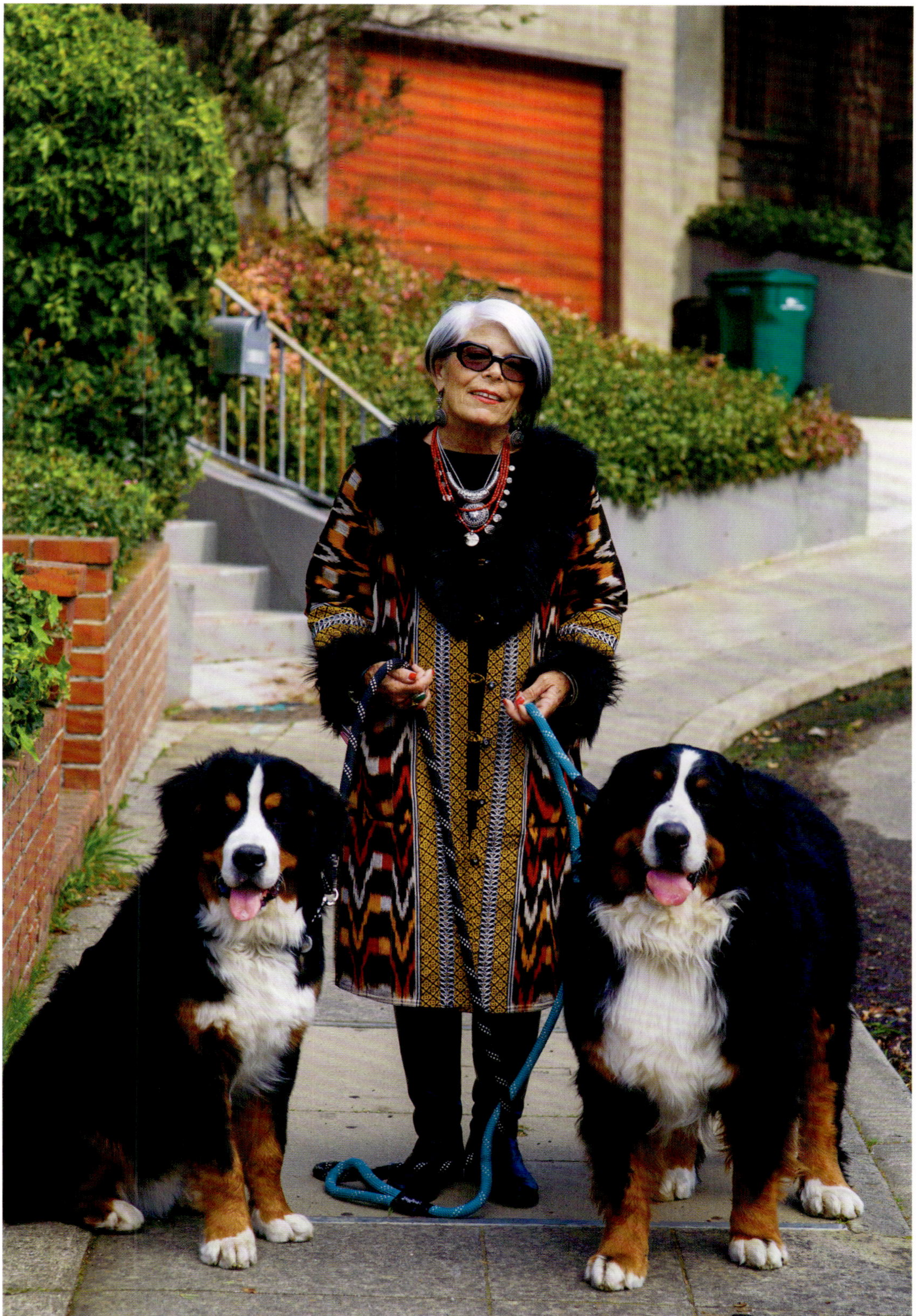

Brooks and Gracie

Gracie was scared to death when we first got her. She's a rescue and was left alone in a crate for days on end by her previous owners. It took us a long time to understand how to make her feel comfortable, but now she is about to turn three and we are very attached. I have a big birthday coming up and I don't want to leave her. I'll have to find a place to go where we can celebrate together. Gracie has become such a lover. She's just the sweetest. She follows us around 24-7 and we have to train her so she's not constantly licking one of our faces. I've had dogs my whole life. I live for them, but they live for us, too.

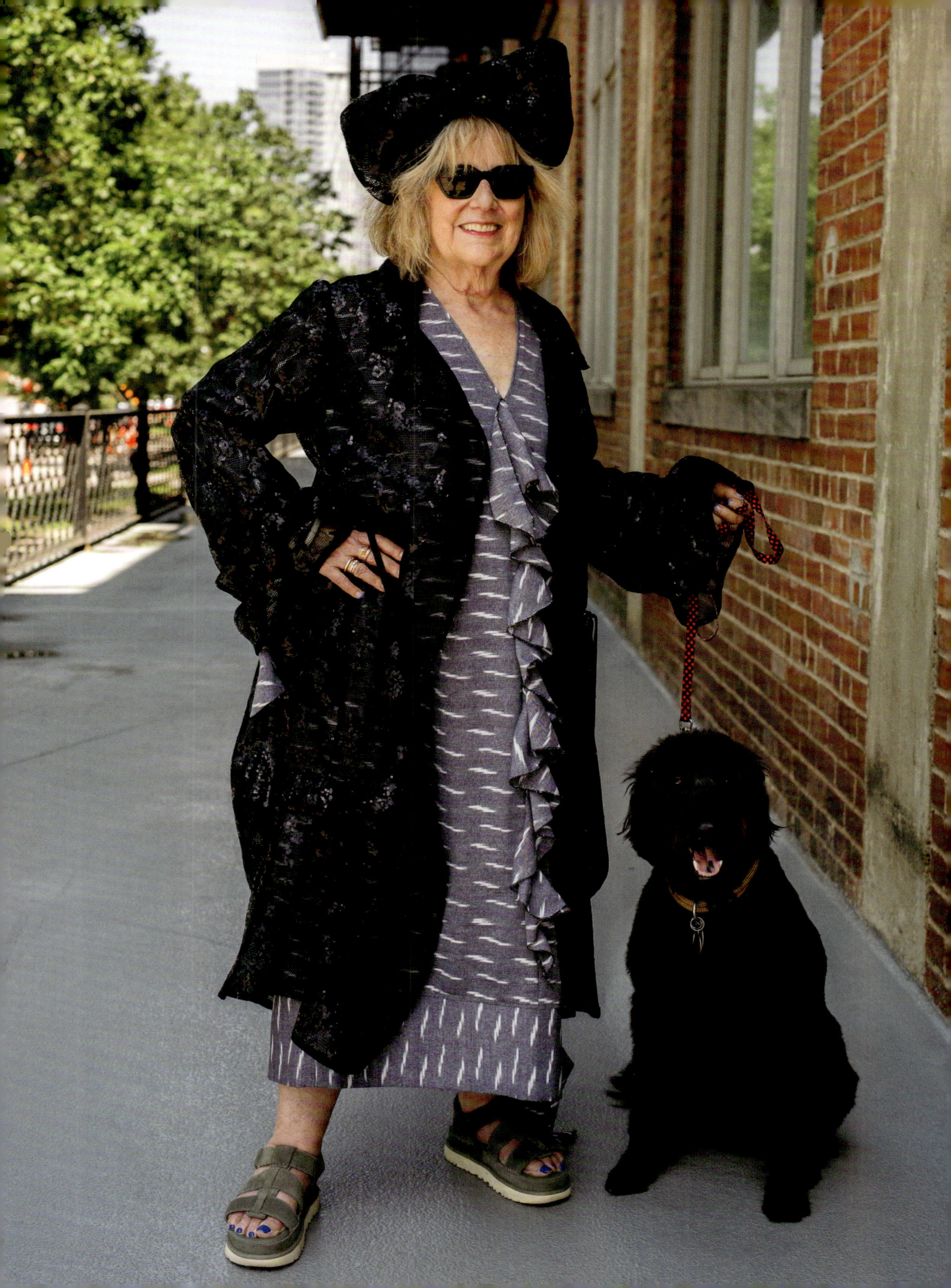

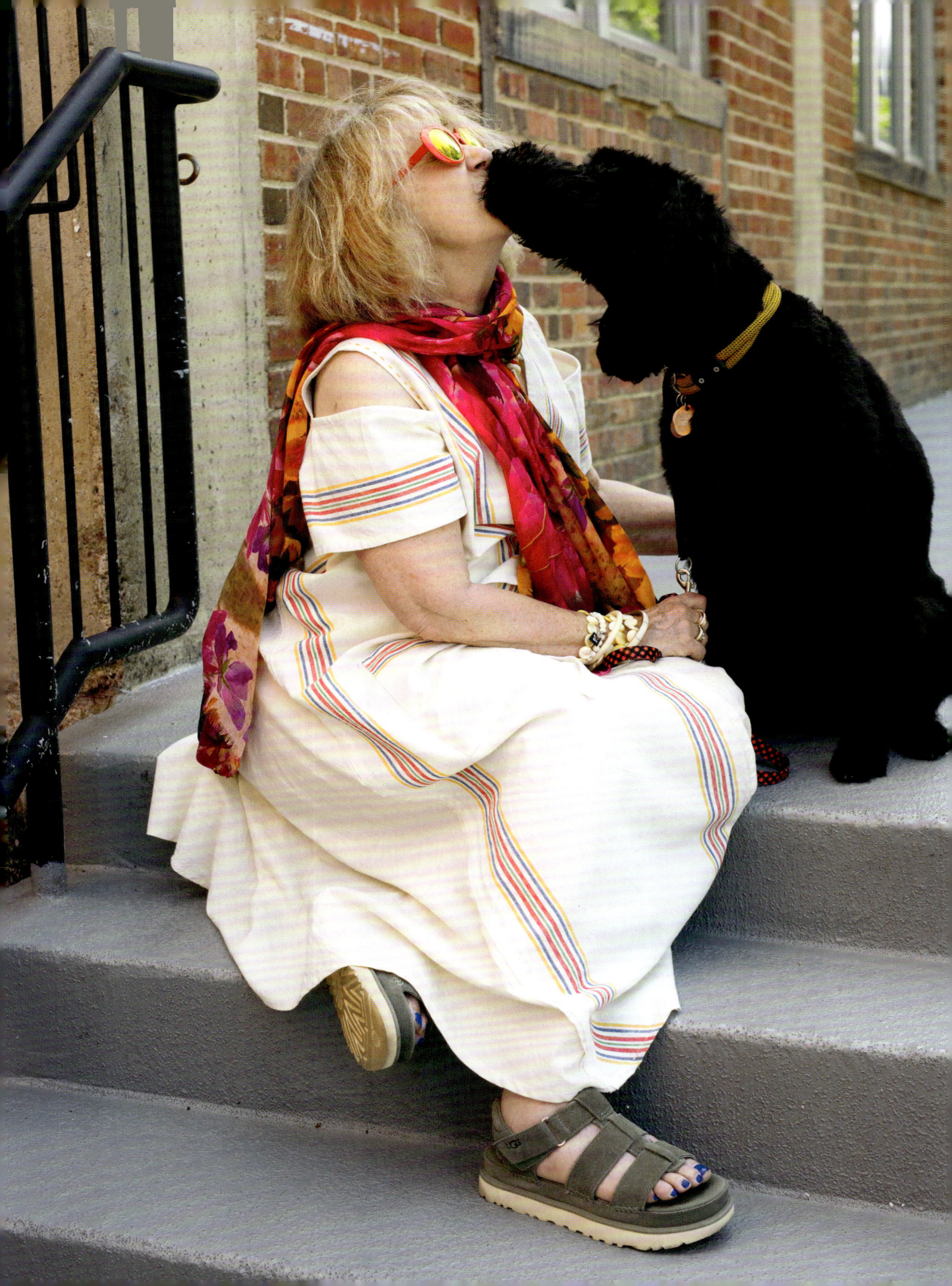

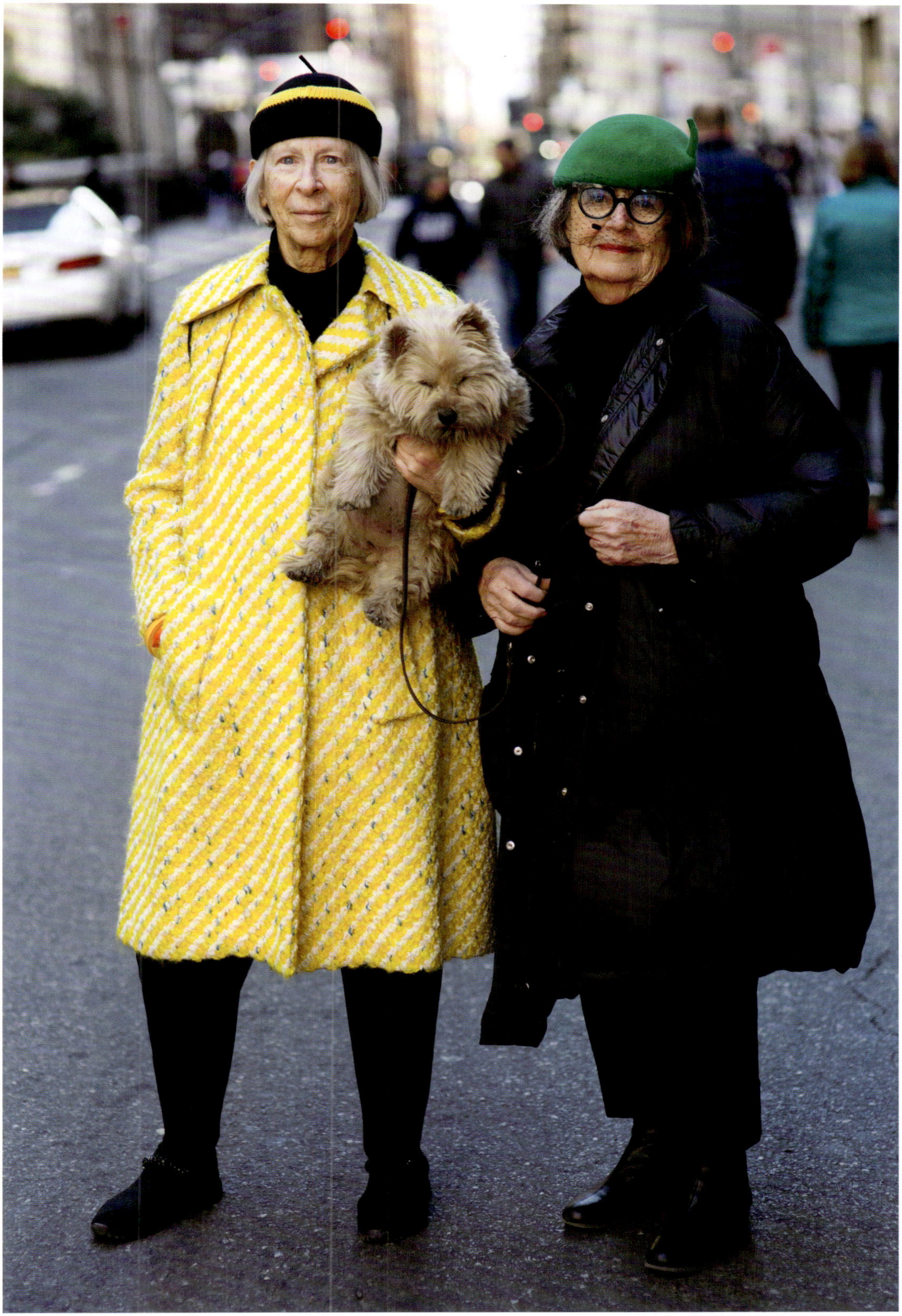

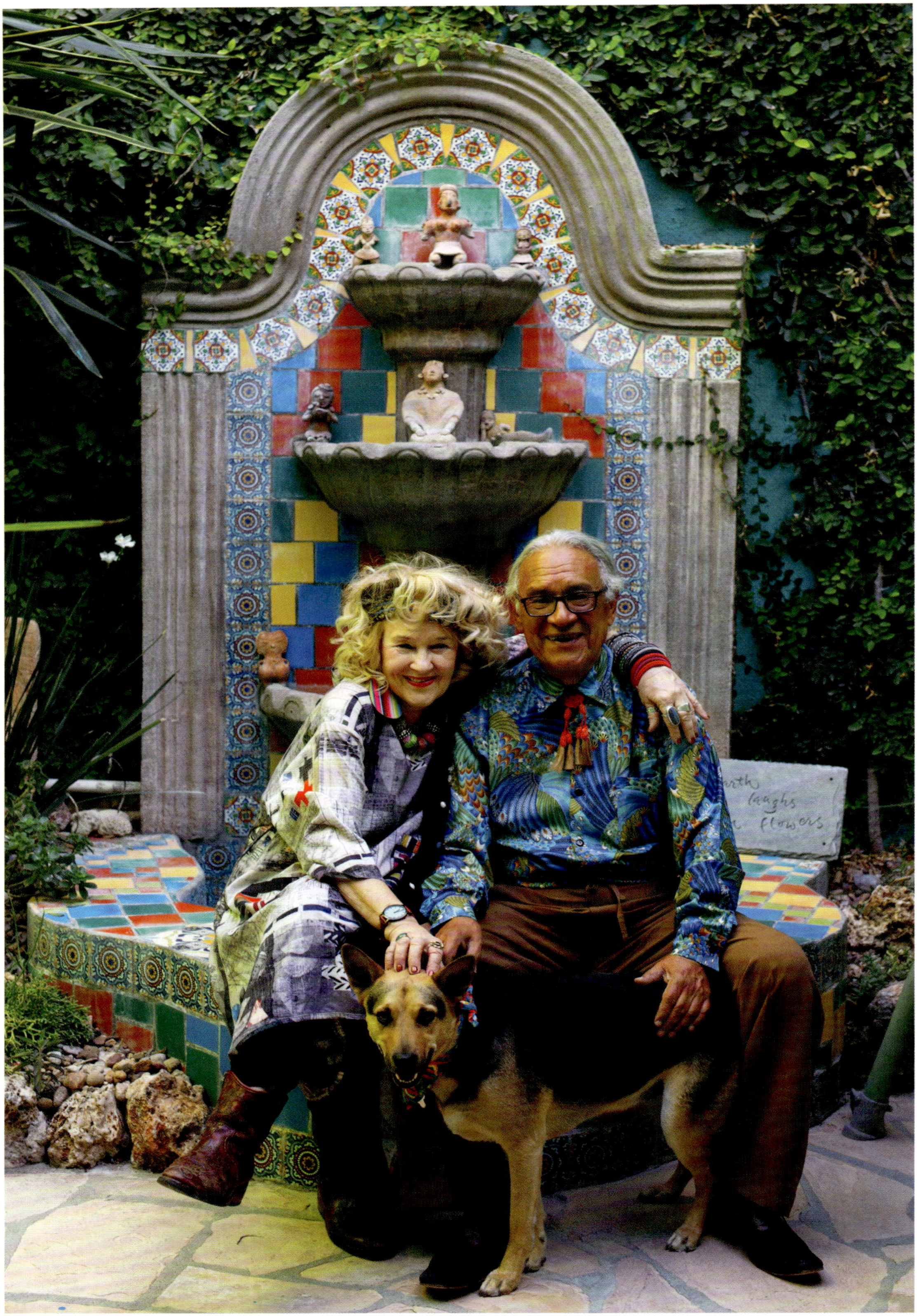
laughs
flowers

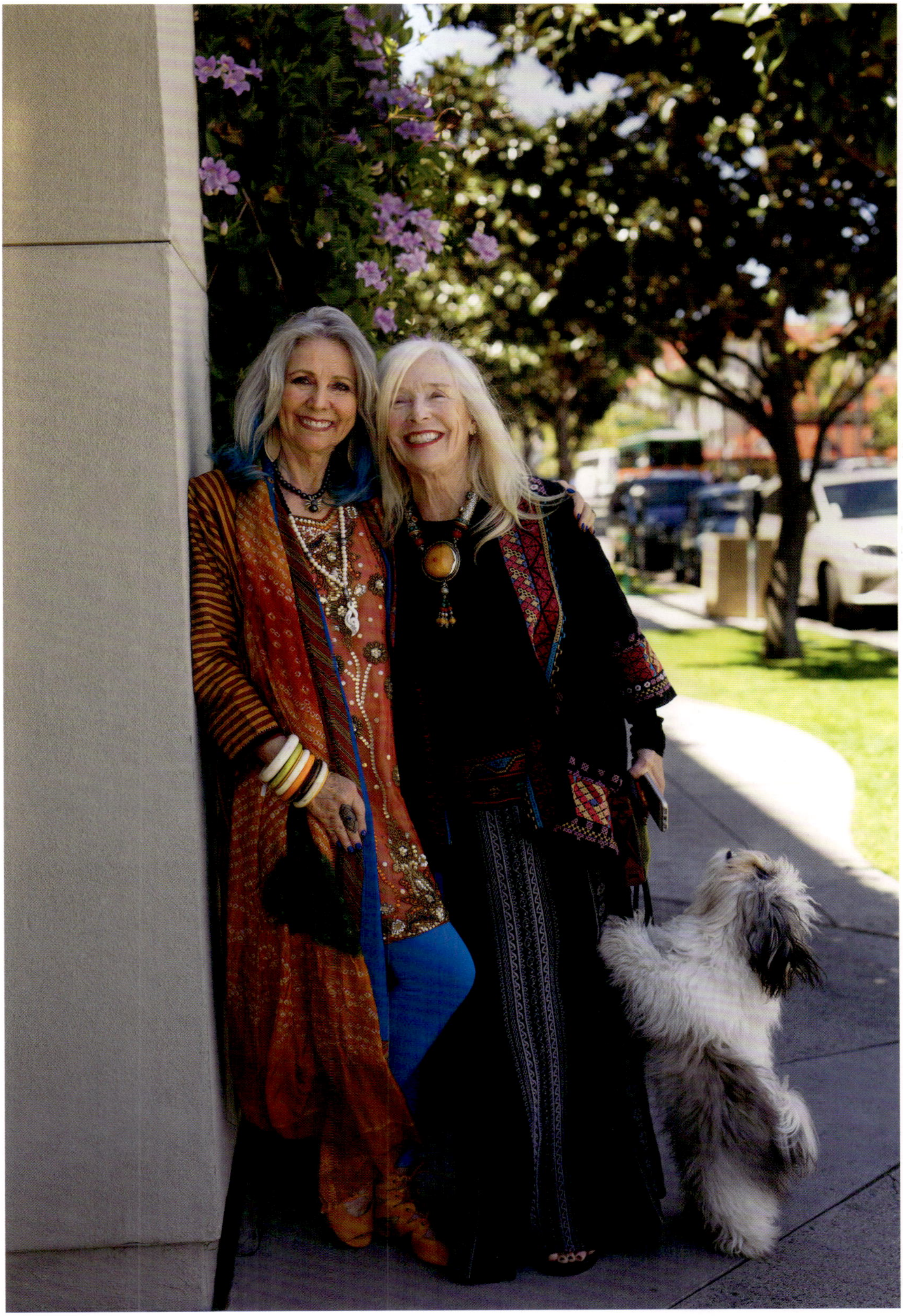

Nazare, Eduardo, and Jack

We lost our best friend Buddy who shared our lives, laughs, and love for fifteen years. Jack came into our lives to help heal my broken heart. He is always ready to follow us wherever we go. He works and plays with us and I can't imagine life without him.

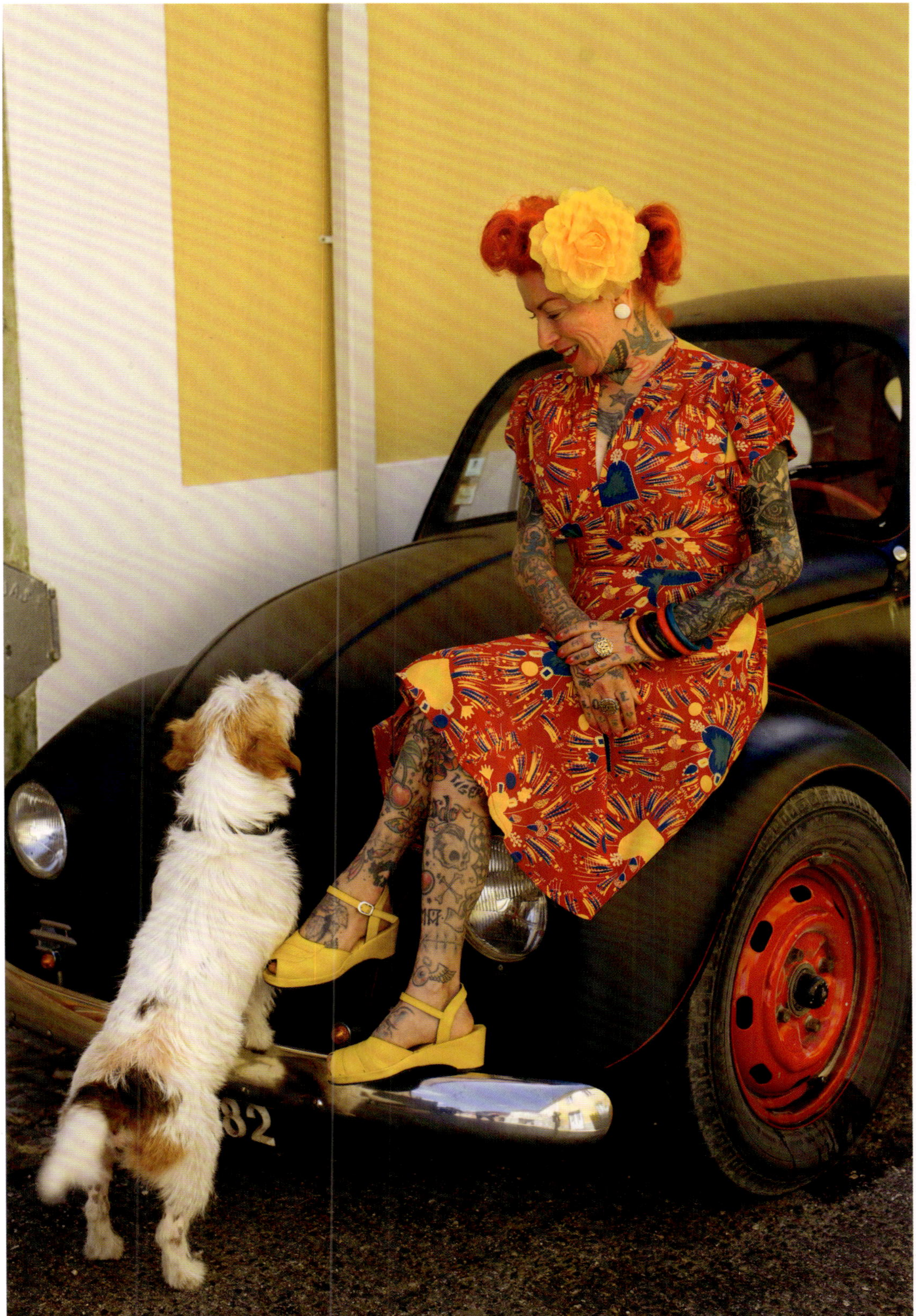

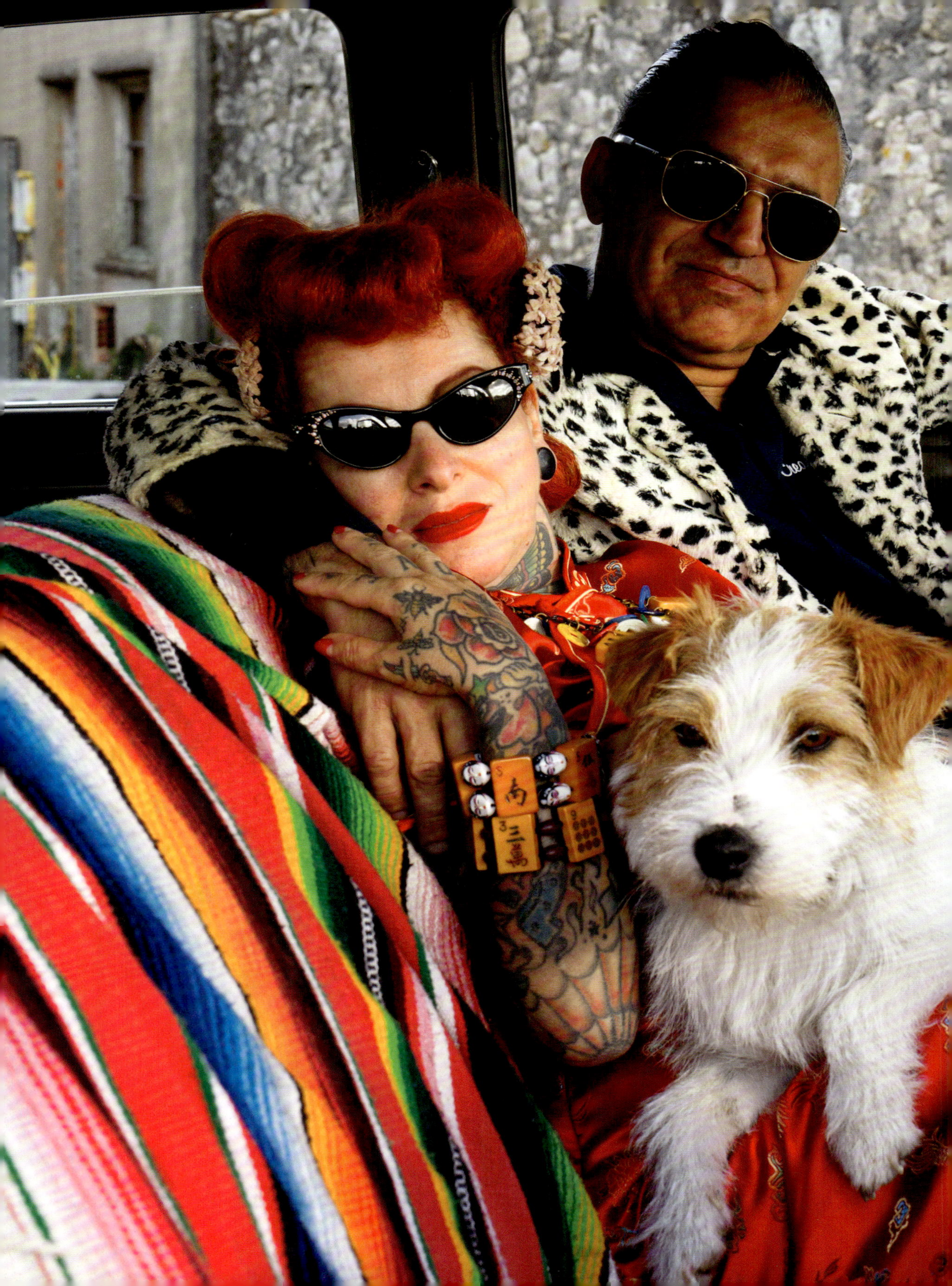

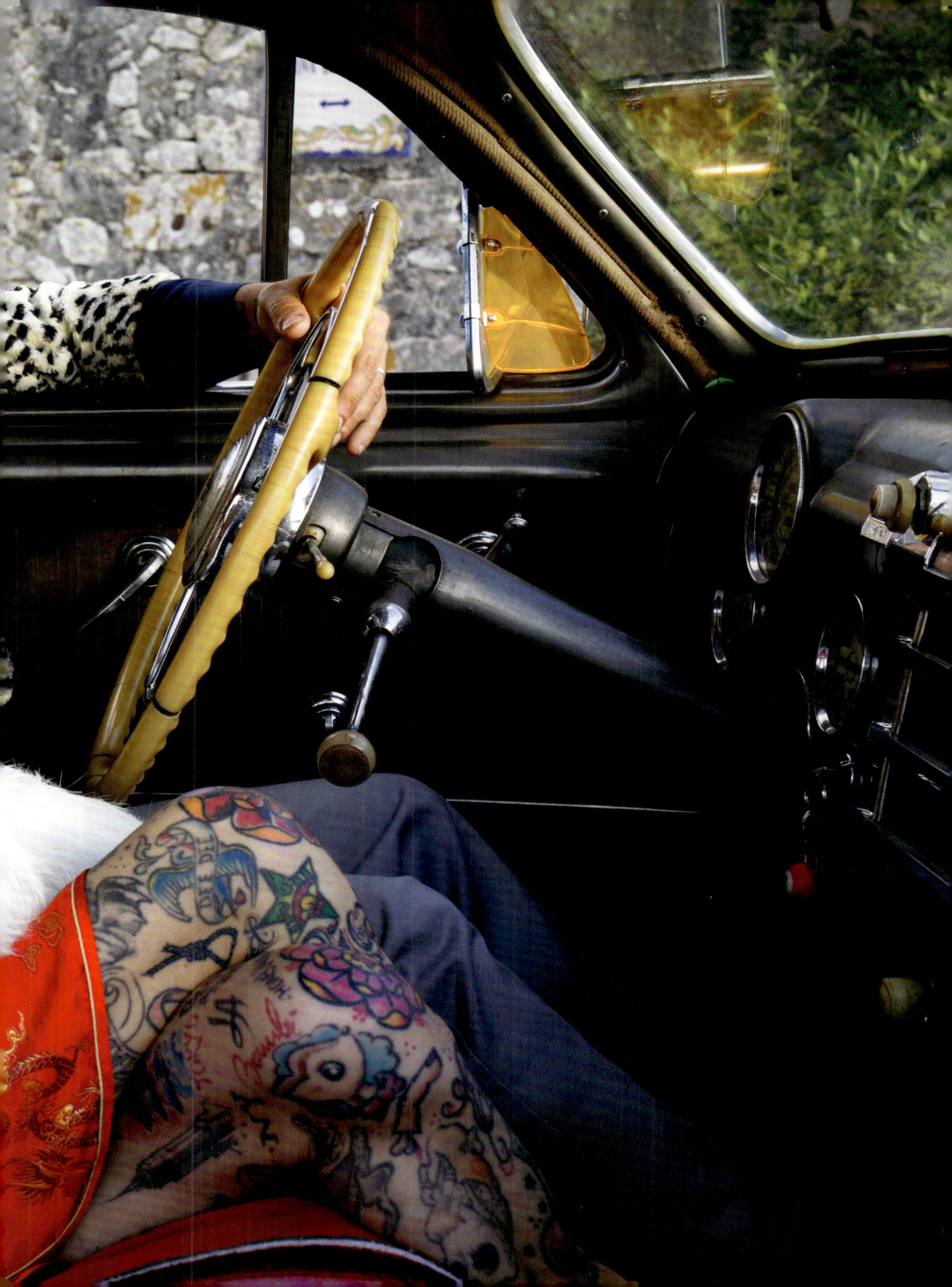

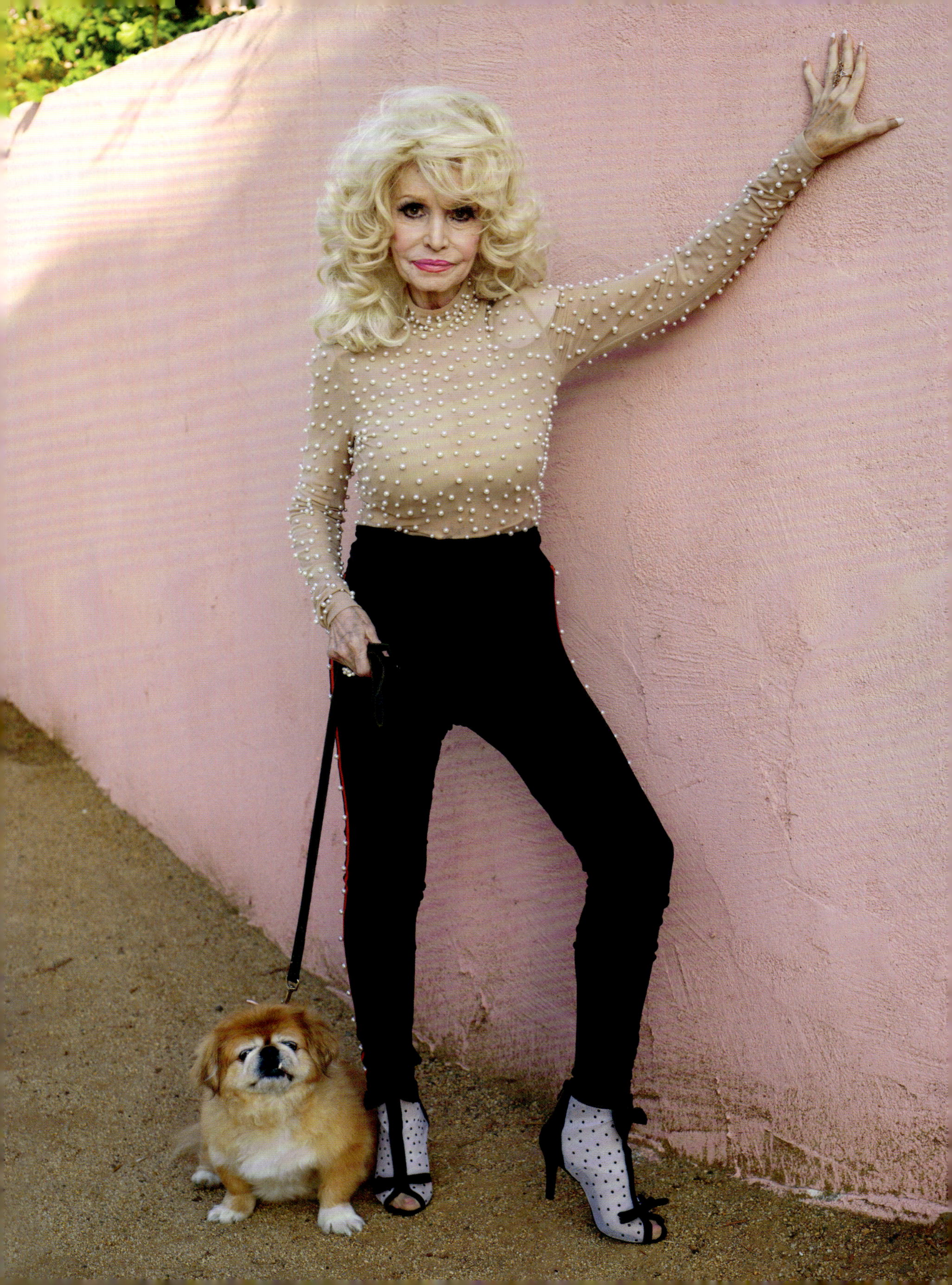

Linda and Jolene

What's not to love about Jolene? I think we are perfect together. I love glamour, and *she's* glamorous. She's just a little sweetie pie and she's got a stubborn streak too, just like me. We are old girls together.

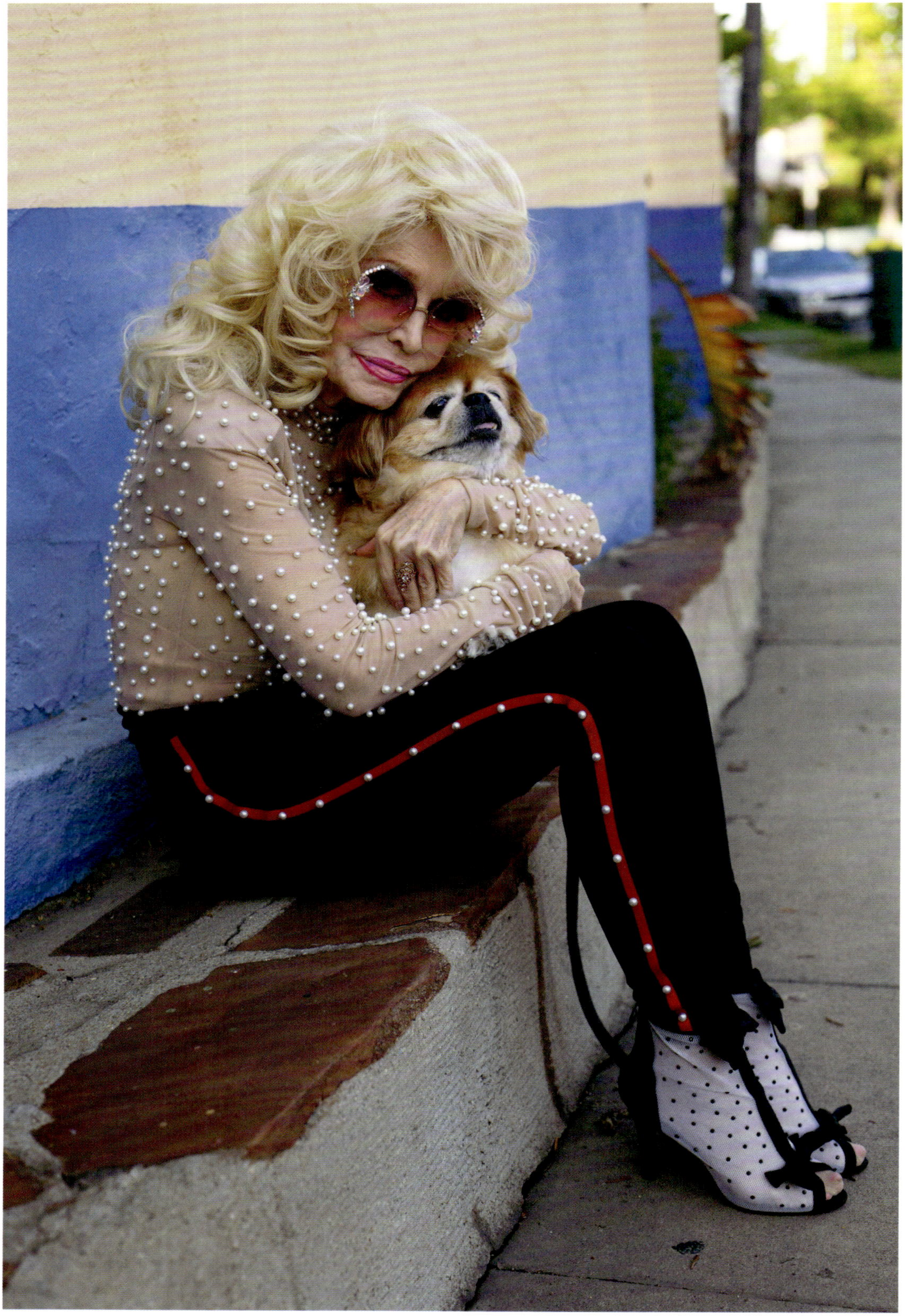

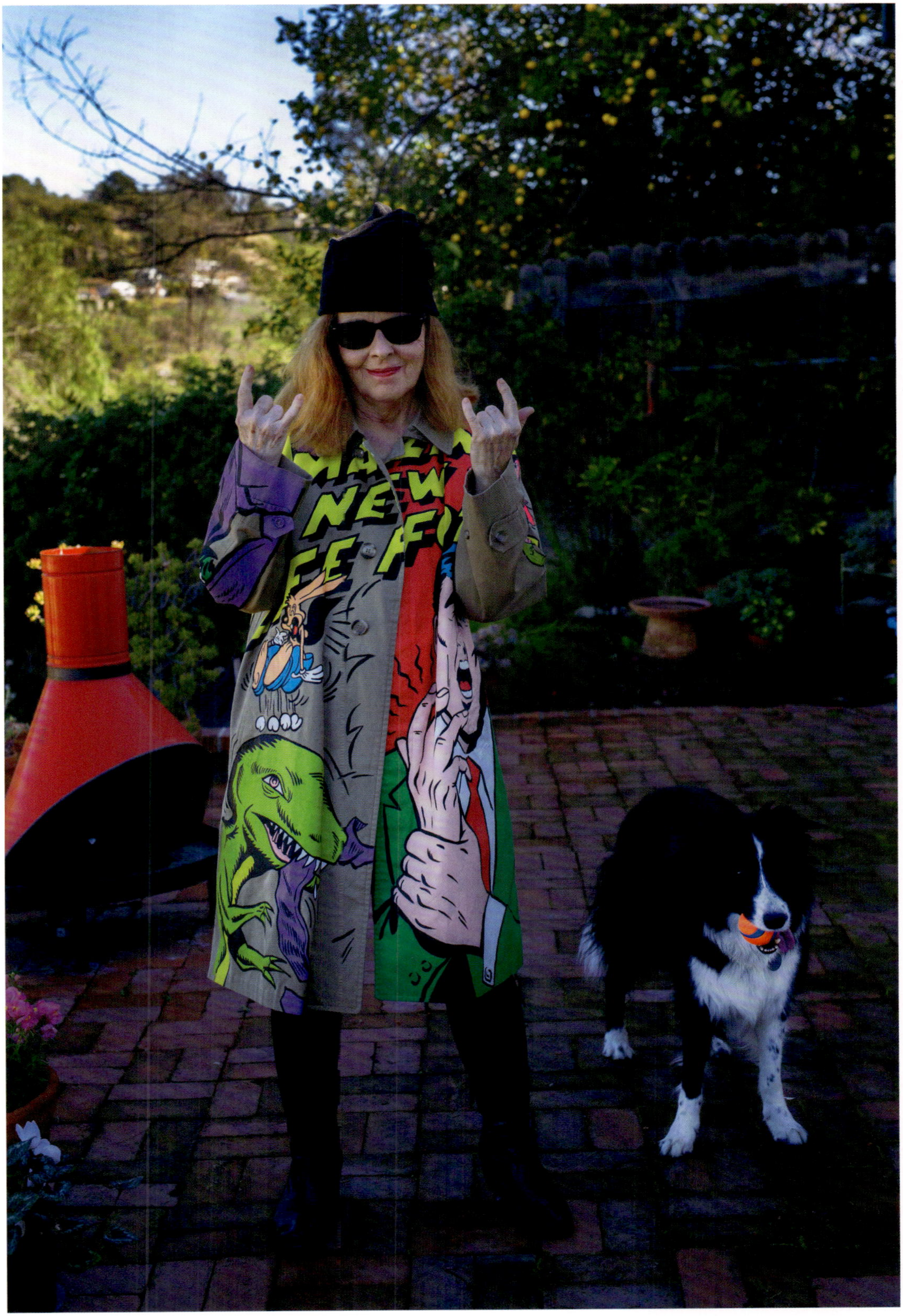
NEW

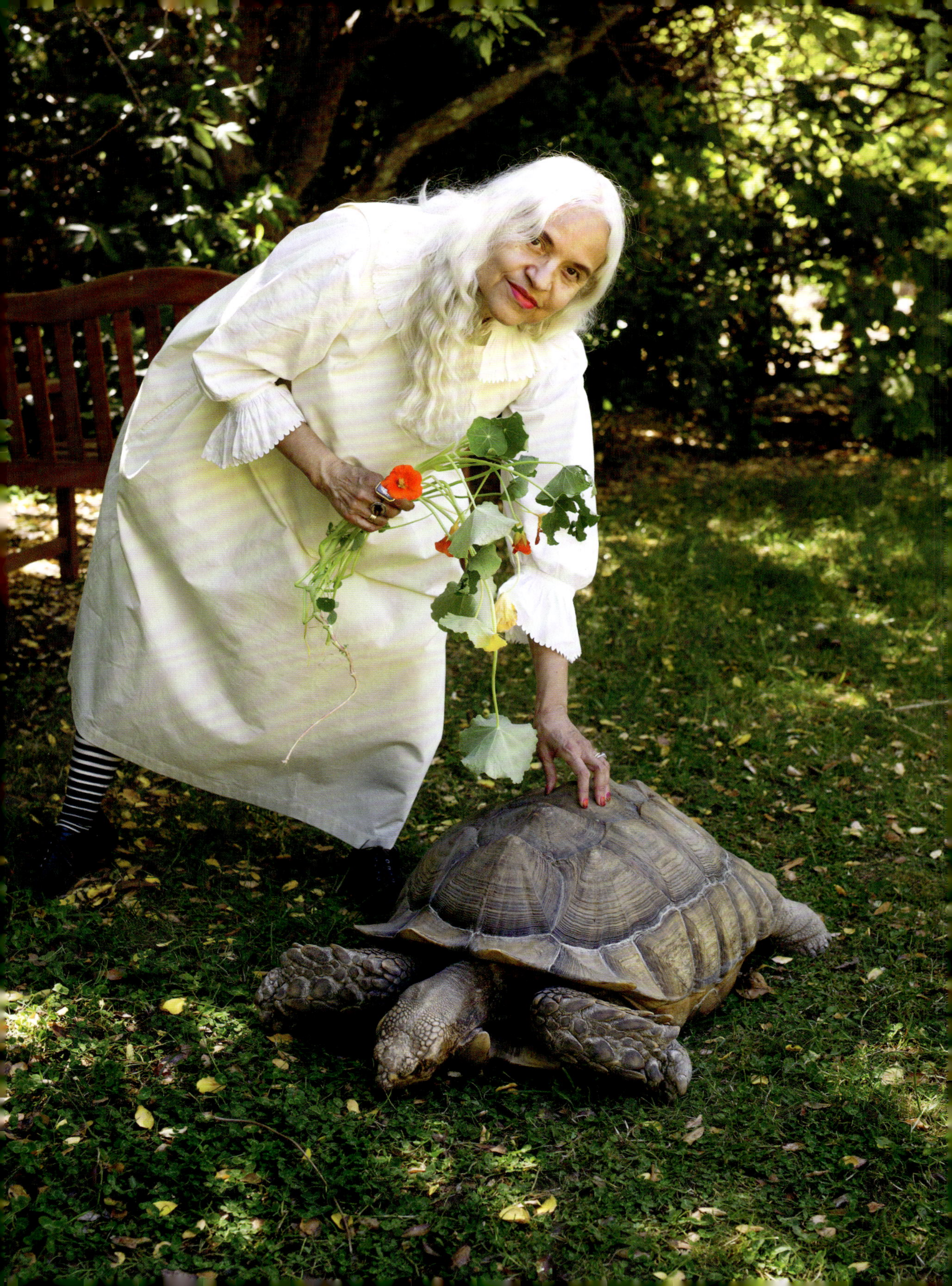

Lauren and Kitty

I adopted Kitty at a pet store as a first wedding anniversary gift for my husband! I wanted to give him something that represented longevity. Needless to say, he was quite surprised. We think Kitty is somewhere between thirty to forty years old. There is something old and soulful about him but he can also be mischievous. He can move furniture around and get tangled in flowering vines in an artful way. He is a vegetarian and would never hurt anyone. Everyone is drawn to him including other creatures—butterflies sit on him, cats visit him, and children love him.

Rory and Elsa

Elsa is my soul mate. She means everything to me. I knew she was coming into my life for years. I always said, "One day I'll have a little black poodle and she will be my heart." She is kind and wise and funny and we are inseparable. I take her everywhere and feel incomplete when we are not together. She is my life. She is me and I am her.

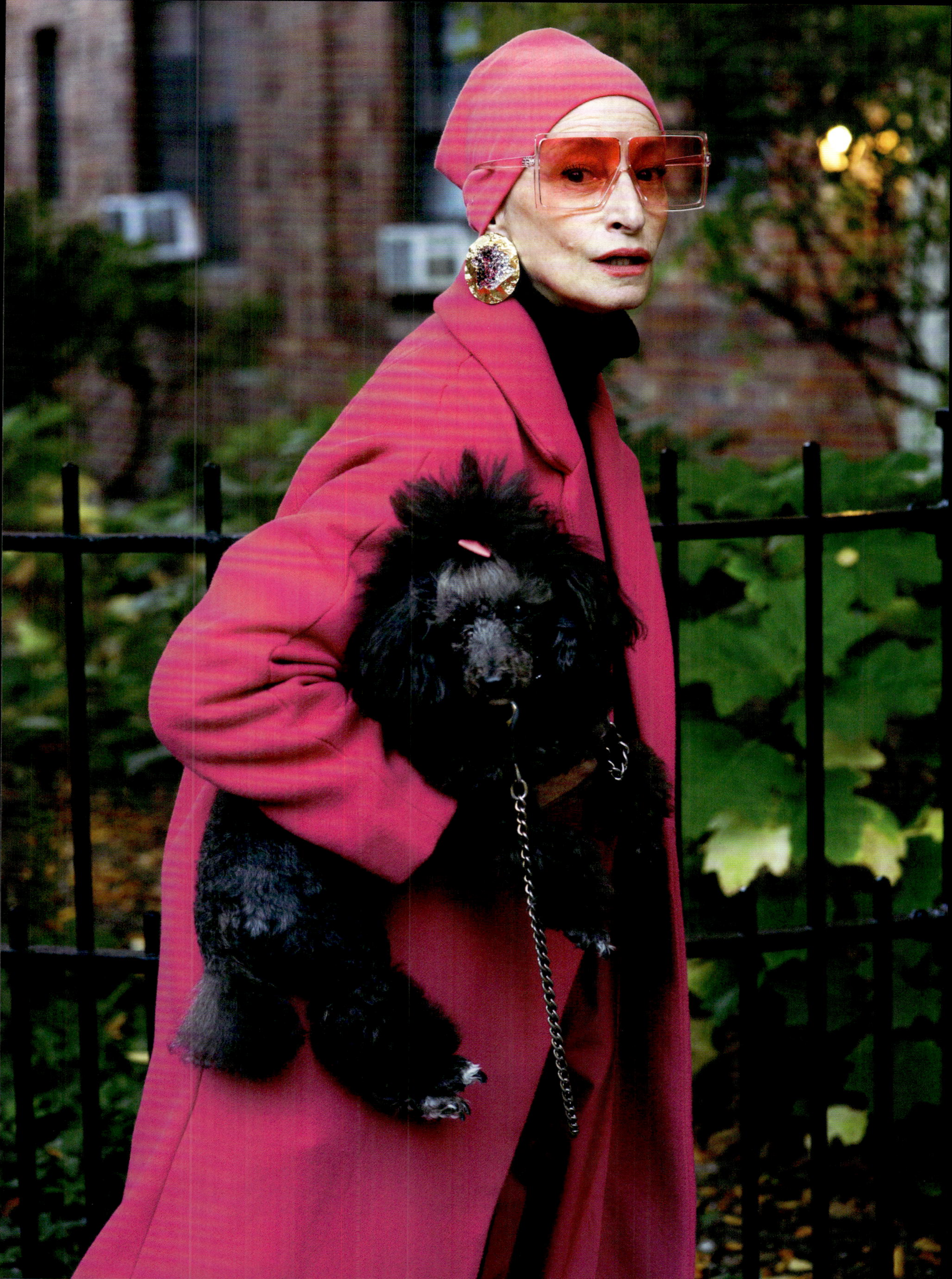

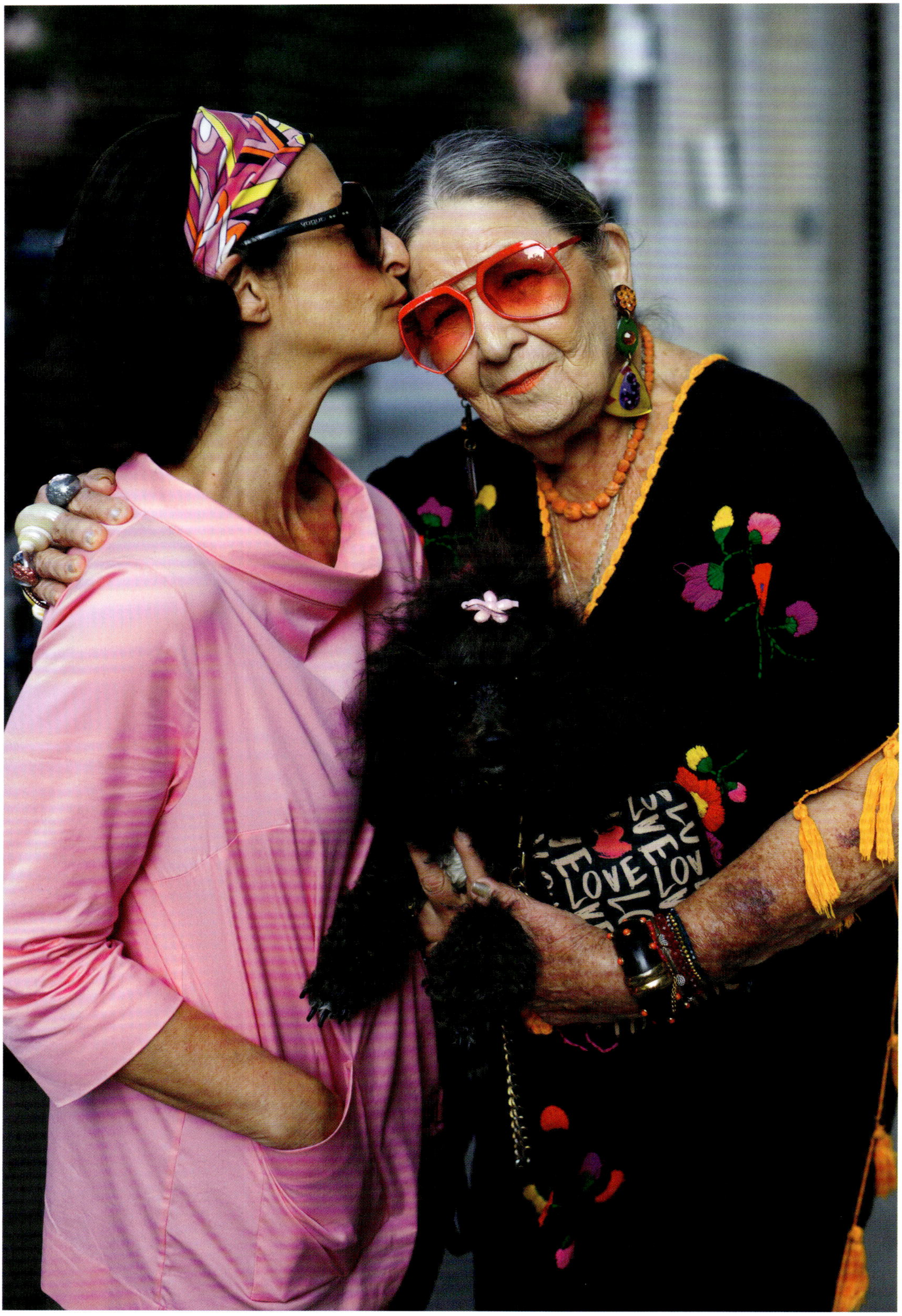
LOVE

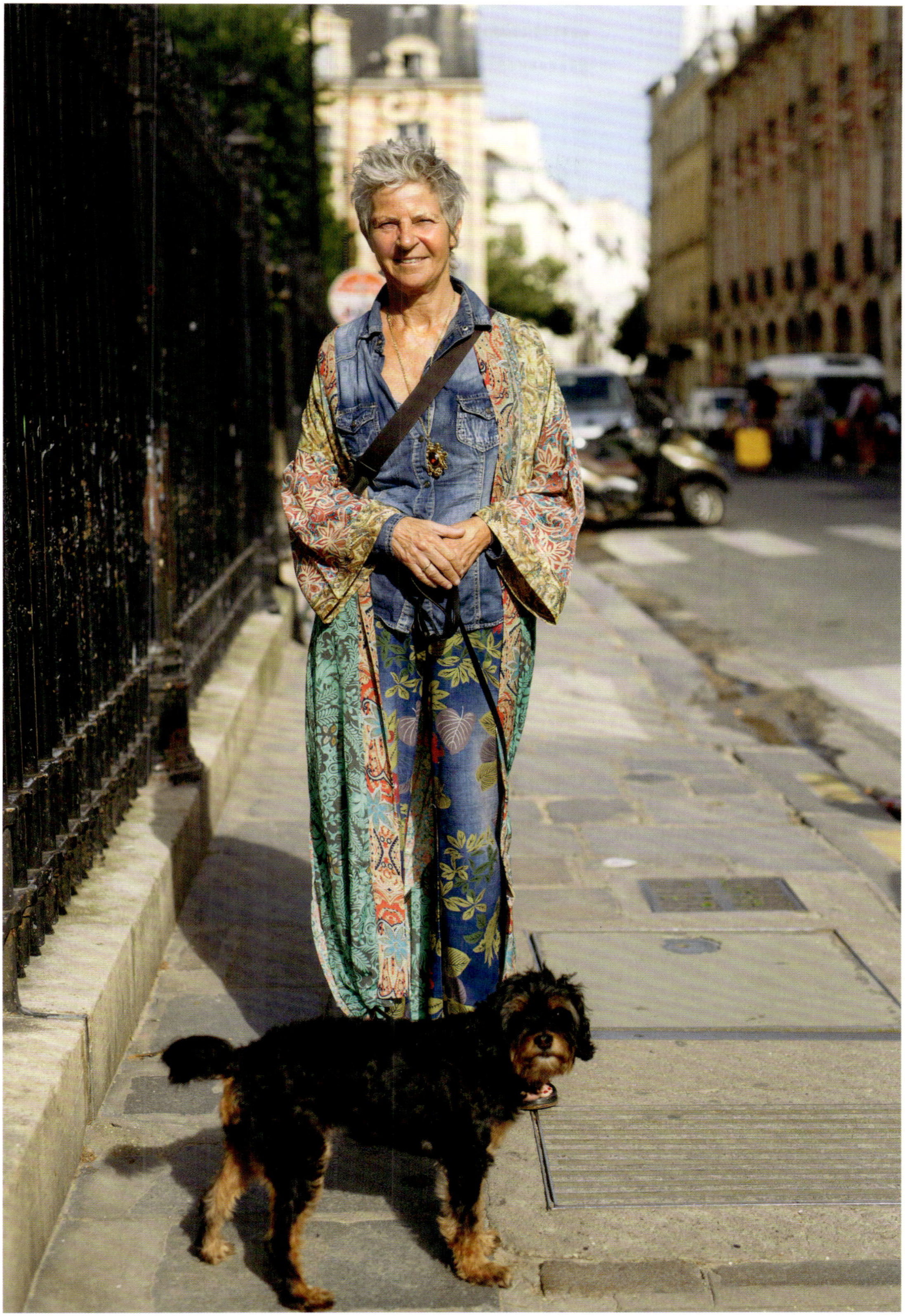

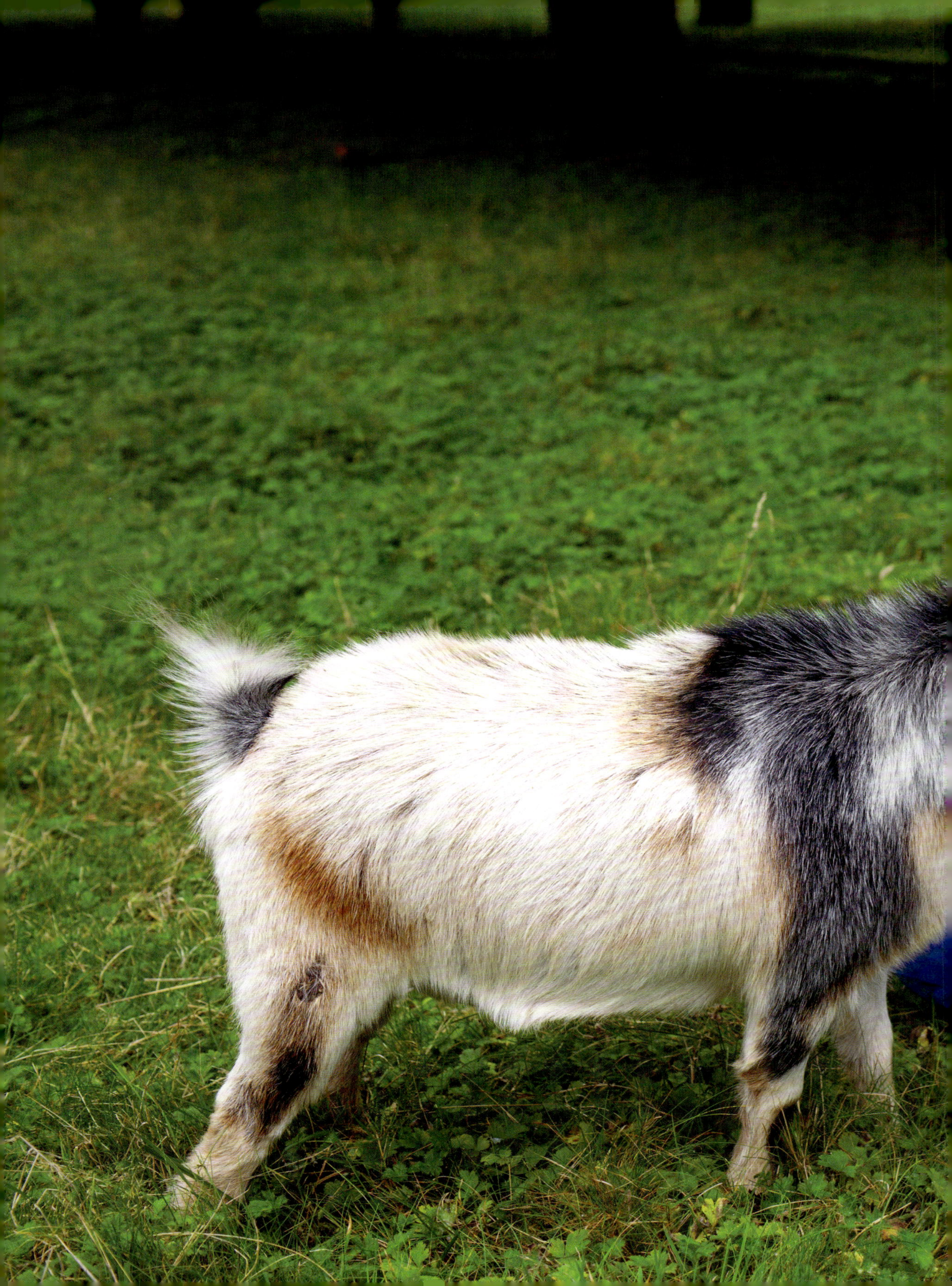

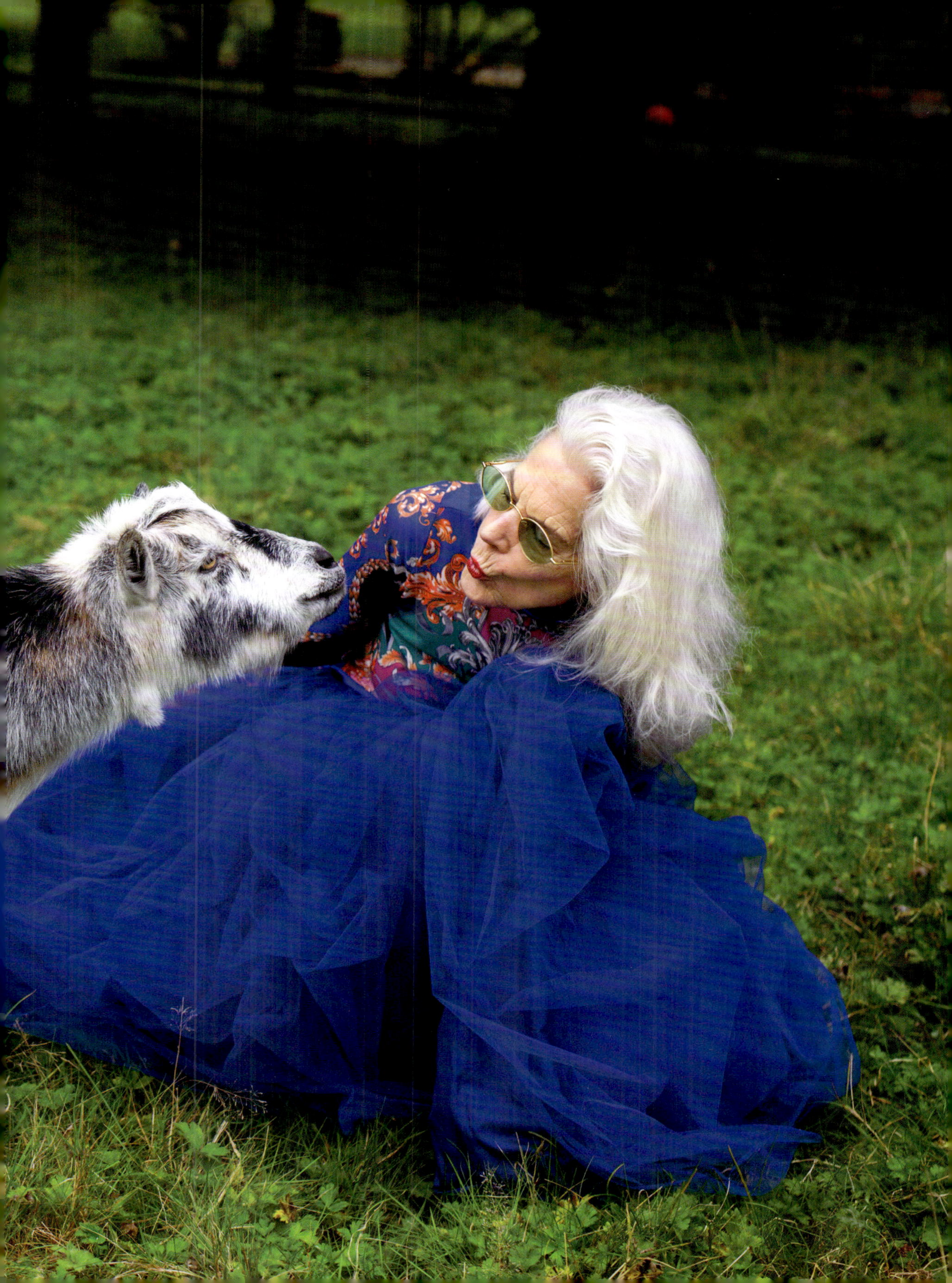

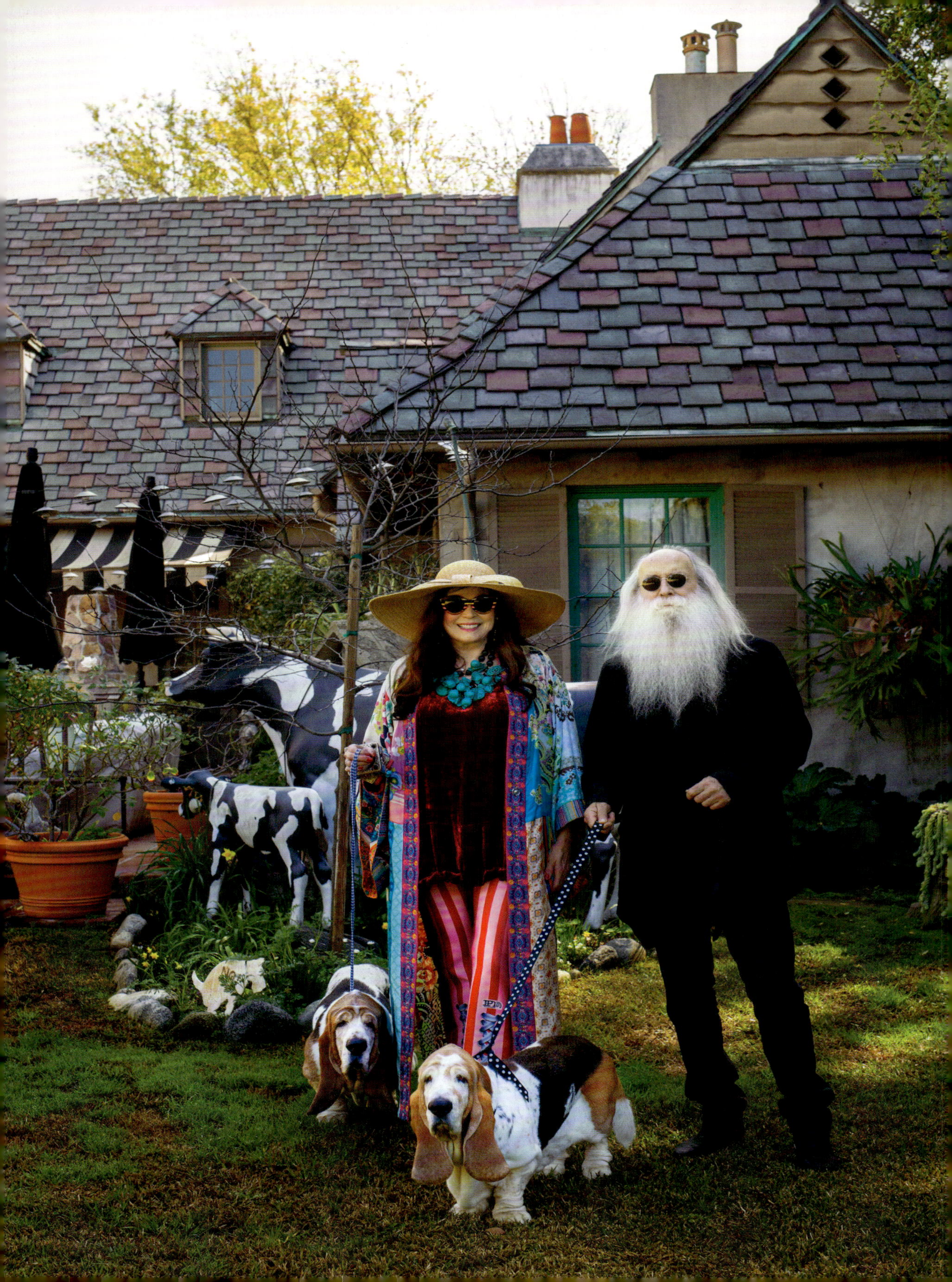

Maureen, Leland, Chumley, and Mr. Peabody

I call them my boyfriends, but they are really my best friends. My deepest love is for them and my husband. They make me smile daily with their sweetness and quirkiness. Mr. Peabody can't go out of the house without carrying one of his many toys. Sometimes he manages to get two or three in his rather large mouth! Bassets were originally bred as scent and hunting hounds, but the only things these guys are hunting are treats and toys. They have over 40,000 fans on Facebook!

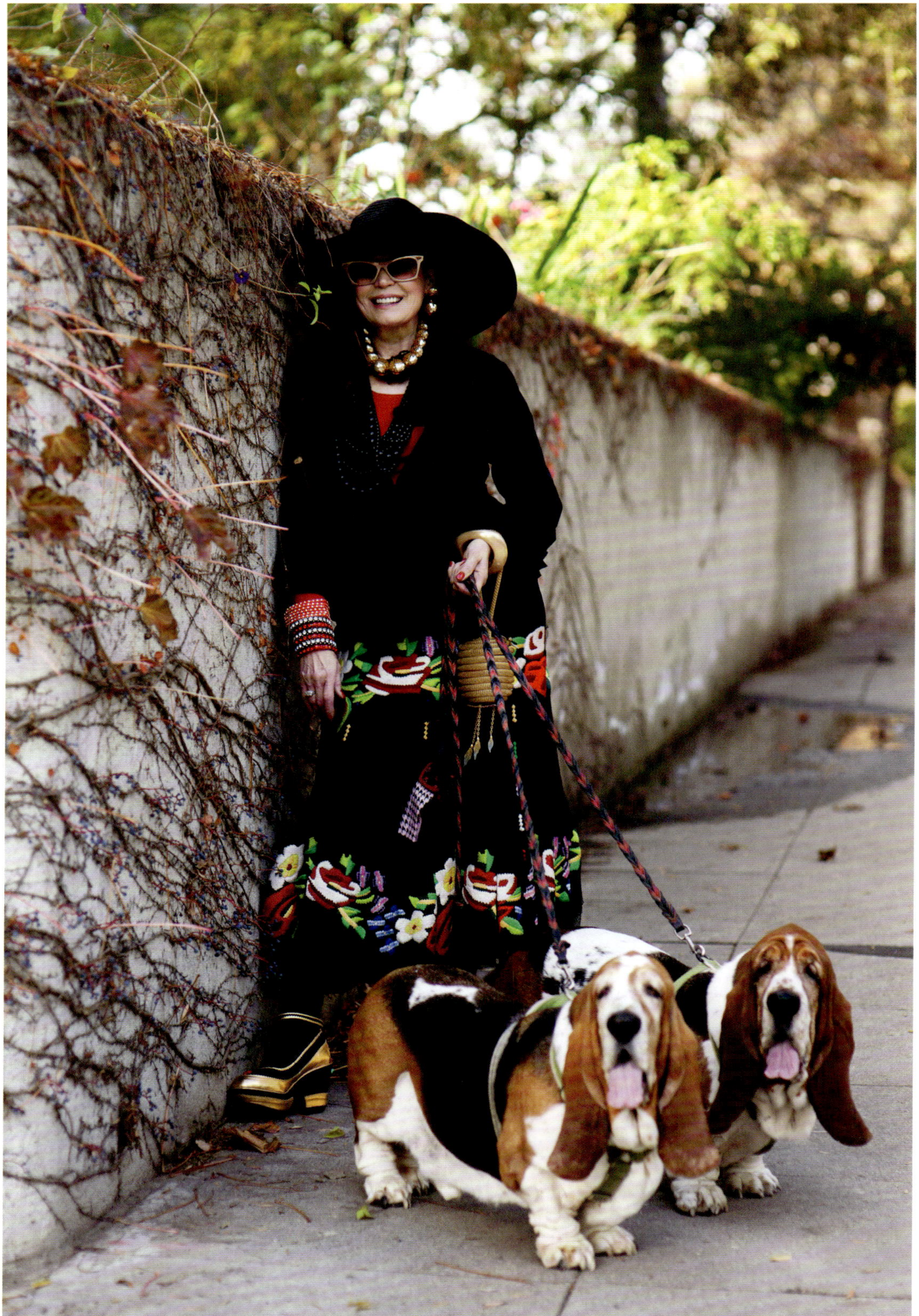

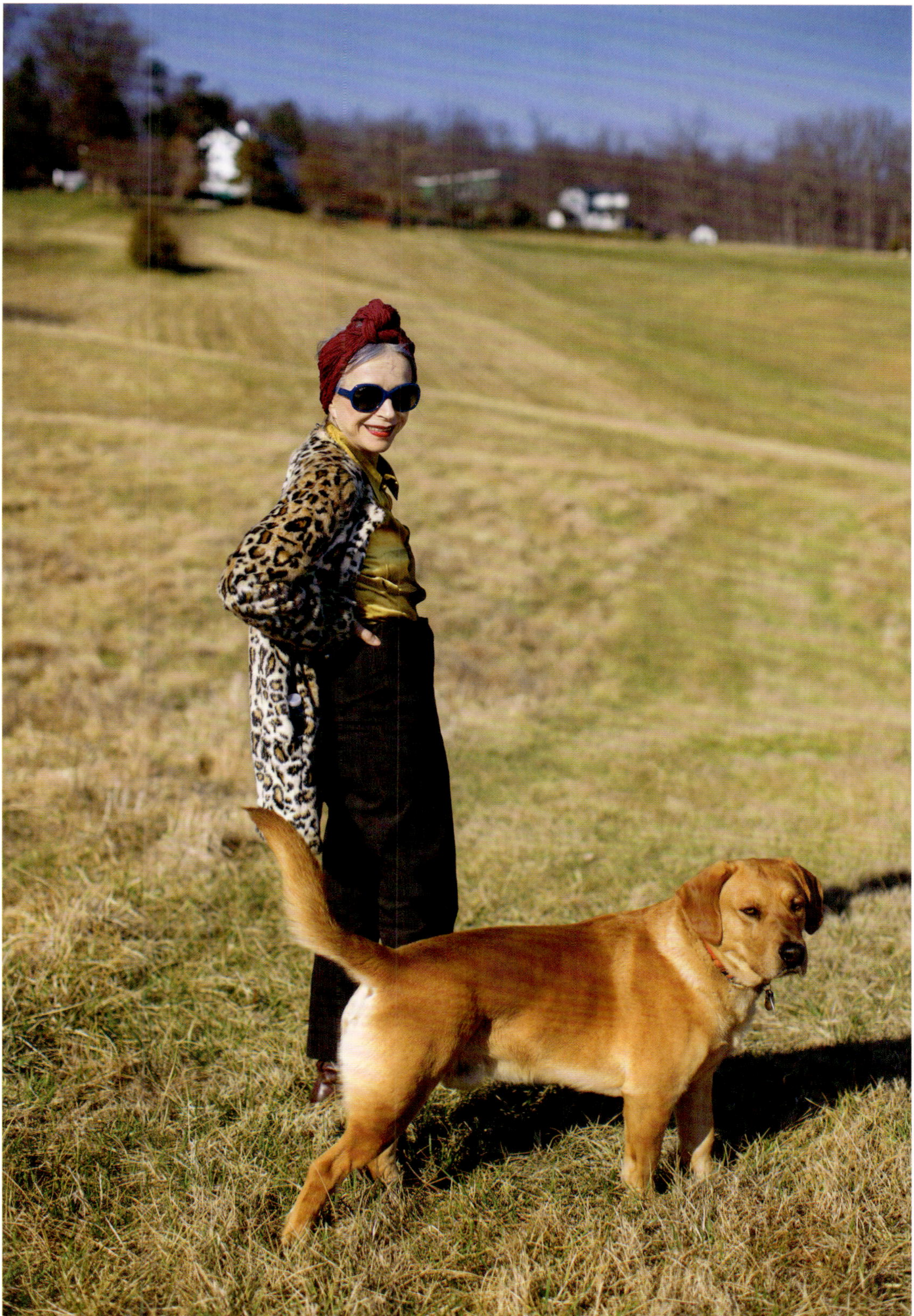

Linda and Lil Buddy

After our old kitty passed at nineteen years old, I promised my husband that we would have no more kitties. It was just too hard. Then, one cold November night, we began to hear this horrible crying coming from underneath the porch. It took us a few days of searching before an orange streak came running out and passed me, only to hide again. I started luring him out with goat's milk every day. After several weeks, he finally came up onto the porch. One magical day I got on my hands and knees and this lovely spirit reached out his little paw and touched my hand. It was so, so sweet. It was electric. I think it was probably the first time he had ever had a connection like that.

Our Little Buddy is a survivor—he must have gone through so much. He's been taking care of us for nine years now. We don't know how he found us or how he knew we needed him. We have never had a little soul come into our lives like that. I have connected to cats ever since I was a little girl, but Little Buddy is our special golden treasure. He's my little kitty muse.

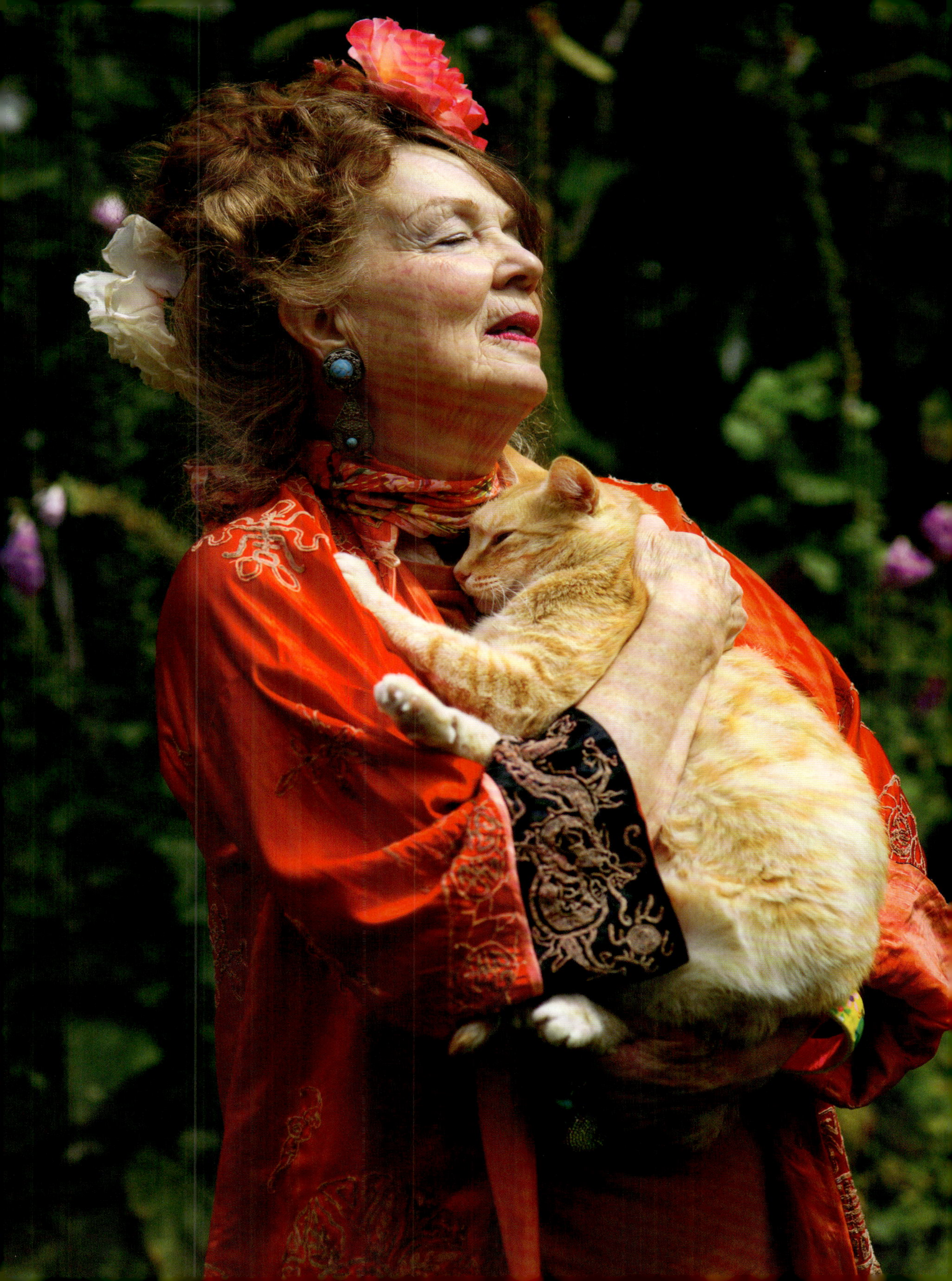

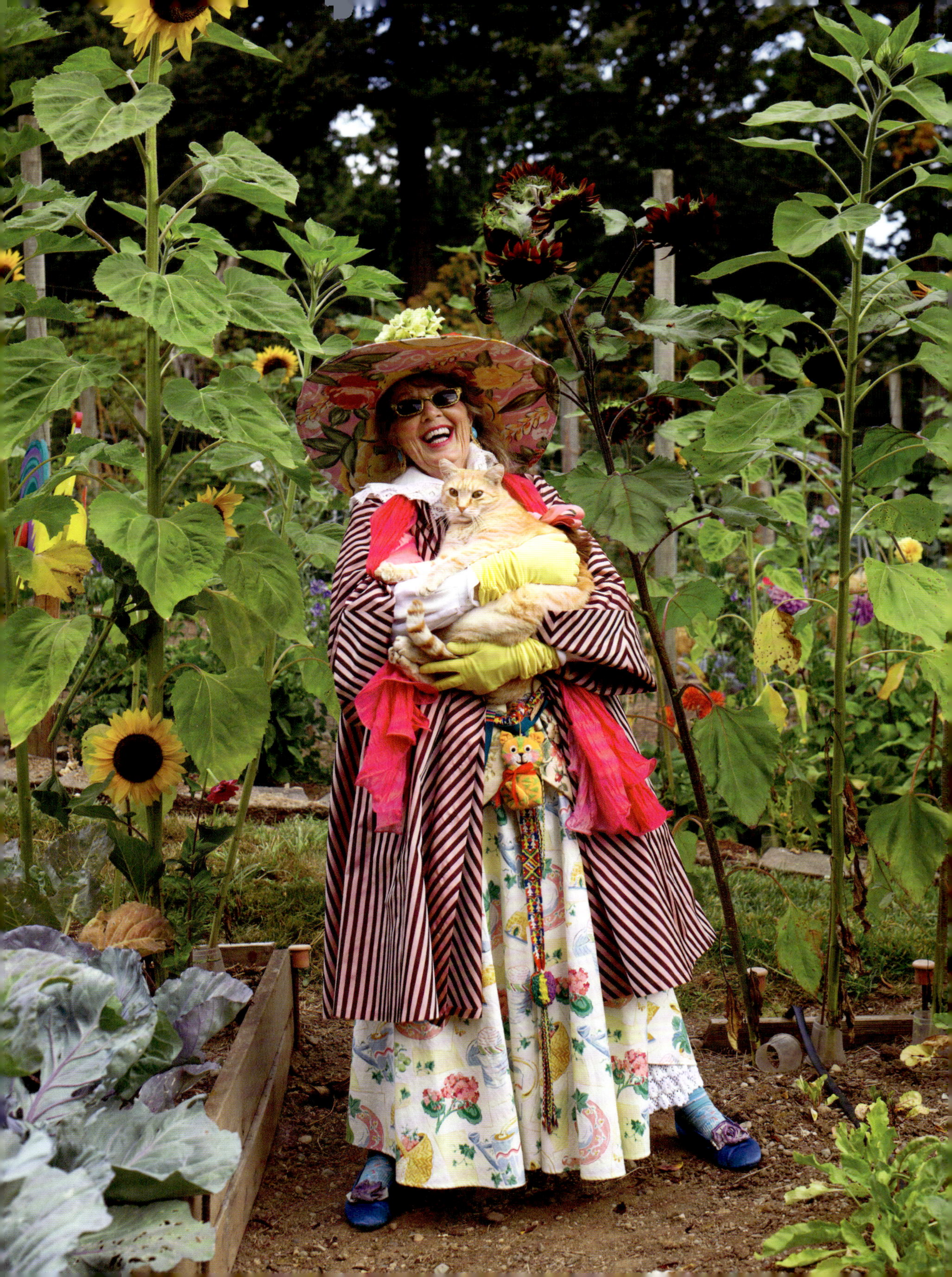

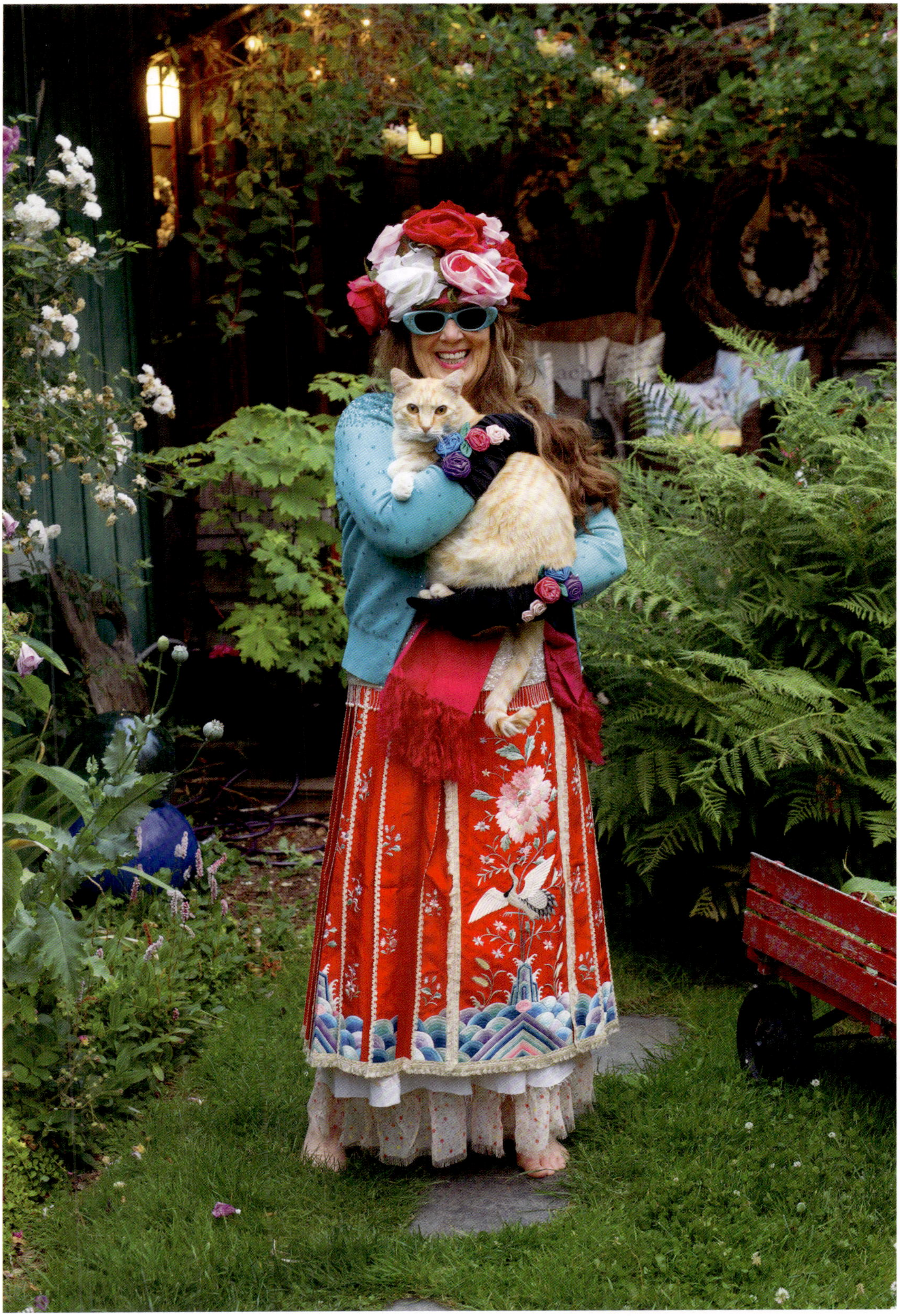

Tutti and Tiggy

When I first met my granddog, a rescue mutt, I was gobsmacked. I'd expected a cute, fluffy mini doodle. Instead I had a medium, shorthaired, American Staffy-kelpie mix who didn't fit in my handbag and didn't like cuddles. Fast-forward ten years—she still doesn't love cuddles, but we see her very often, and she's such a joy. When she dives into the sea she comes up glistening and looking like a baby seal. She may not love cuddles, but she loves to be close. Sometimes she accidentally bites me and I treasure every tooth mark. She's our furry granddaughter and I couldn't love her more if I'd given birth to her myself.

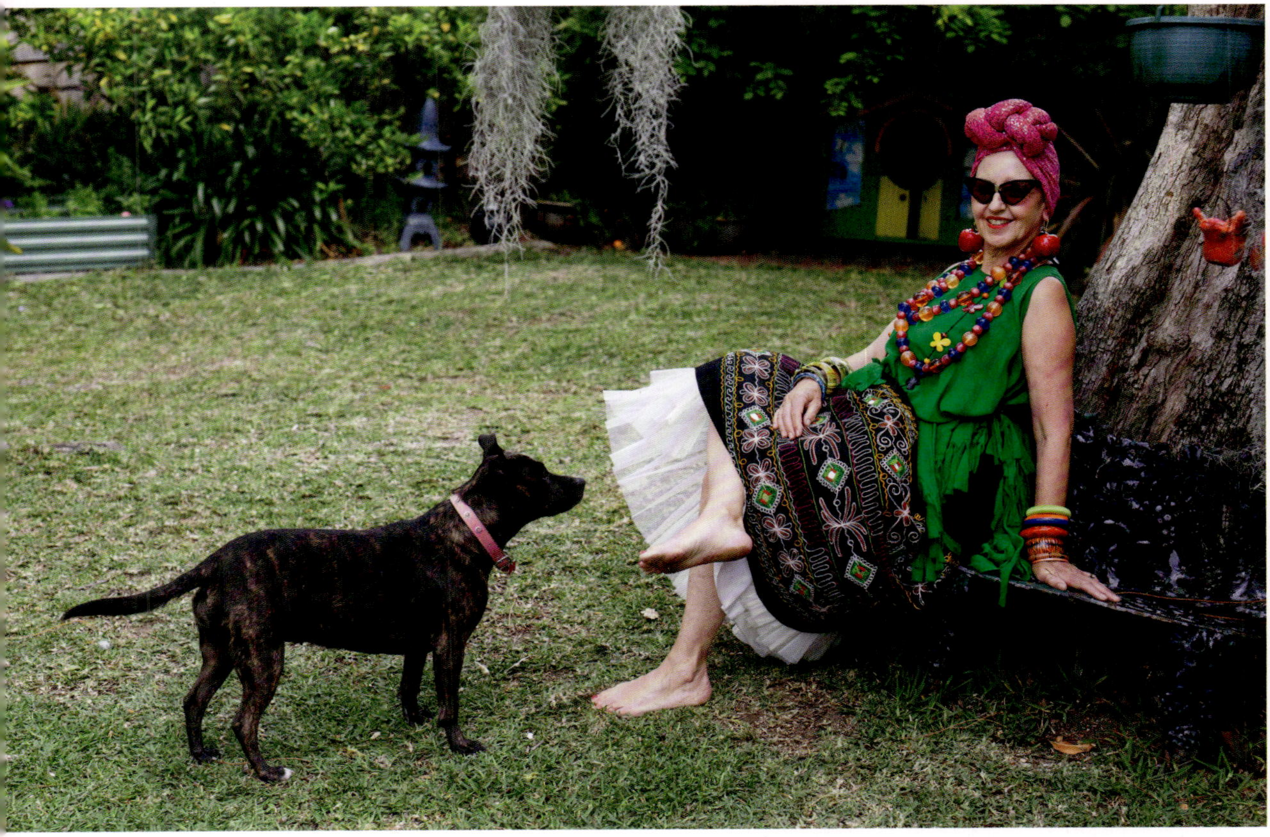

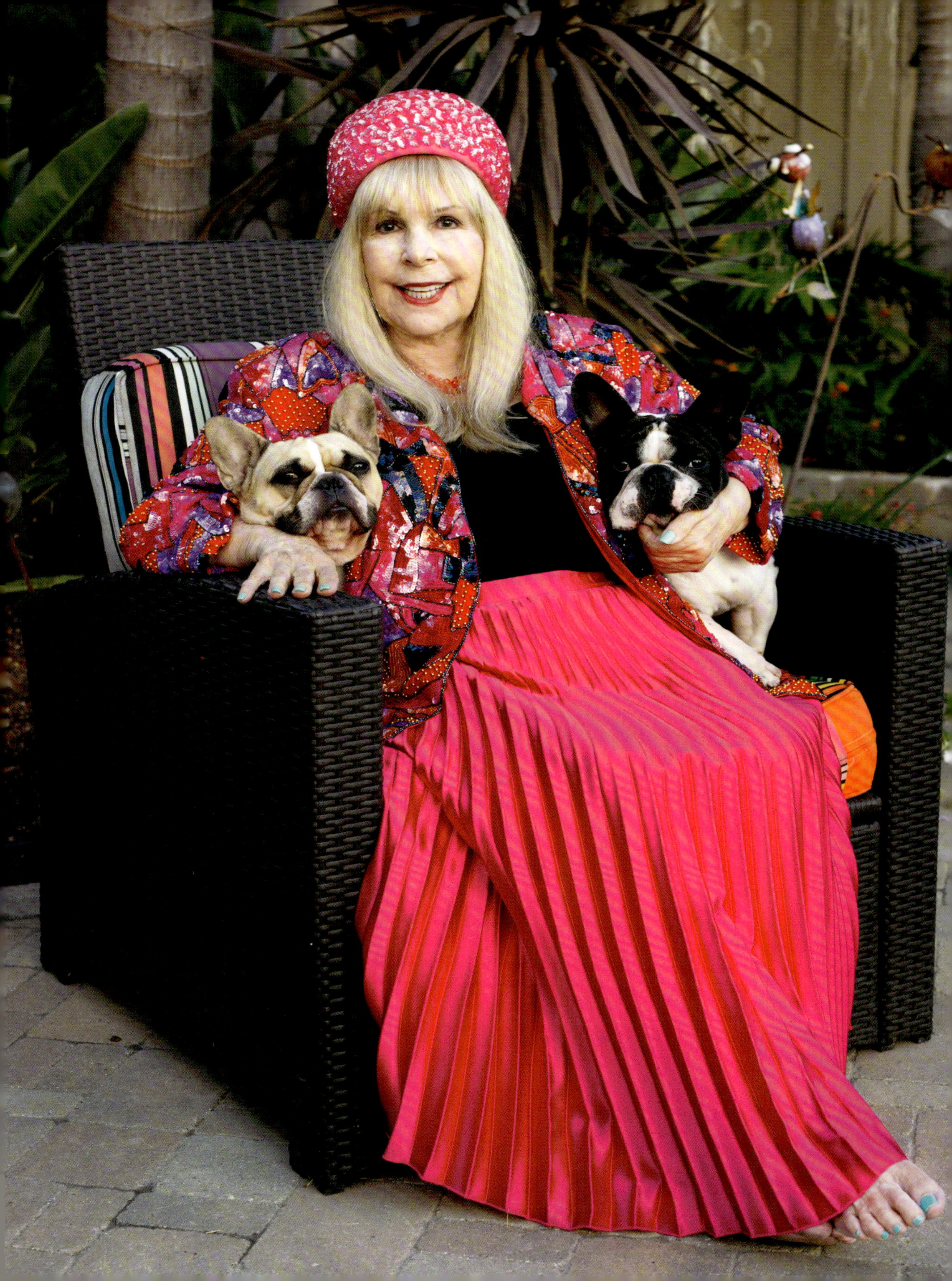

Mom, Little, and Cooper

Frenchies are your best friends. They are like little people. When I talk to them they understand everything and even talk back. When I leave the house I can't wait to return home to find my two little babies waiting by the door. Even though their mommy doesn't like to go out in the sun, I love to watch Little and Cooper taking their daily sunbaths by the pool. I have had dogs all my life. They have always comforted me during hard times.

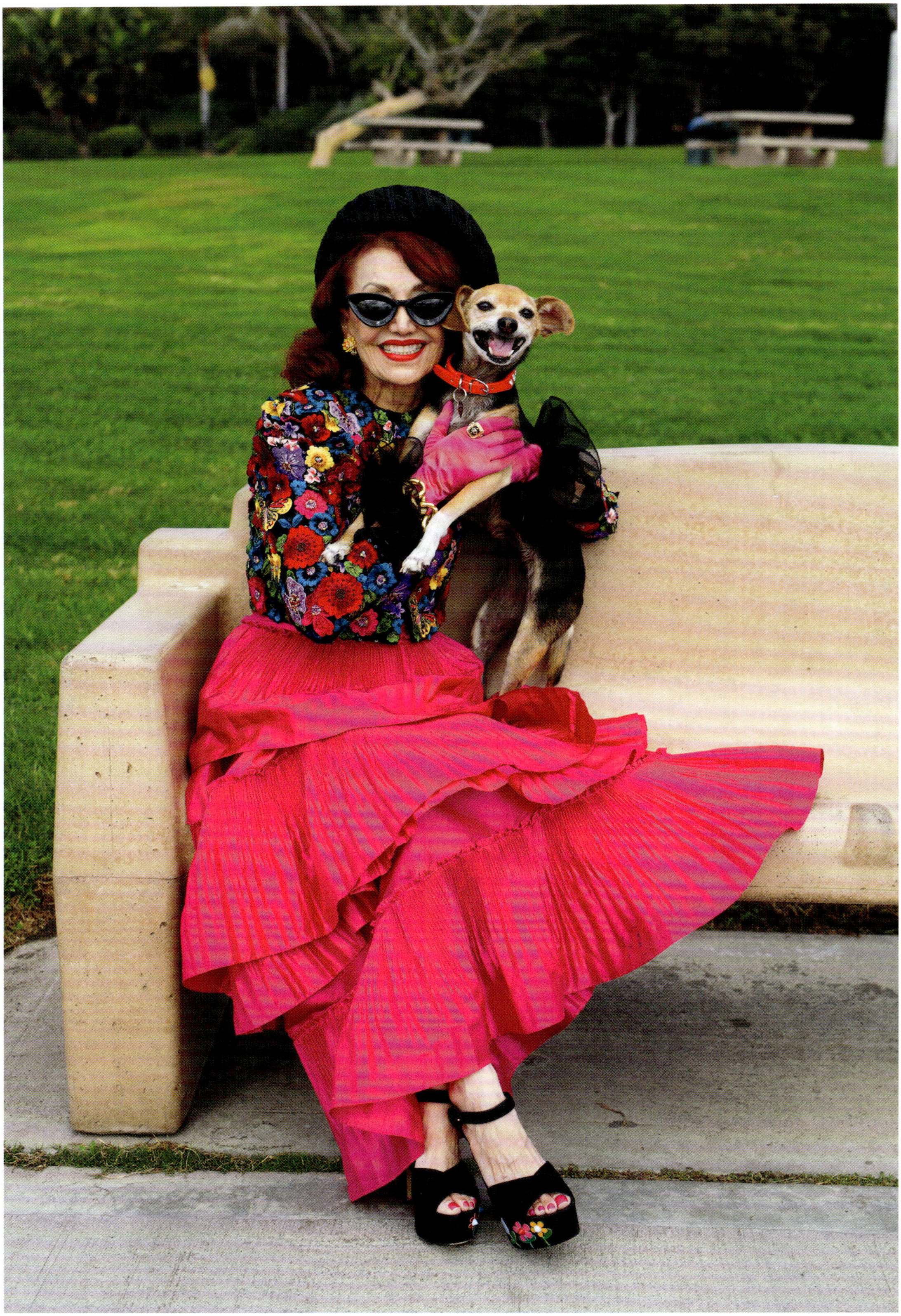

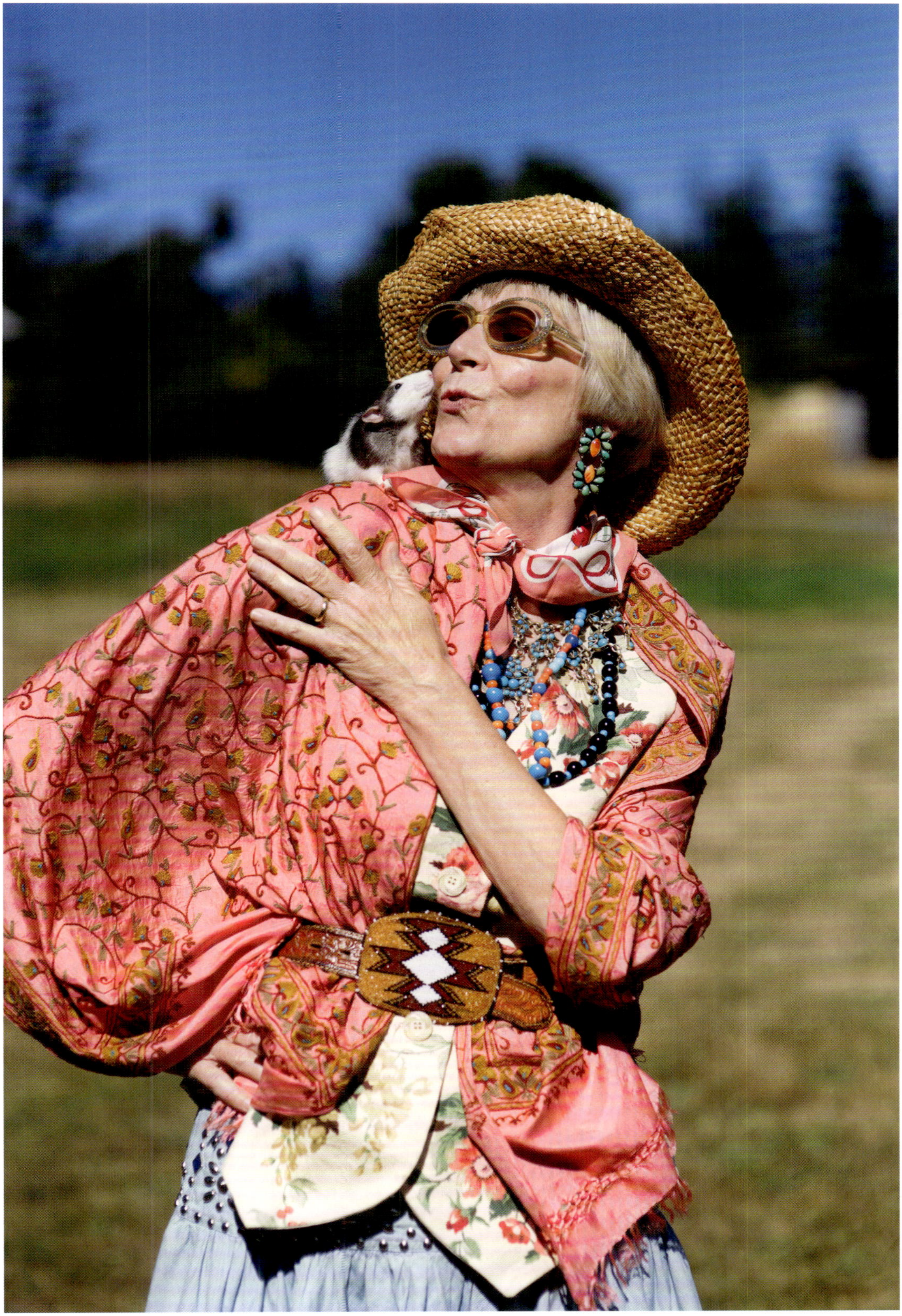

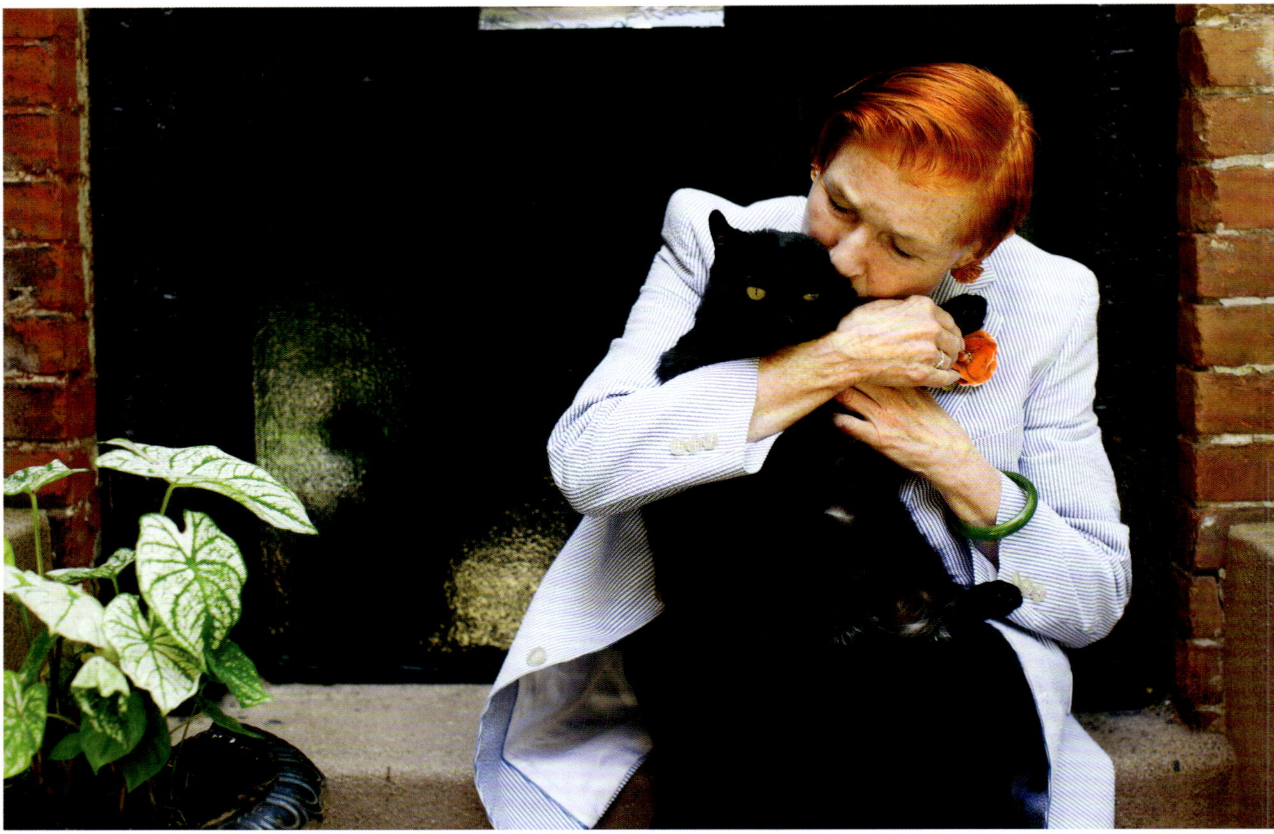

Alice and Oberon

I love Oberon not only for his "I'm the king" attitude. I love him for surviving the streets of Manhattan to become a cat that rules the roost in a small apartment. I even love him for his huge size, cuddling between Geoffrey and myself in bed at night and giving us less room. When I see him strolling across the floor staring at me with his one eye, I know in his street-cat way he loves me too.

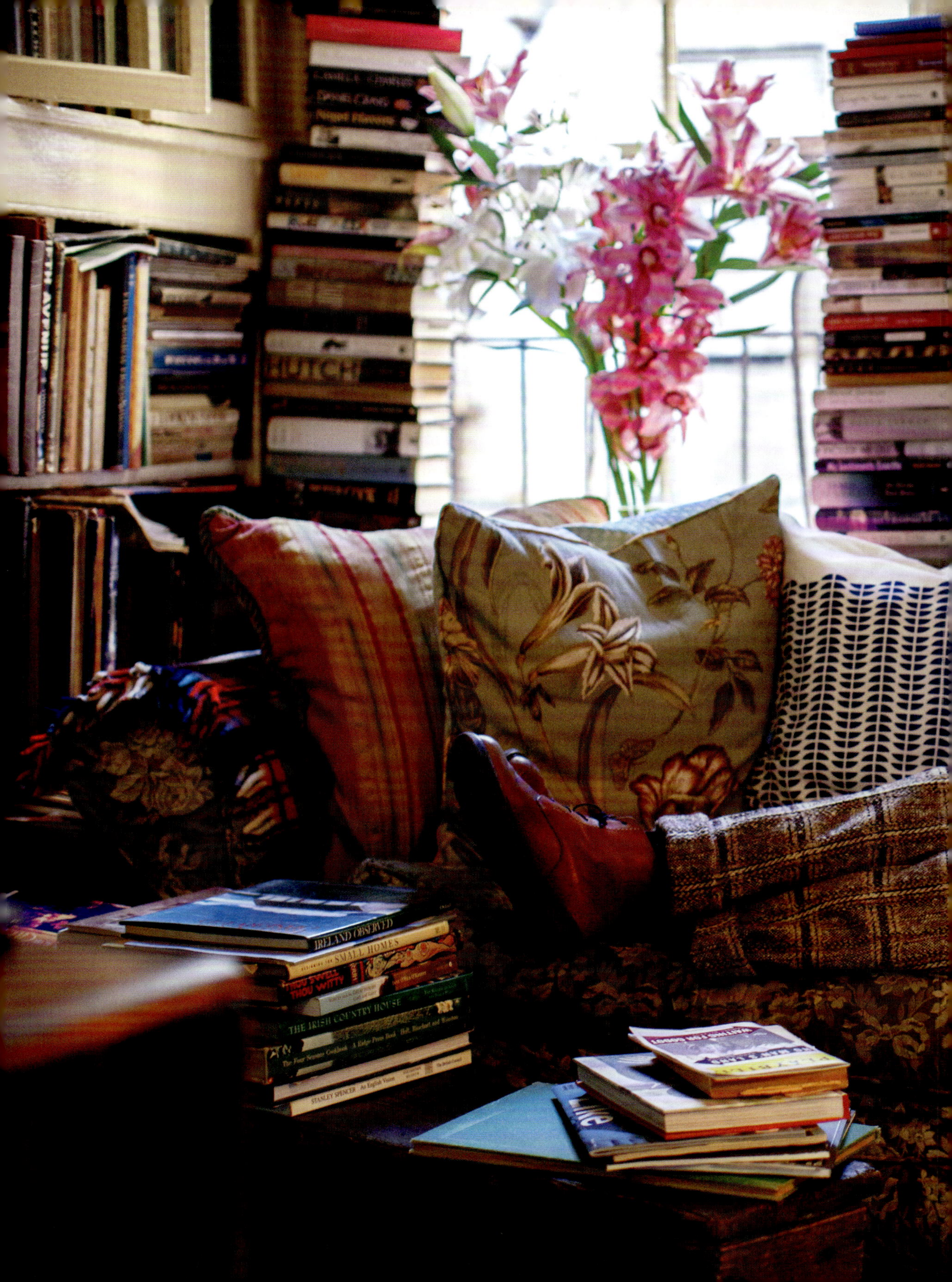
IRELAND OBSERVED
SMALL HOMES
THE IRISH COUNTRY HOUSE
STANLEY SPENCER An English Vision

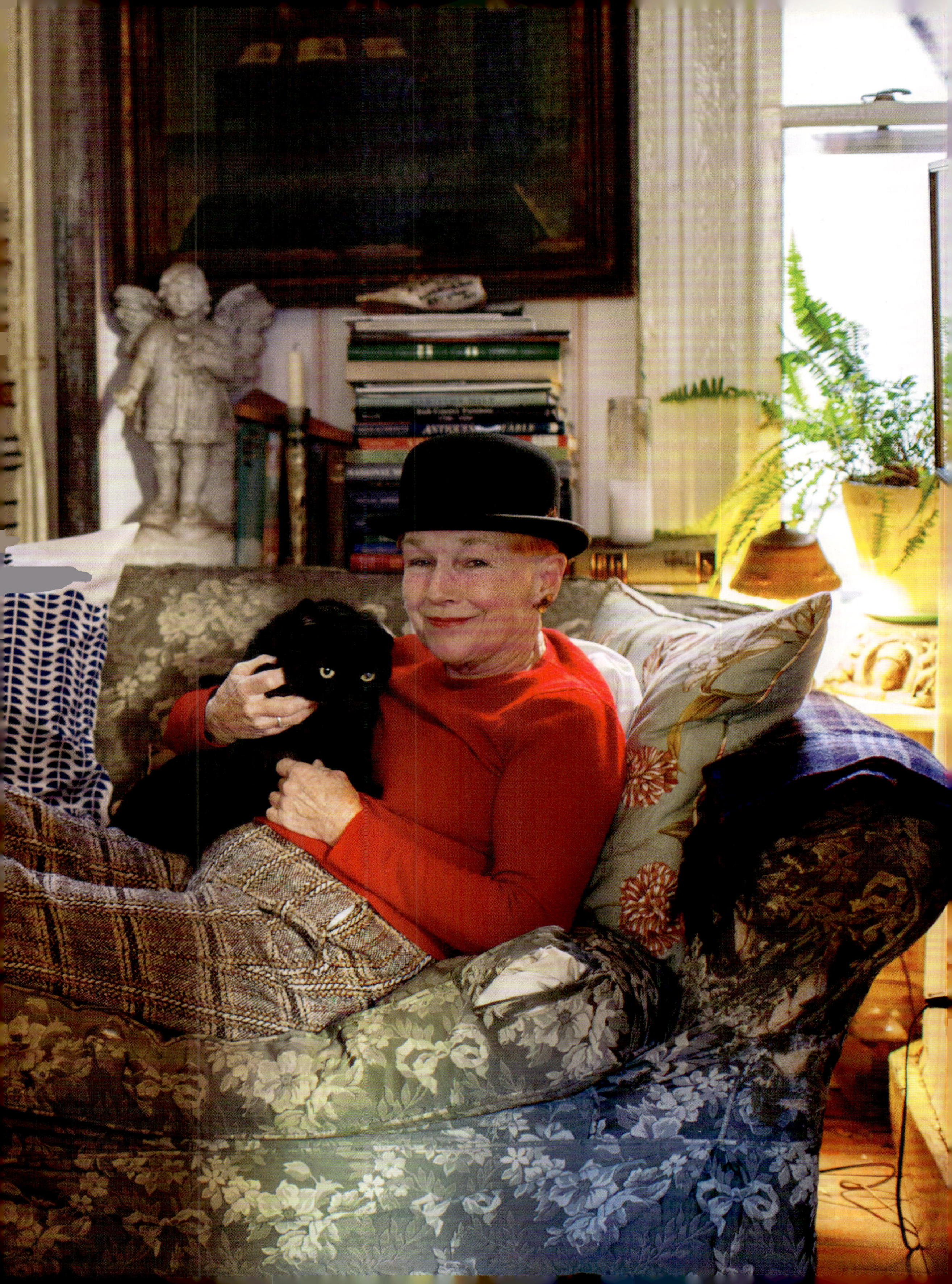

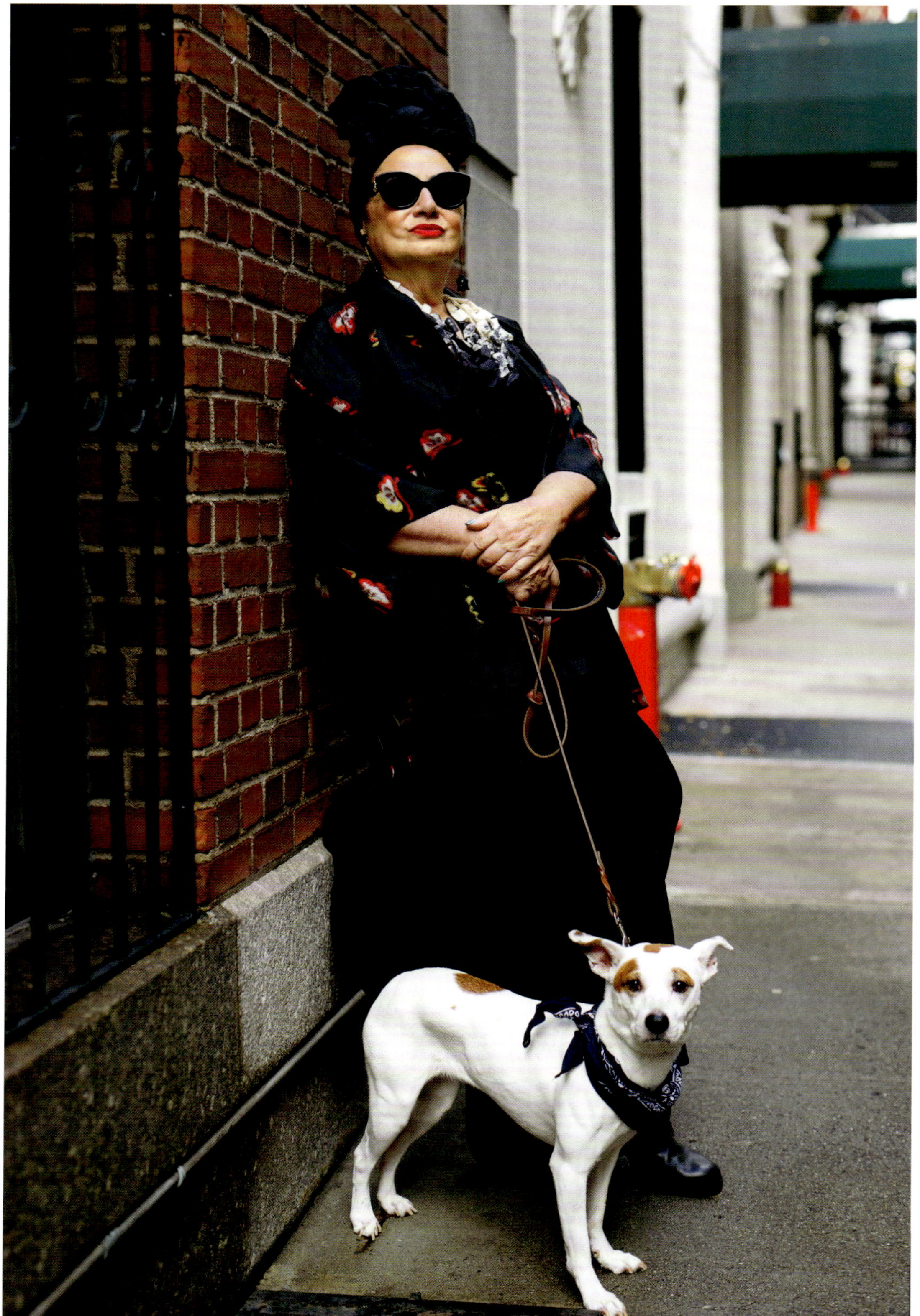

Rebecca and Mia

I lost my partner a year and a half ago. Mia is our dog. We adopted her together. When he passed away, I still had her love and connection. Mia's quite a magical little girl. She's neurotic, but aren't we all? Dogs are like angels; they have something that is so spiritual inside them.

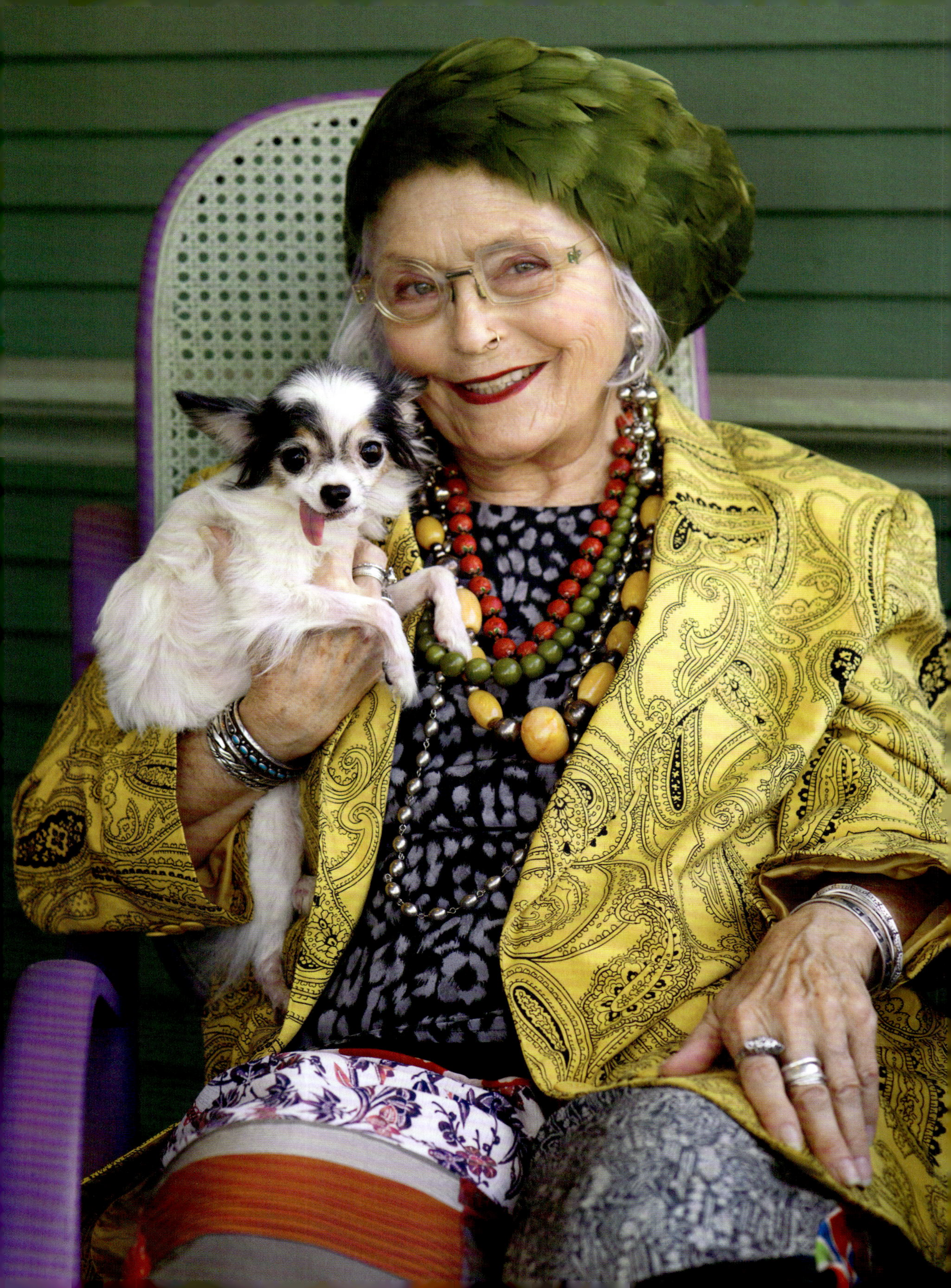

Donna and Dixie Sugar Belle

A dog is the only unconditional love that I may experience in this dimension. Dixie accepts me as I am, no matter what. She allows me to play as a child or cry in bewilderment; she is ever faithful.

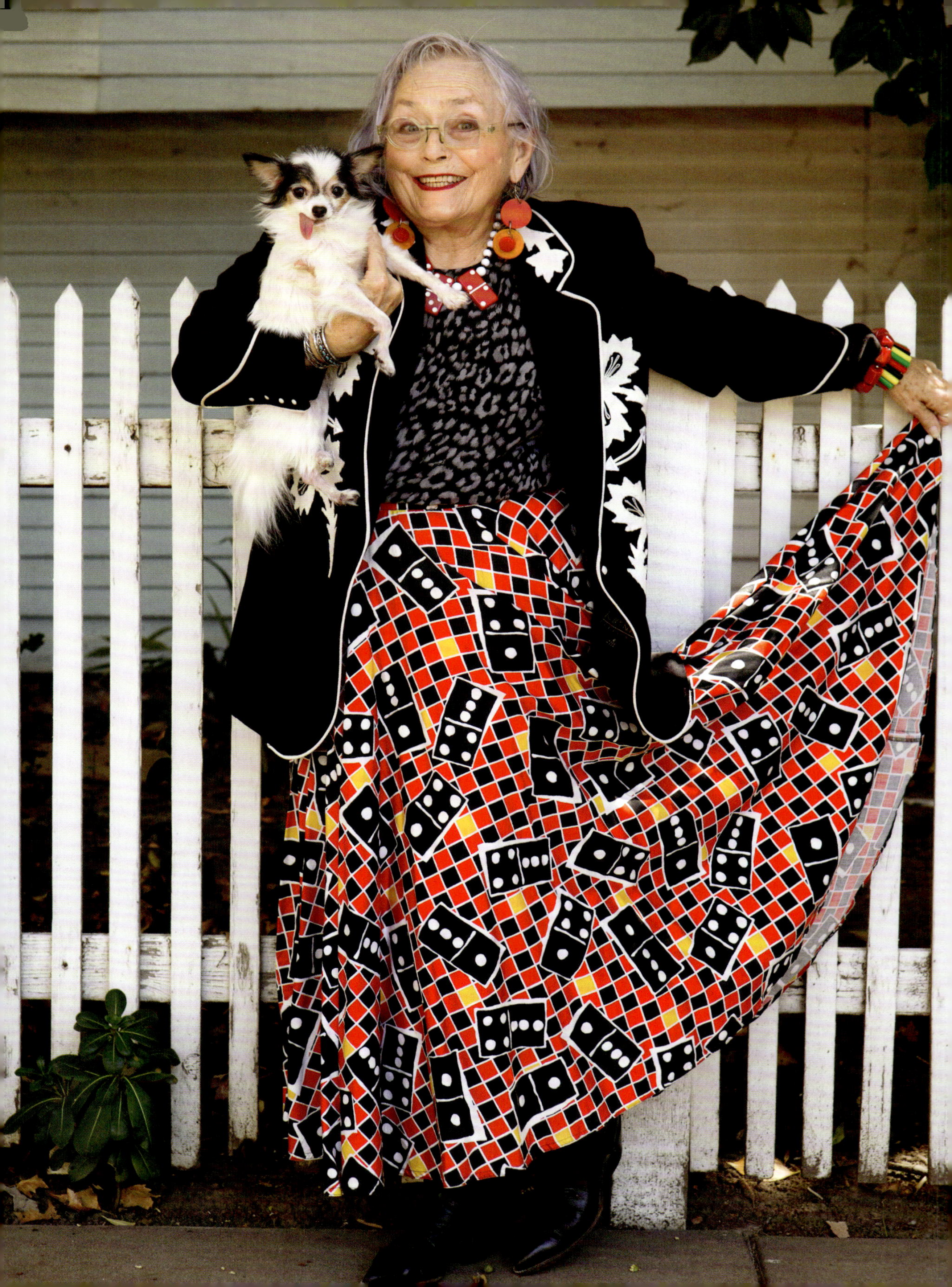

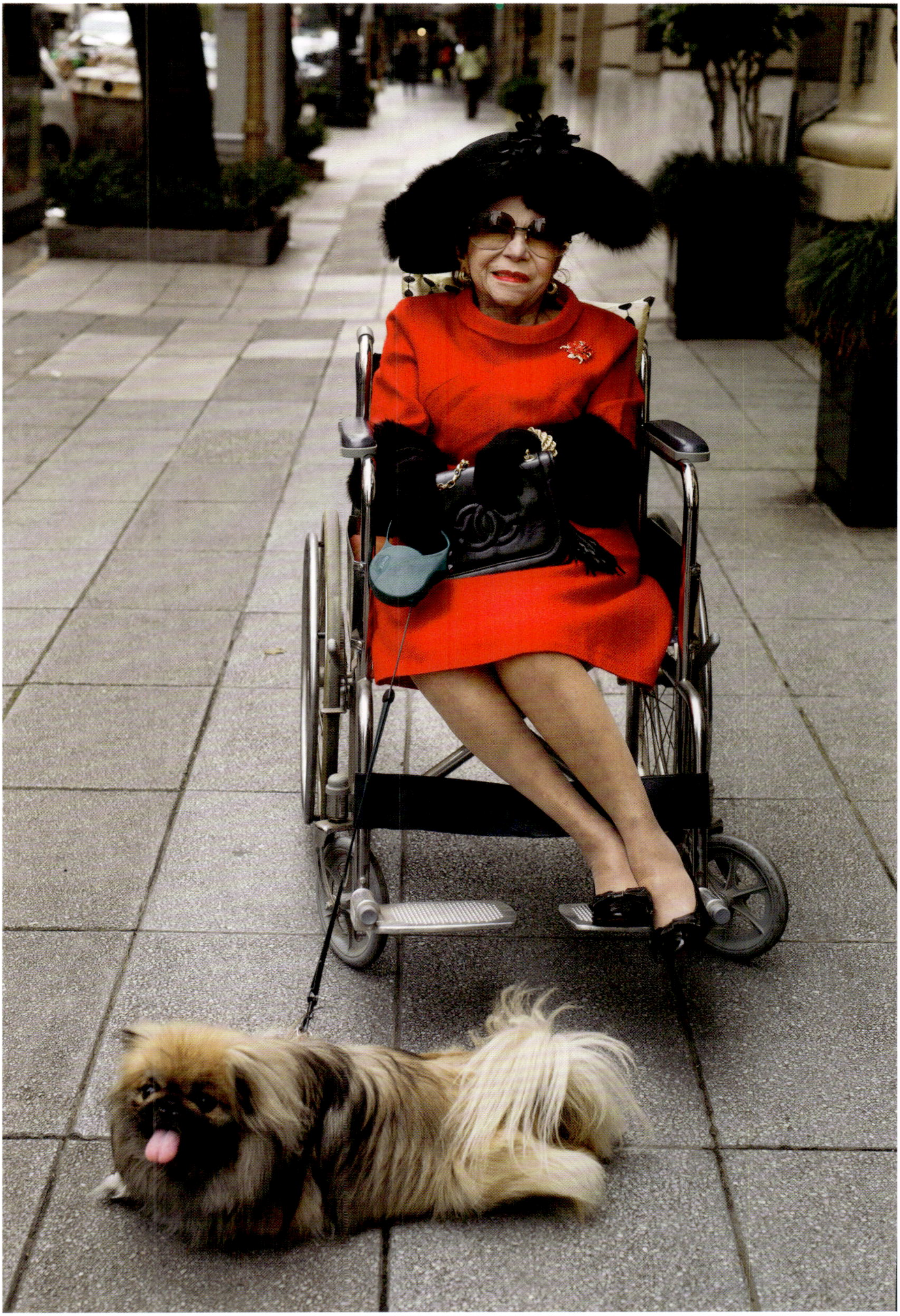

Patricia and Ruby

Ruby Woo (named after my favorite MAC lipstick) is my twelve-year-old miniature French poodle. She goes everywhere with me. When mommy is shopping at Bergdorf, Ruby sits and waits patiently in the middle of the salon allowing everyone to pet her. She has seventeen beds and uses them all. Ruby has a vocabulary of over 175 words. She loves to ride the subway and go in elevators. She brings me enormous joy, laughter, and unconditional love.

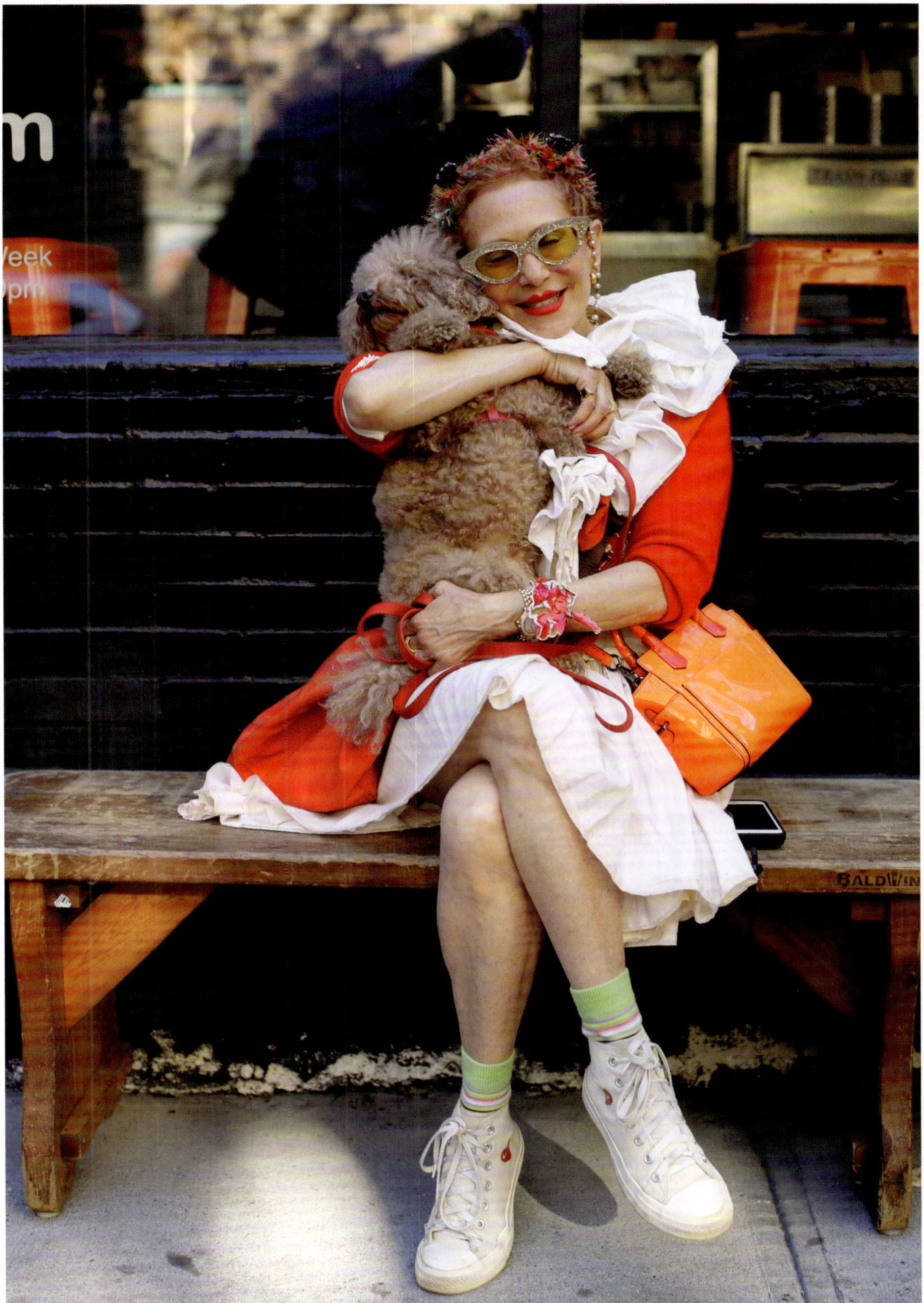

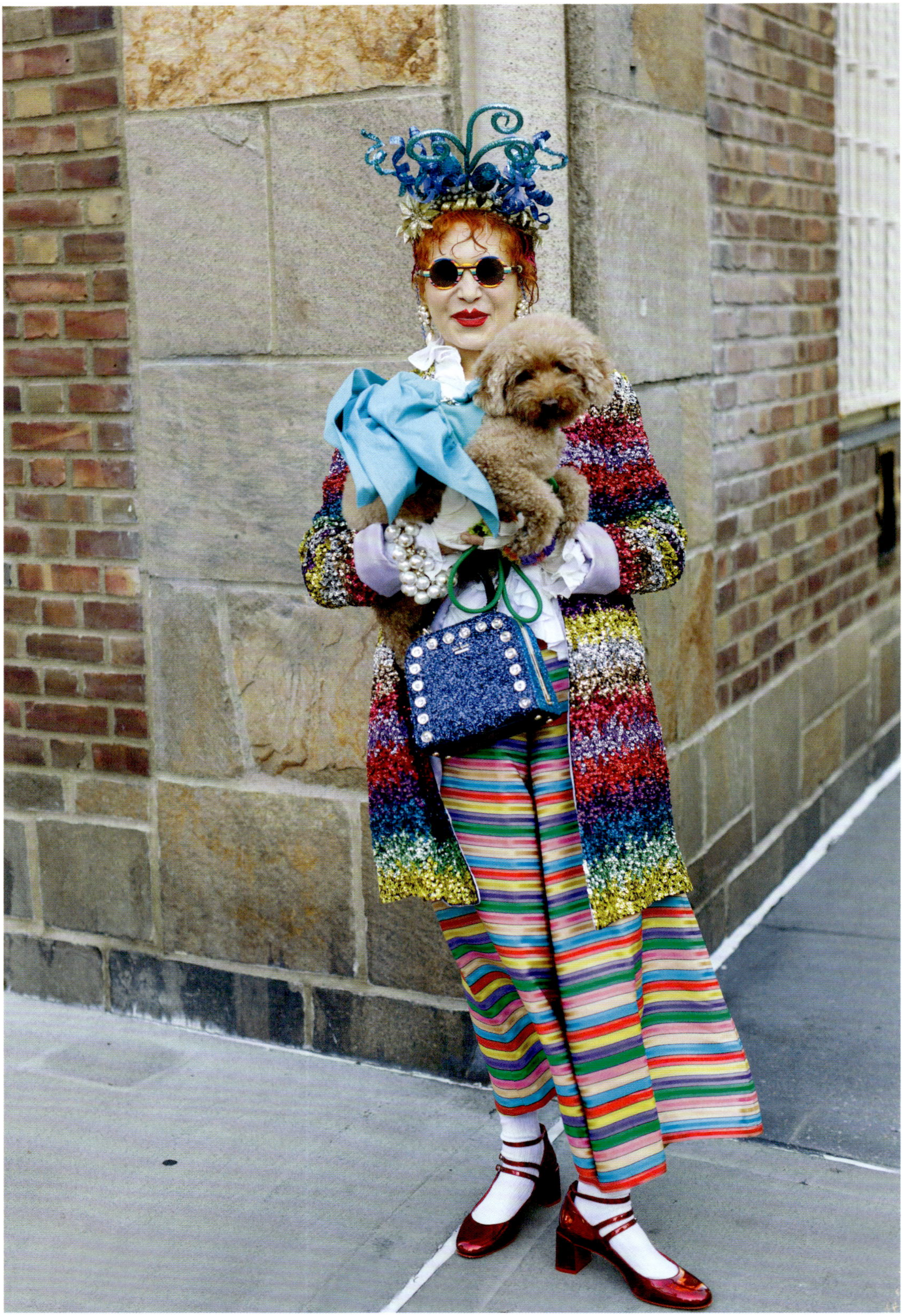

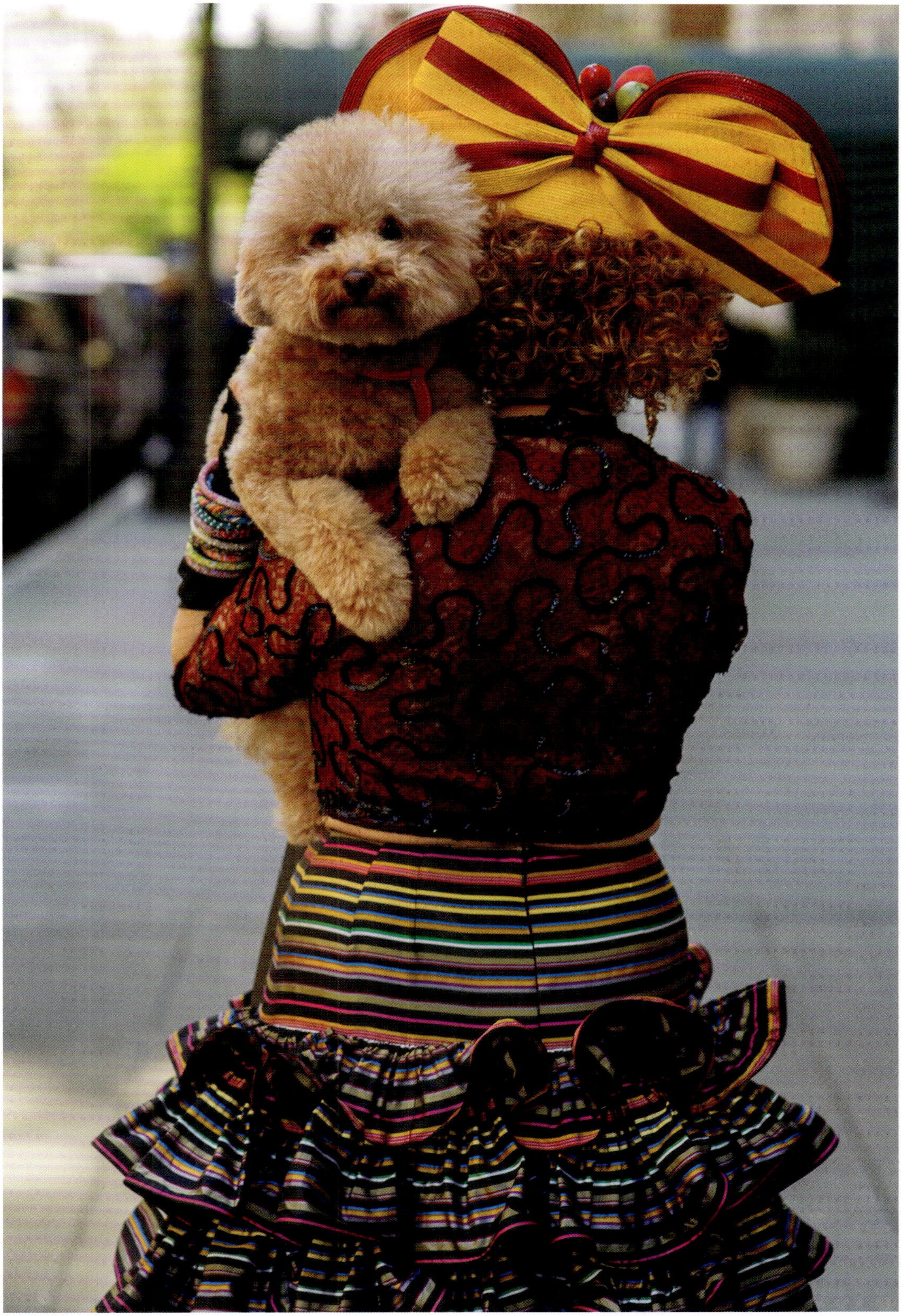

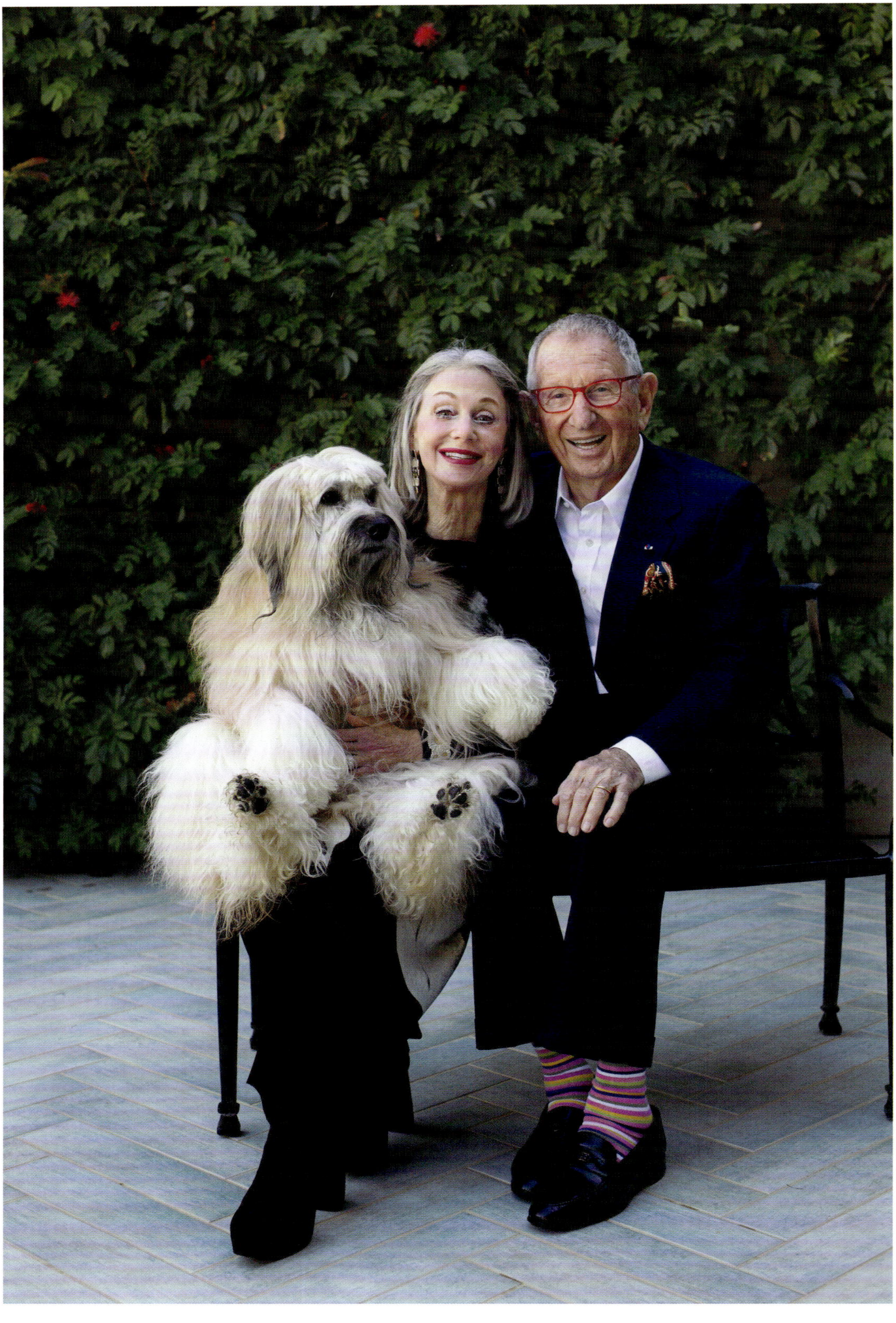

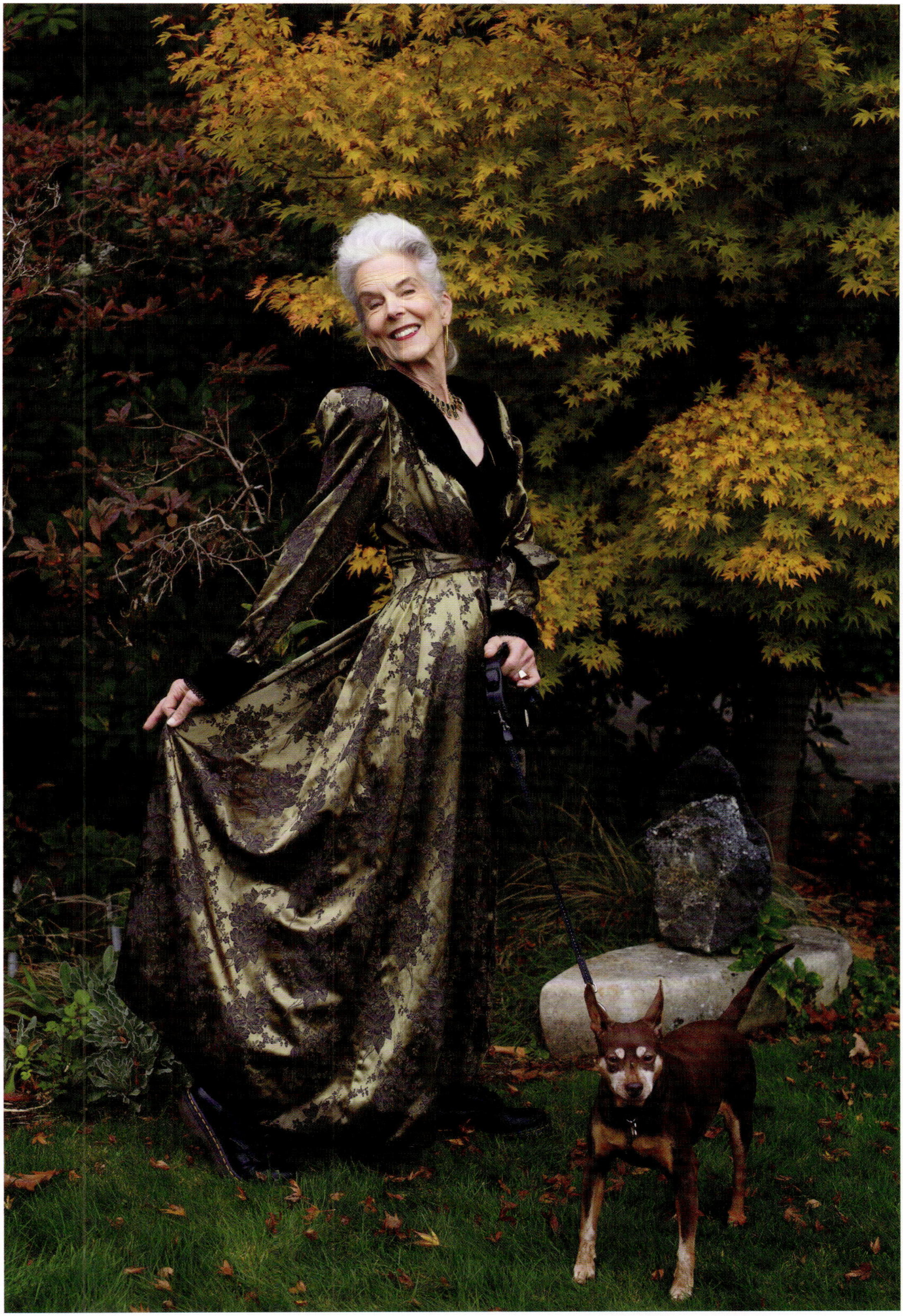

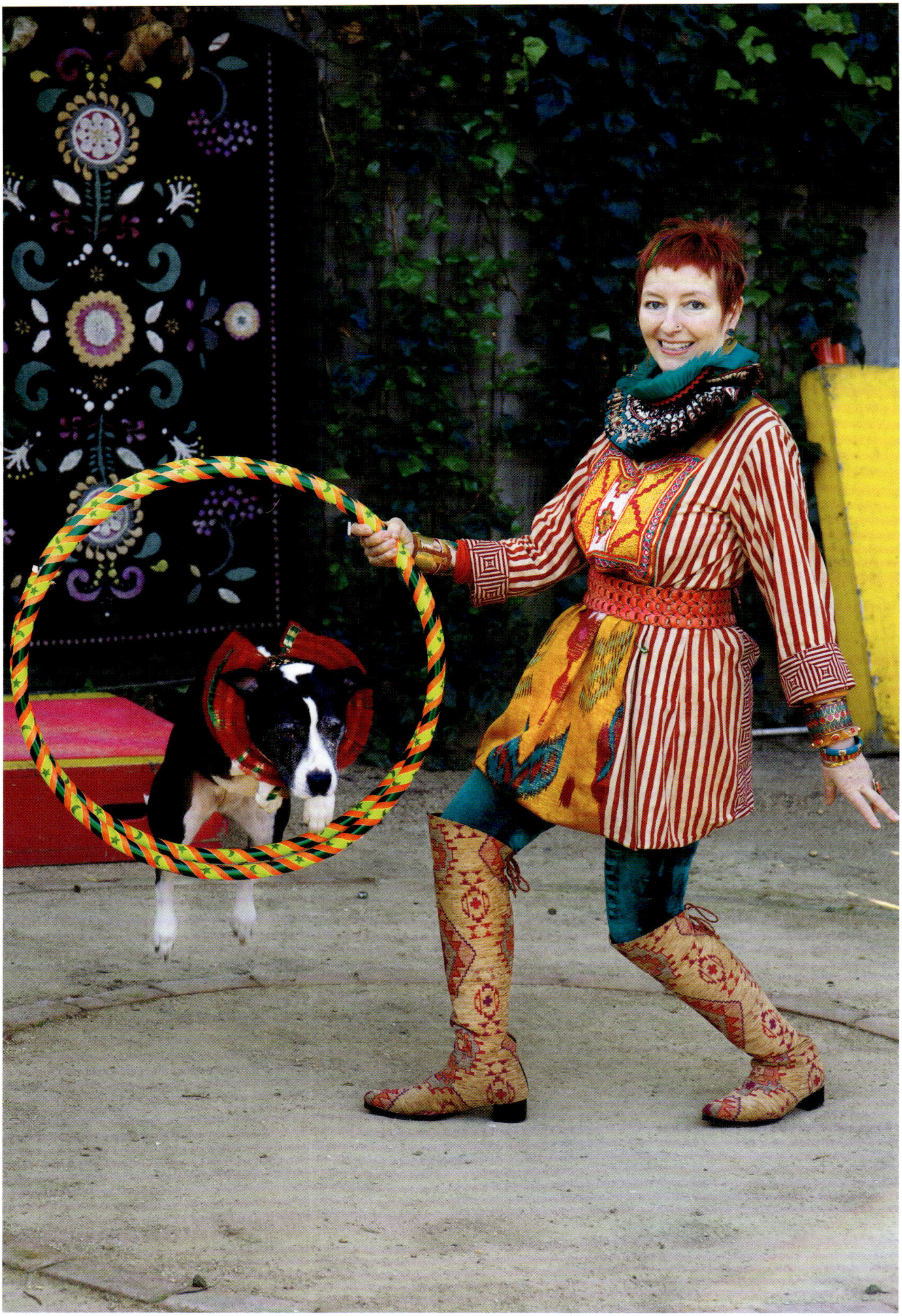

Andrea and Isha

Isha came into my life in 2013. Little did I know that rescuing her was as much about rescuing me. It's a two-way street, and we are happily inseparable. This once shy and timid Staffordshire terrier truly blossomed after attending Oakland's Canine Circus School. After six years of classes & consistent practice, she is a champ in hoop jumping, ball balancing, leg weaving, and more.

I can't imagine life without this amazingly talented, loyal, friendly, smart, and sweet dog. She has boosted my sense of who I am as her mother. She is as much of a daughter to me as one could ever imagine.

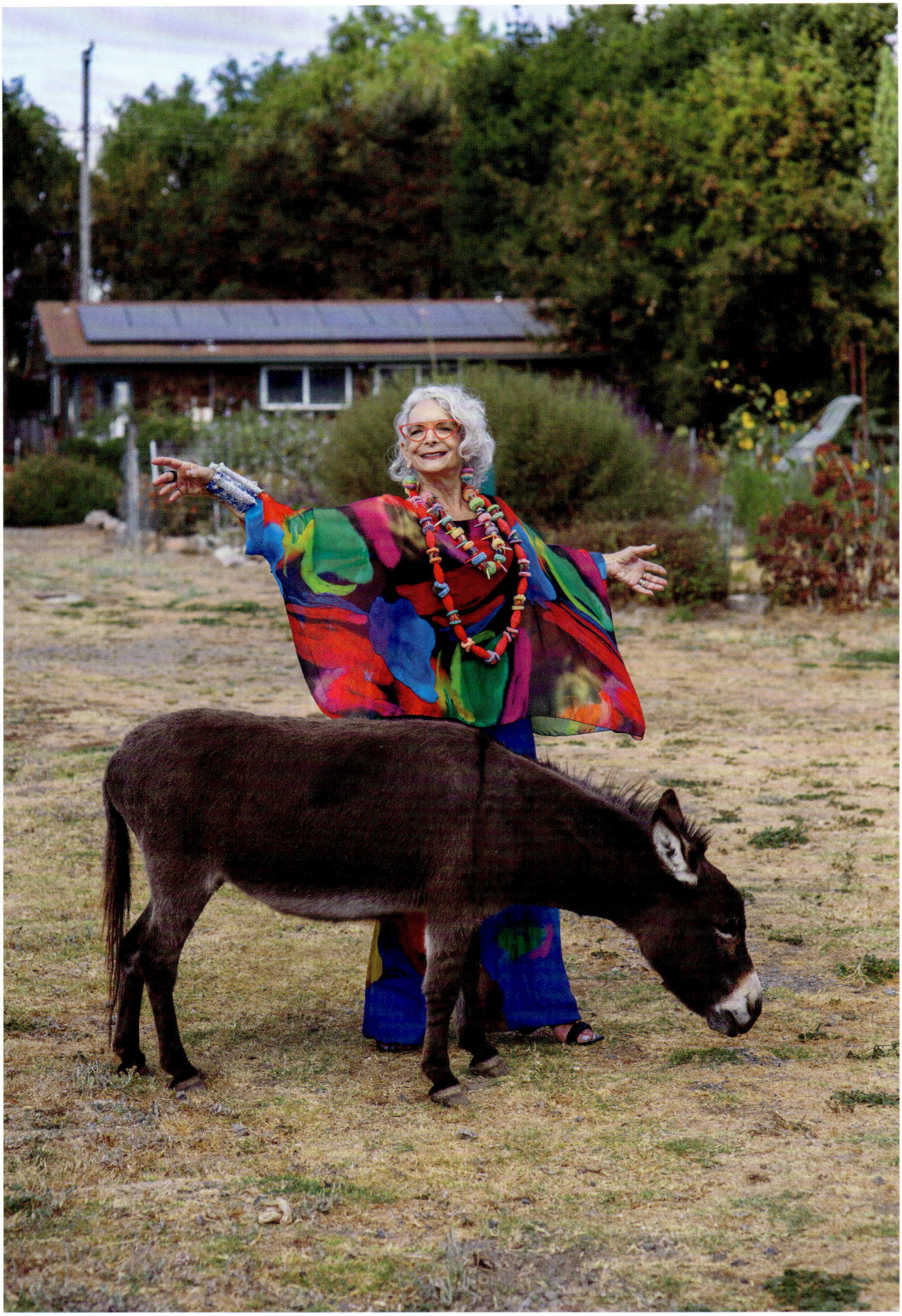

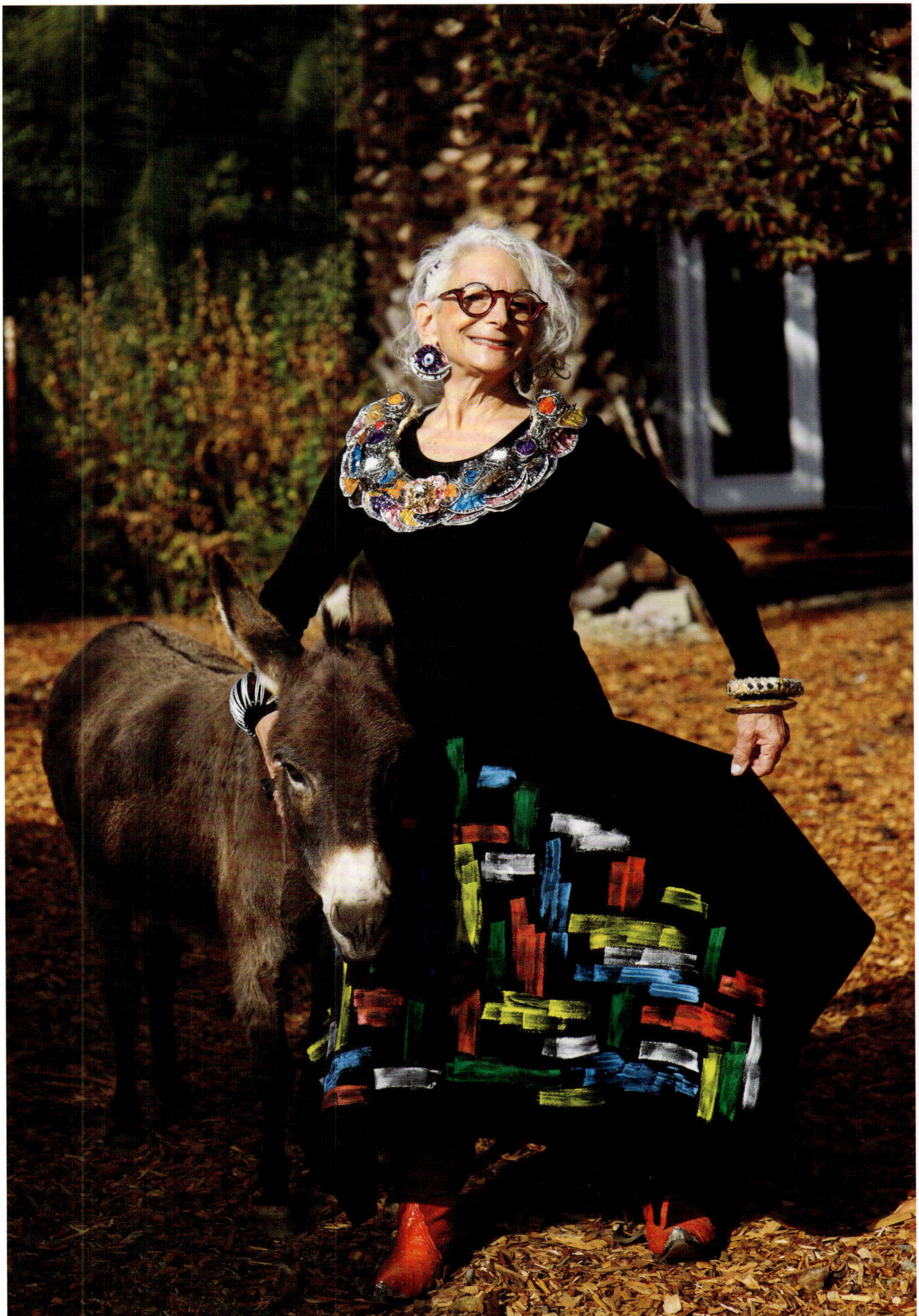

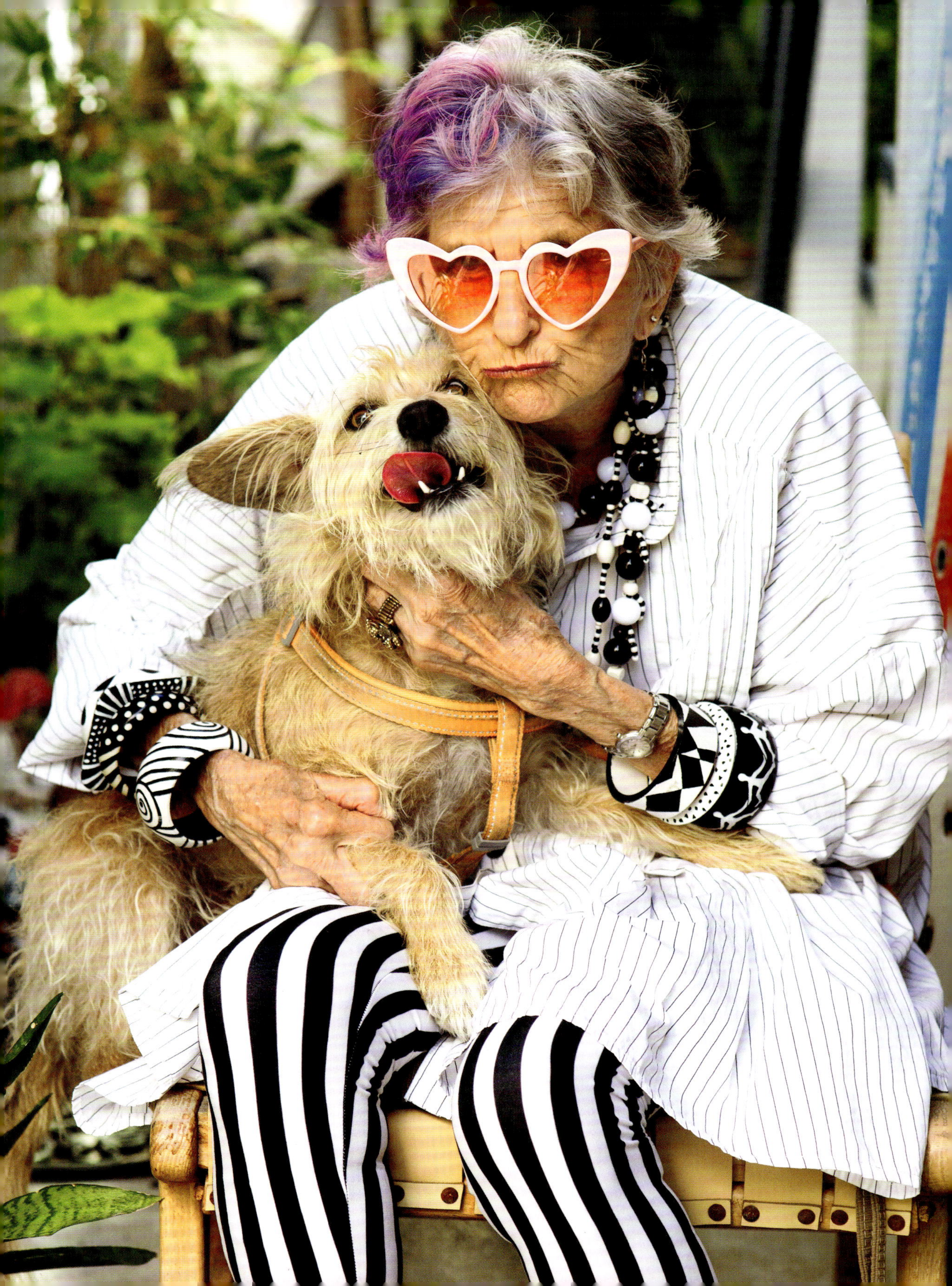

Jackee and Lucky

Lucky loves to play and to go for walks, which is good for ninety-two-year-old me. We are so lucky to have her and she is lucky to have us. Of course, she is the boss and makes the rules, but she is a sweetheart.

Ellyn Anne and Pepper

When it comes to our pets, analytics support the likelihood that we will outlive them. After having assisted three beloved canines transitions into doggie Heaven and experiencing the heartbreak of losing them, I'd taken the stance of no dogs henceforth. Yet here I am, happily eating those words.

My daughter-in-law and son adopted Pepper, a senior pup whose future was looking bleak. Without certification of her age, the guesstimate puts Pepper at ten or twelve years old. In human speak, she is sixty to seventy years old, and—as with her human counterparts (including me)—is arthritic, hearing impaired, has tummy problems, and is a nap addict.

I hadn't anticipated that as a part of Pepper's caring team, I would feel such a sense of honor. Perhaps at seventy-five, I see myself through her, and as my marbles begin to scatter, I too will be enveloped in a cocoon of safety and love that will take me from here to eternity.

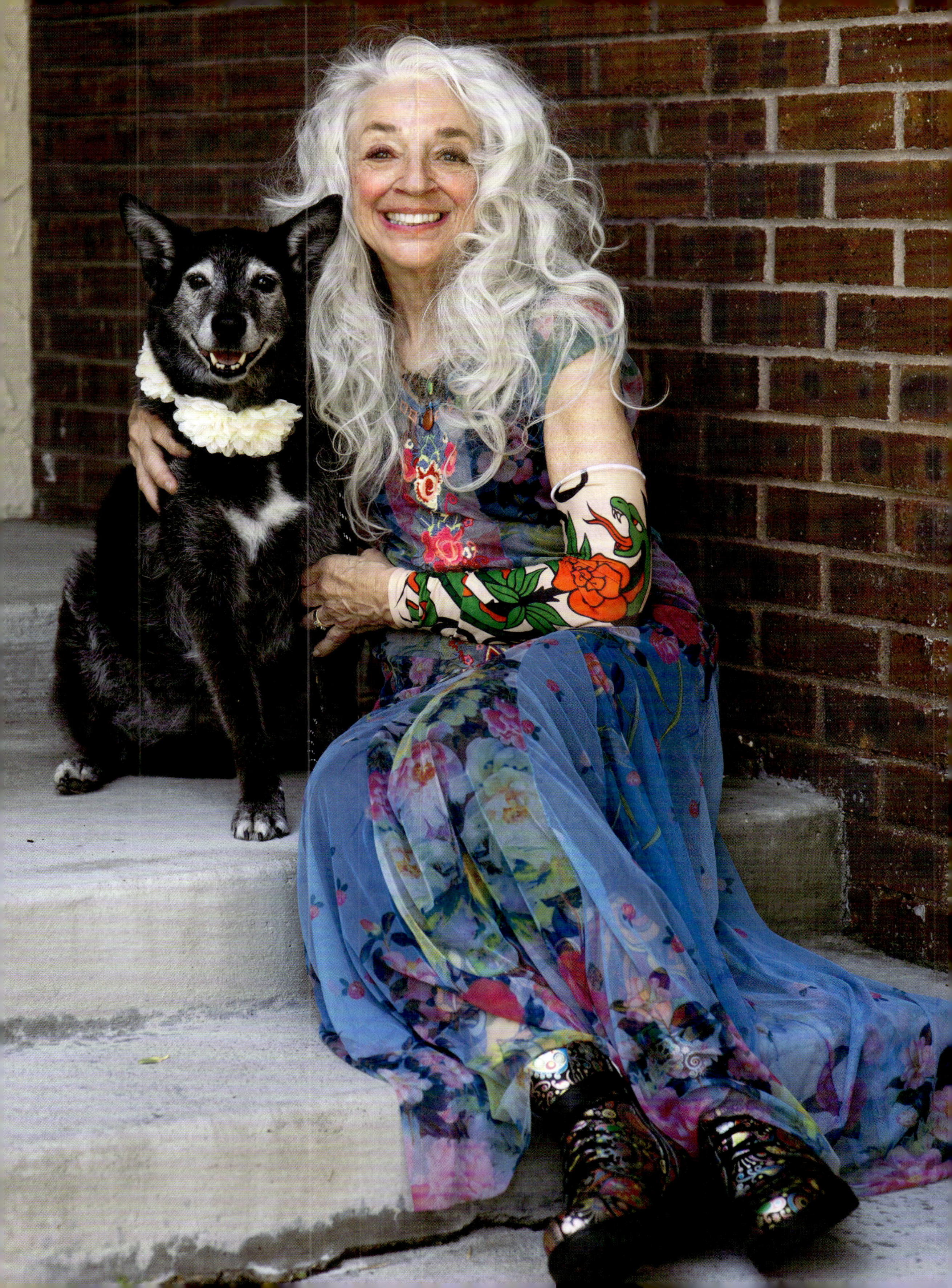

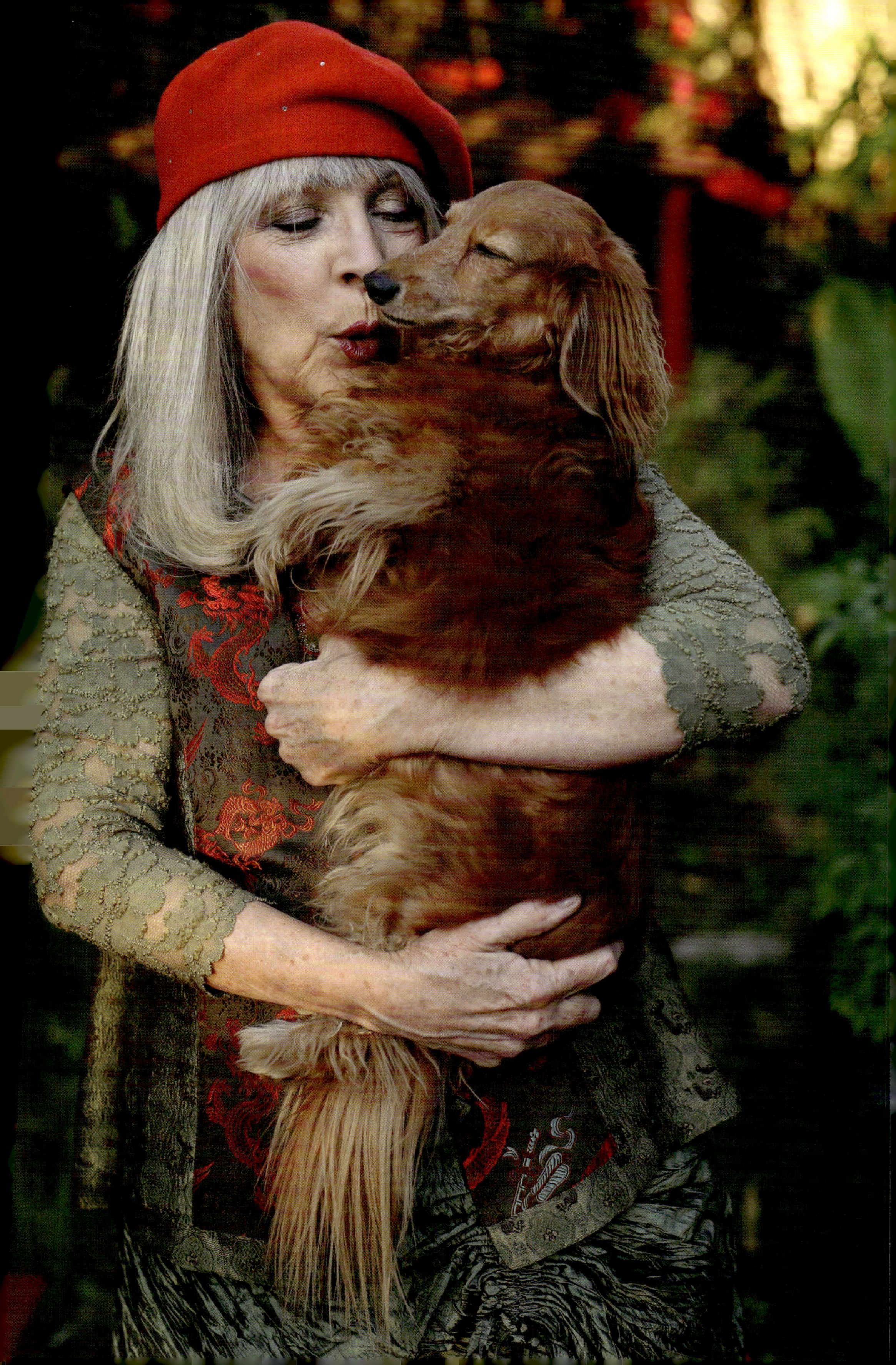

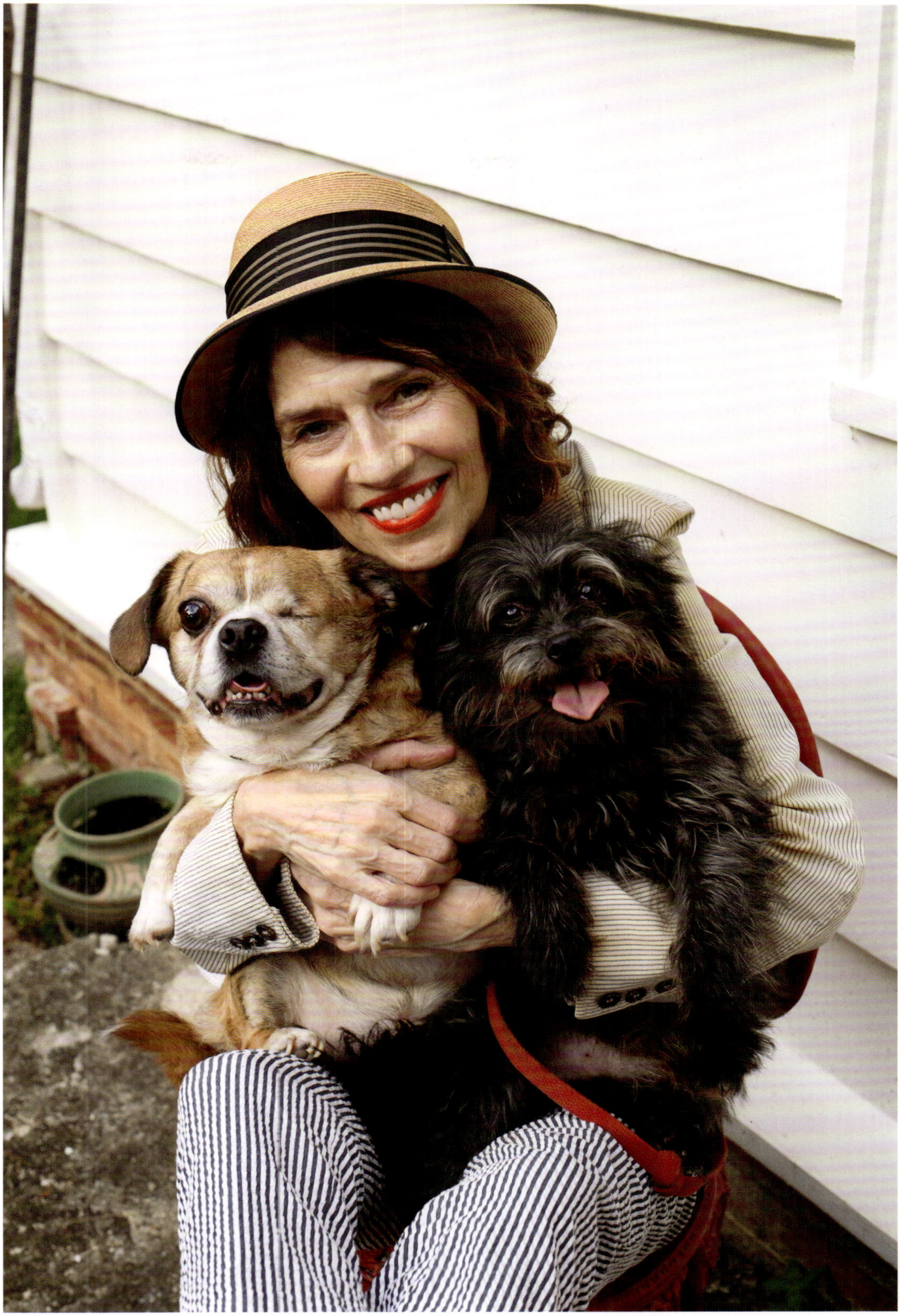

Grandma Pat and Trixie

I adopted Trixie two years ago from A Purposeful Rescue in Los Angeles. She's just the sweetest little thing and I can't imagine life without her! I truly believe my late husband Al sent her to me.

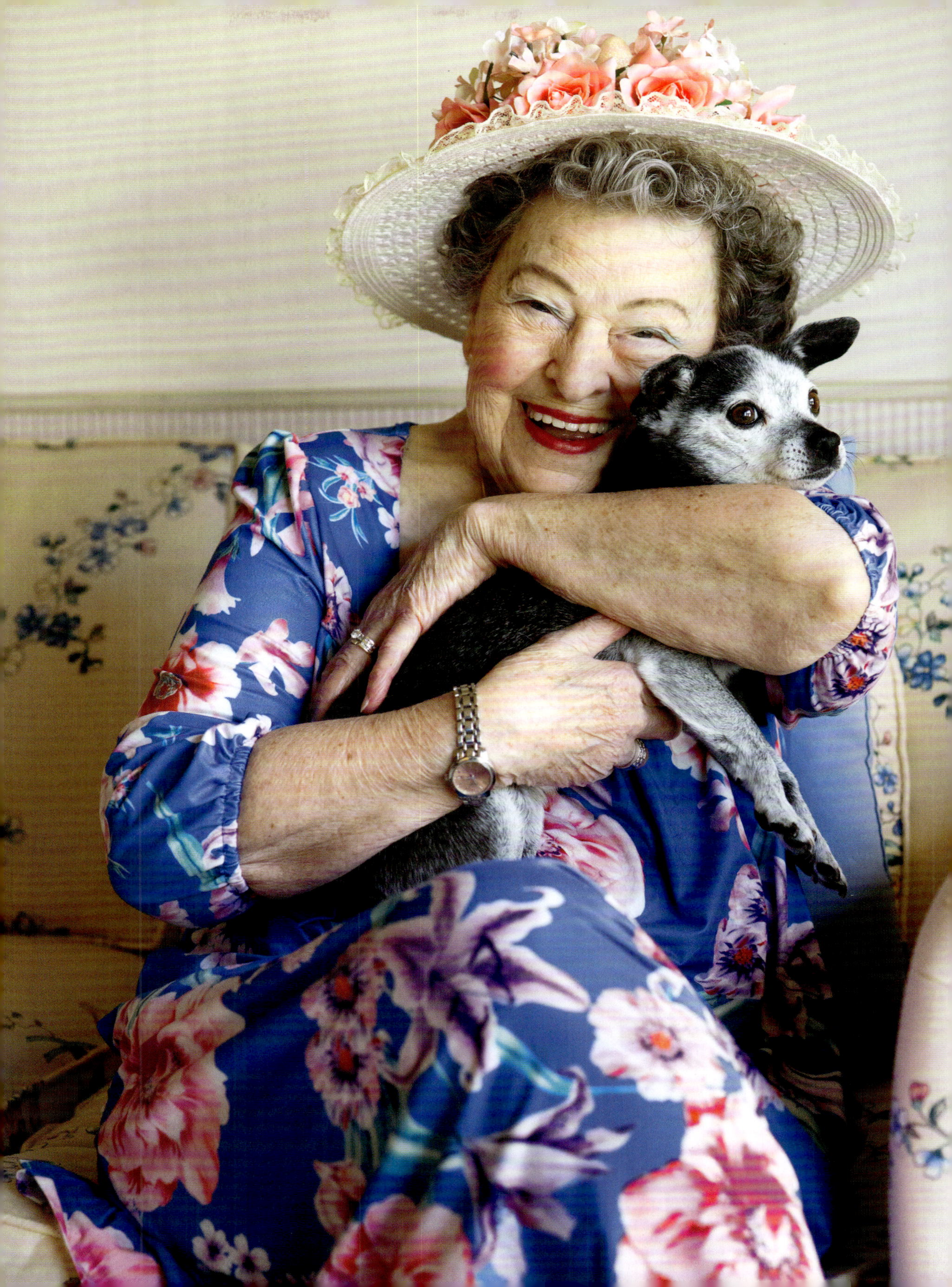

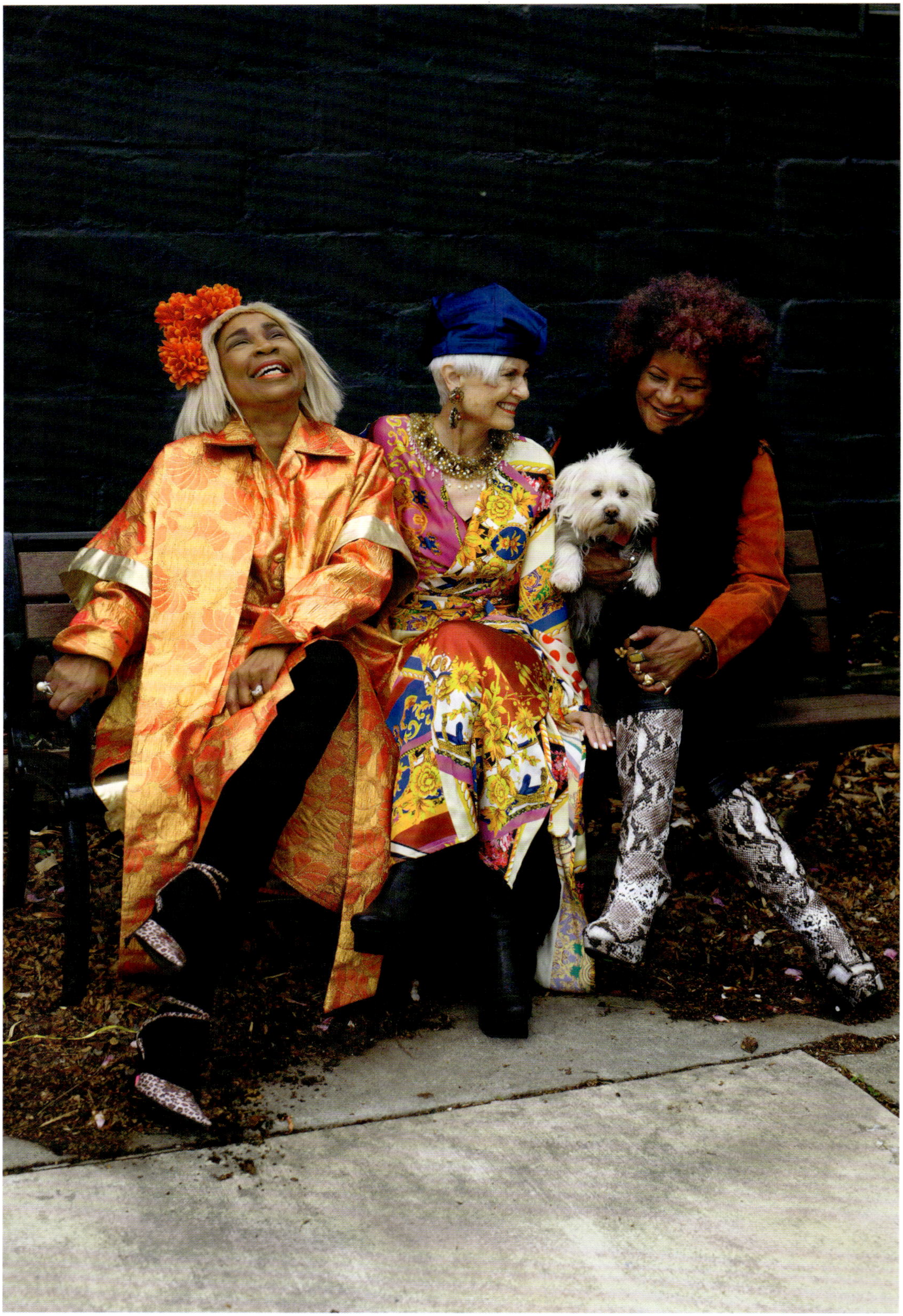

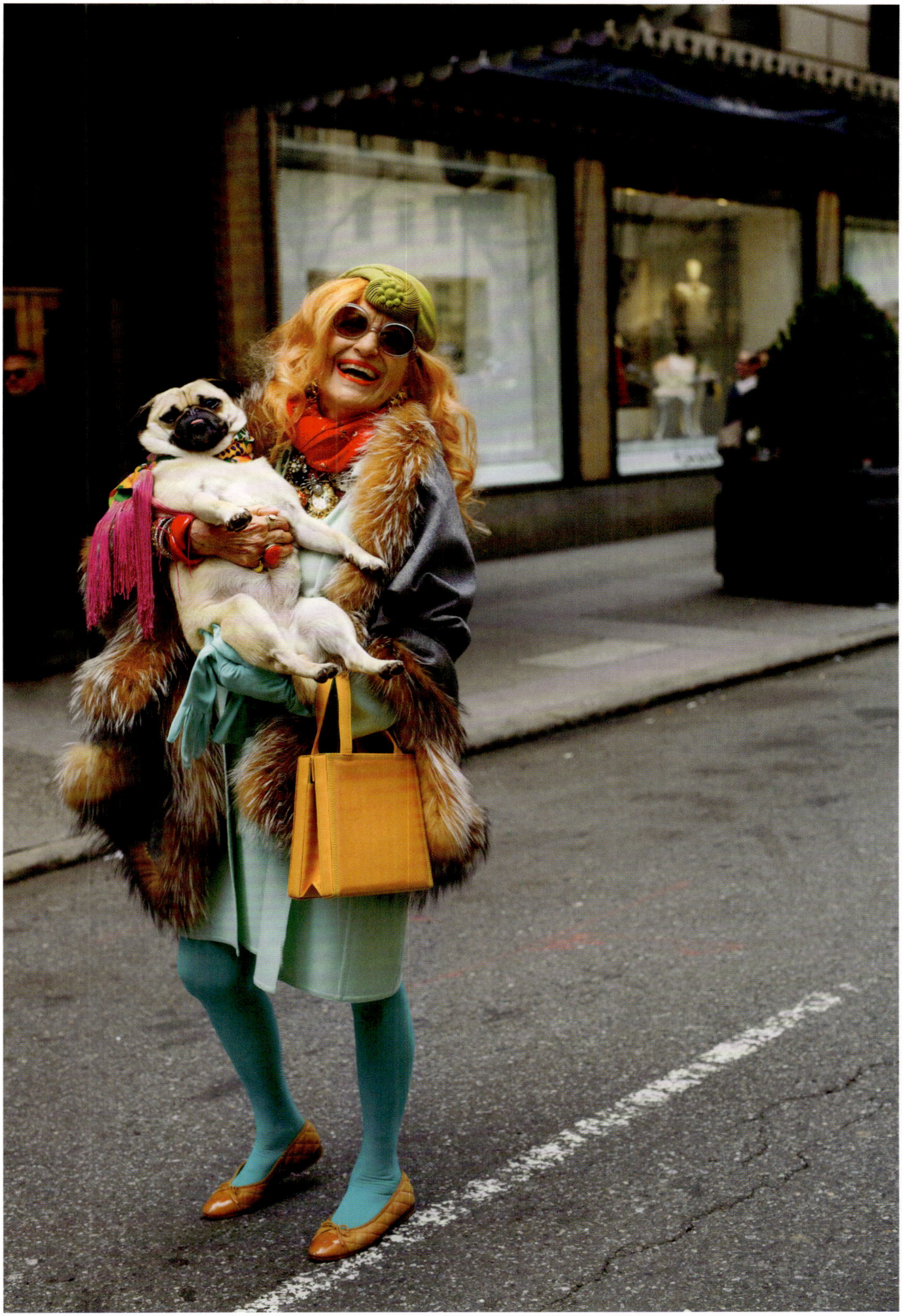

Lauren, Norma Jean, and Isadora

I could not love Norma Jean and Isadora more, even if I gave birth to them myself! They are my sunshine and heart and are there for me no matter what. They don't care about what I wear or look like, make-up or no makeup. It's unconditional love and that's the most anyone can hope for in life. You'll probably never get that from your husband!

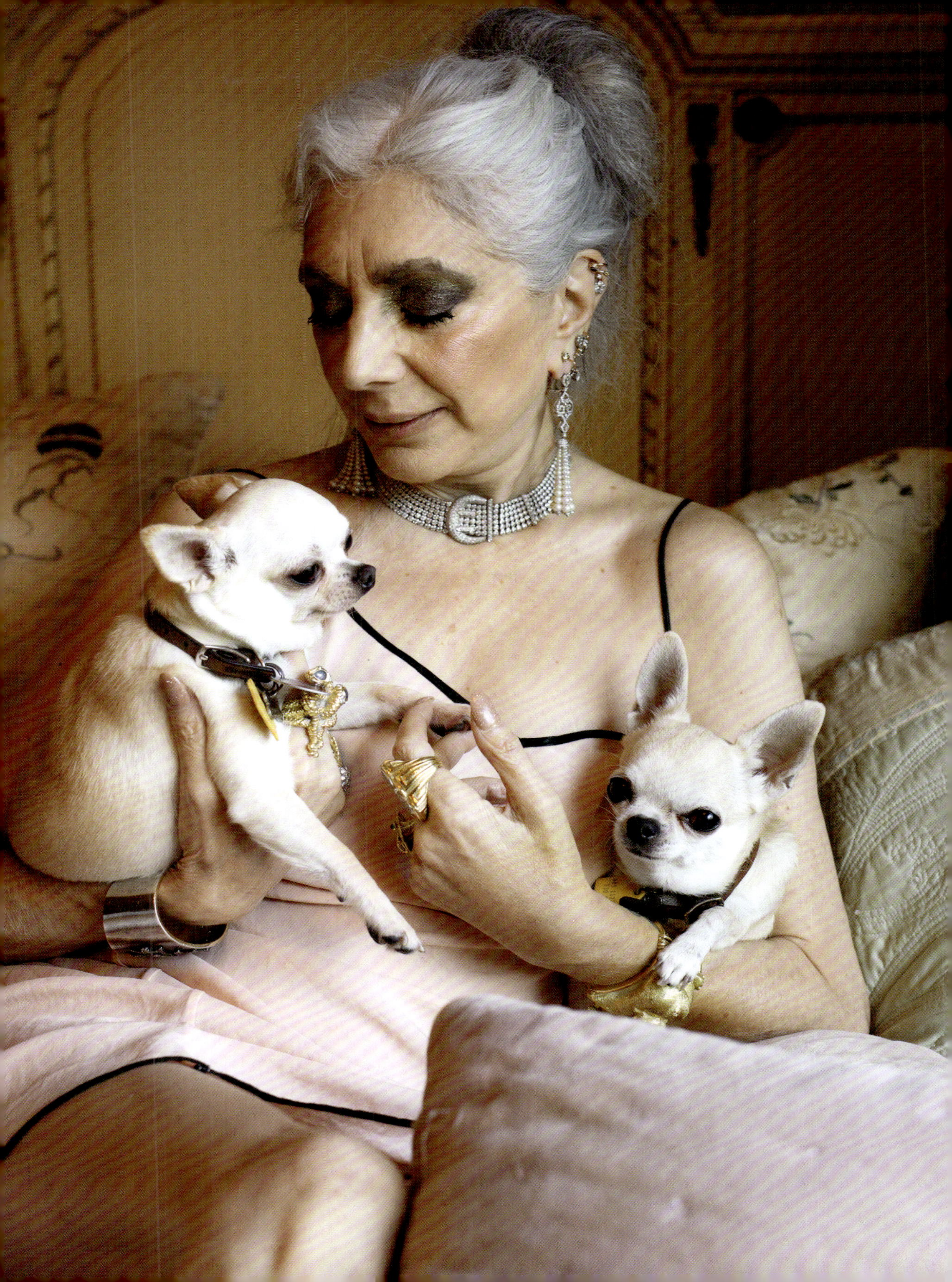

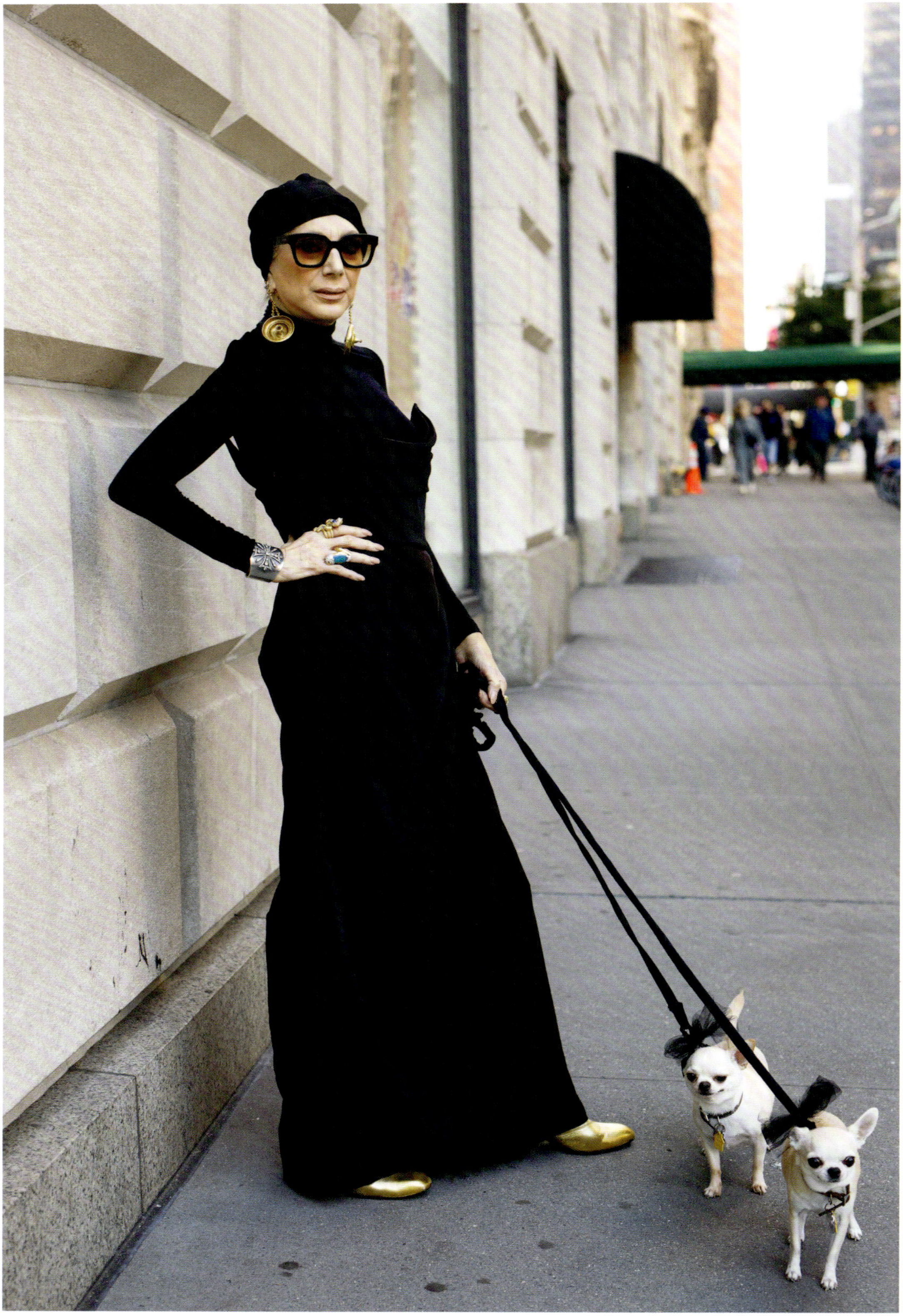

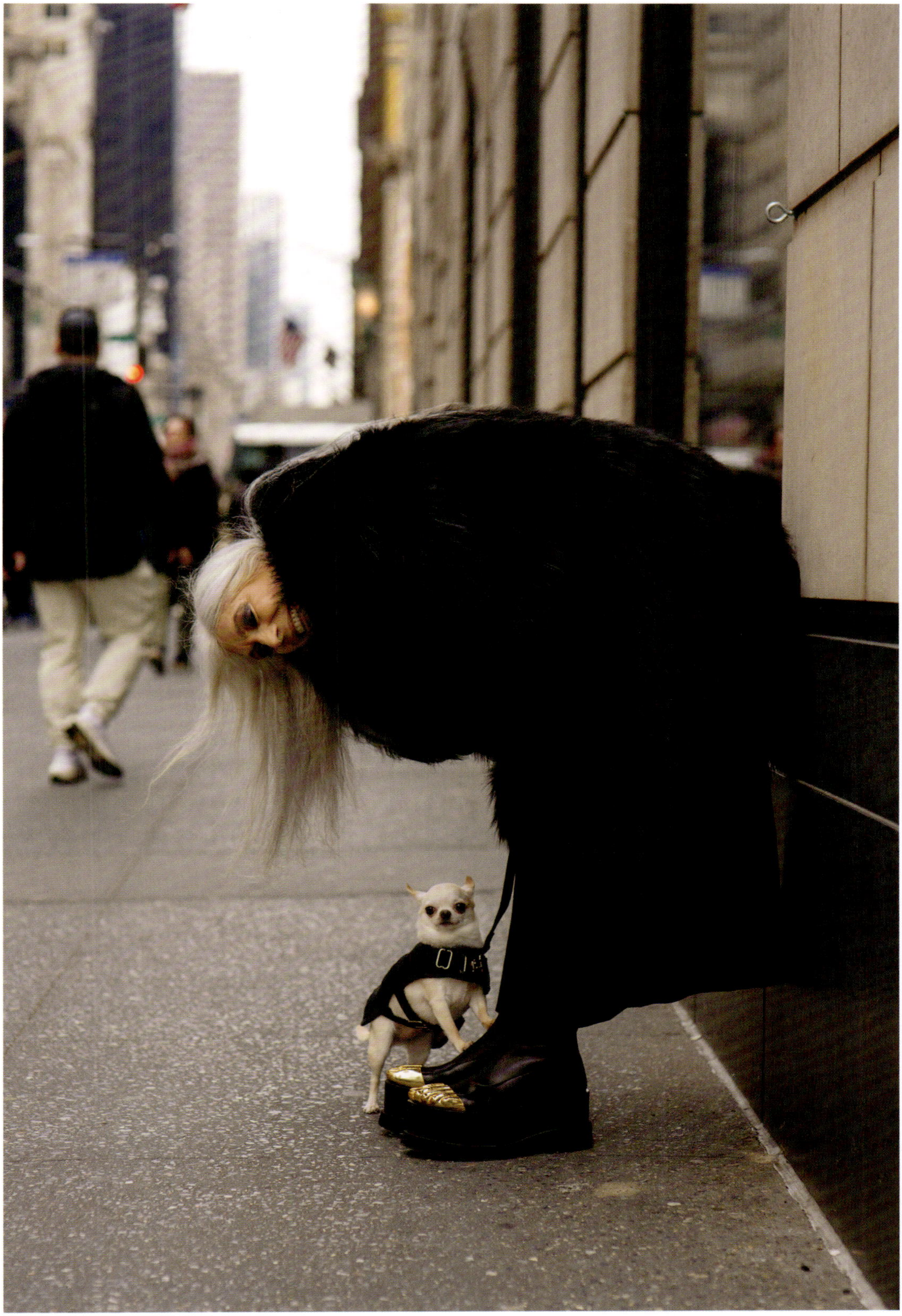

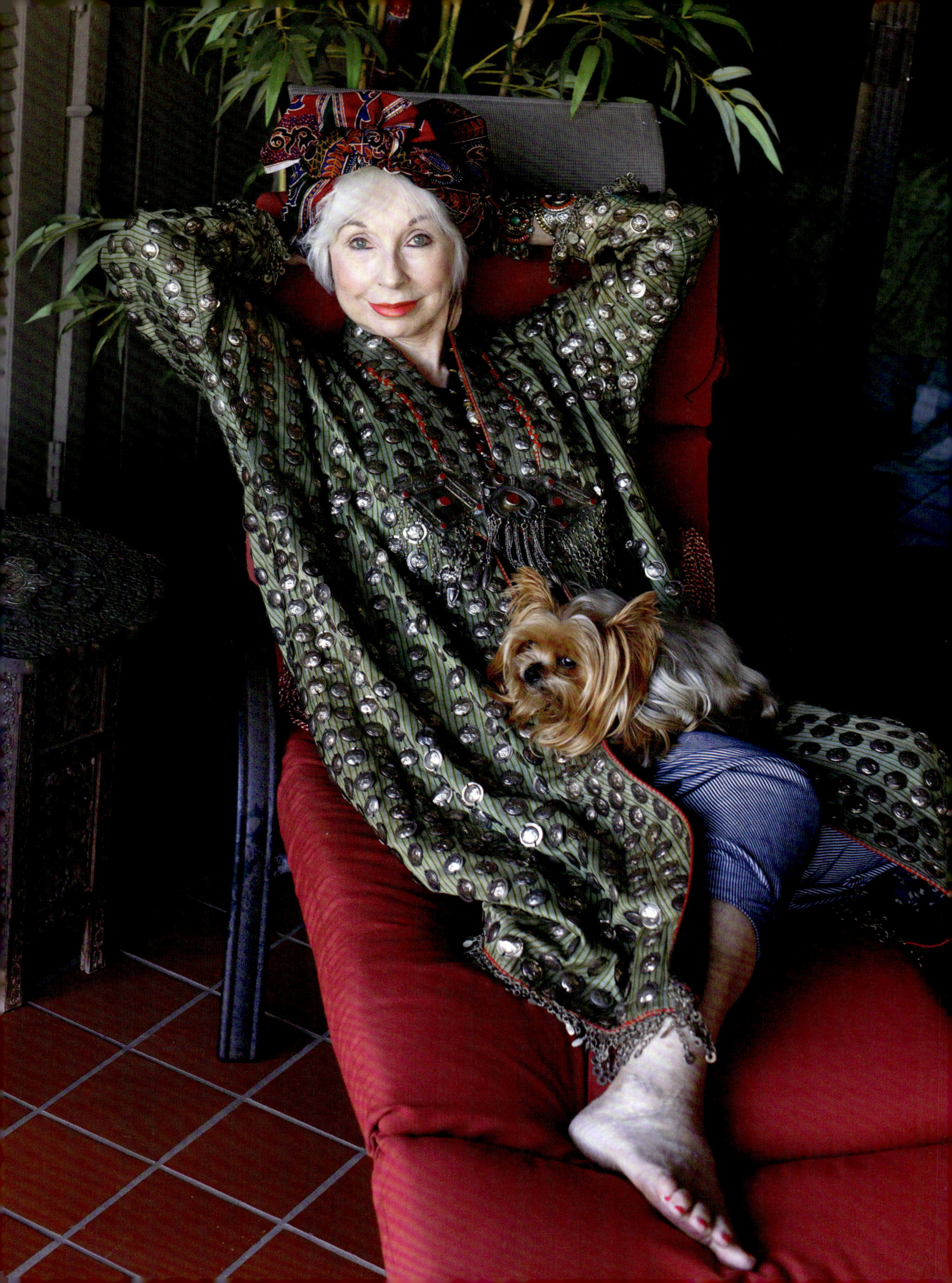

Gretchen and Feather

Feather is my little mink. She's soft as a puff of dandelion and the color of misty gold. She's the perfect accessory! I take her everywhere with me, looped over my arm or peeking out of my bag.

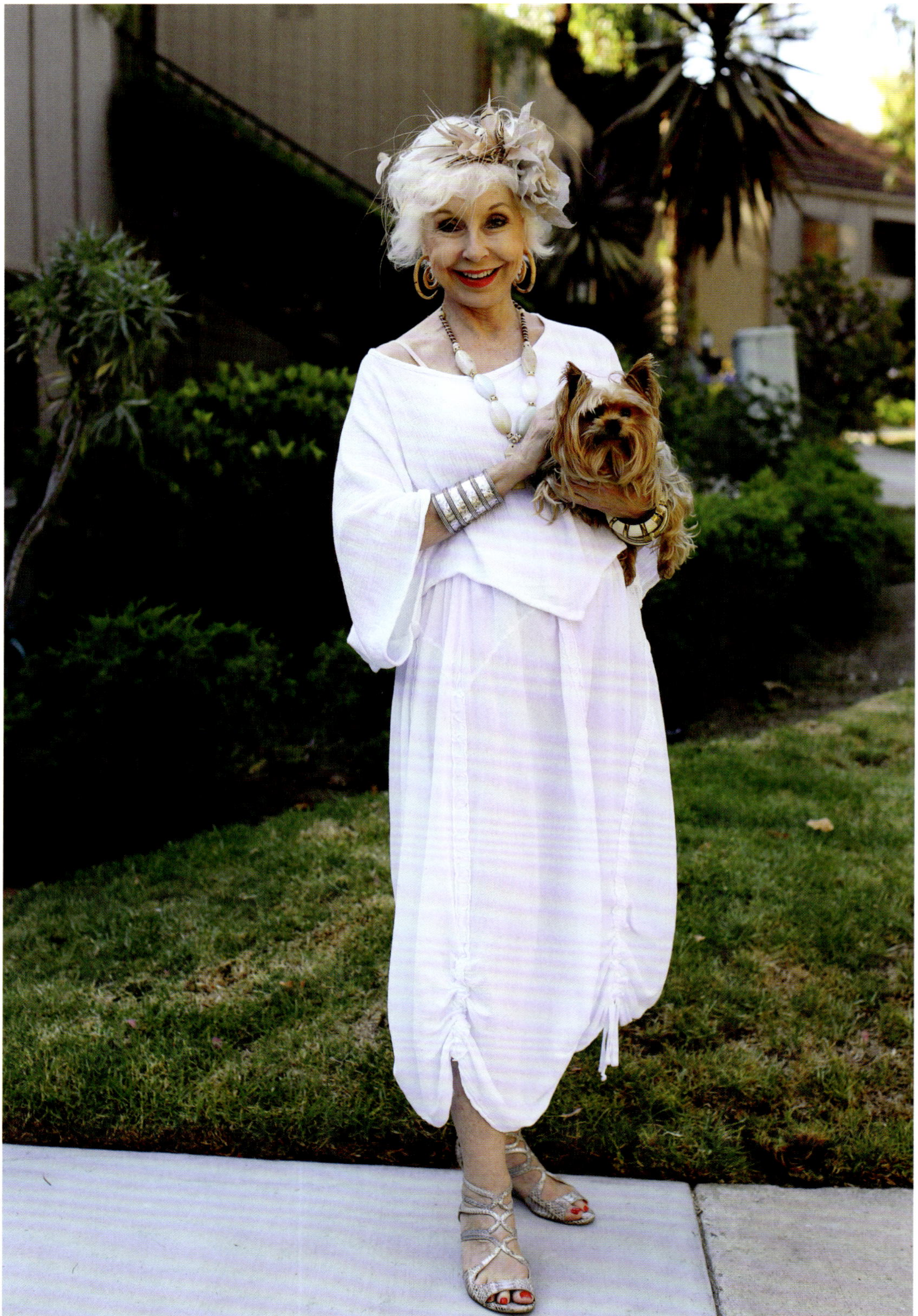

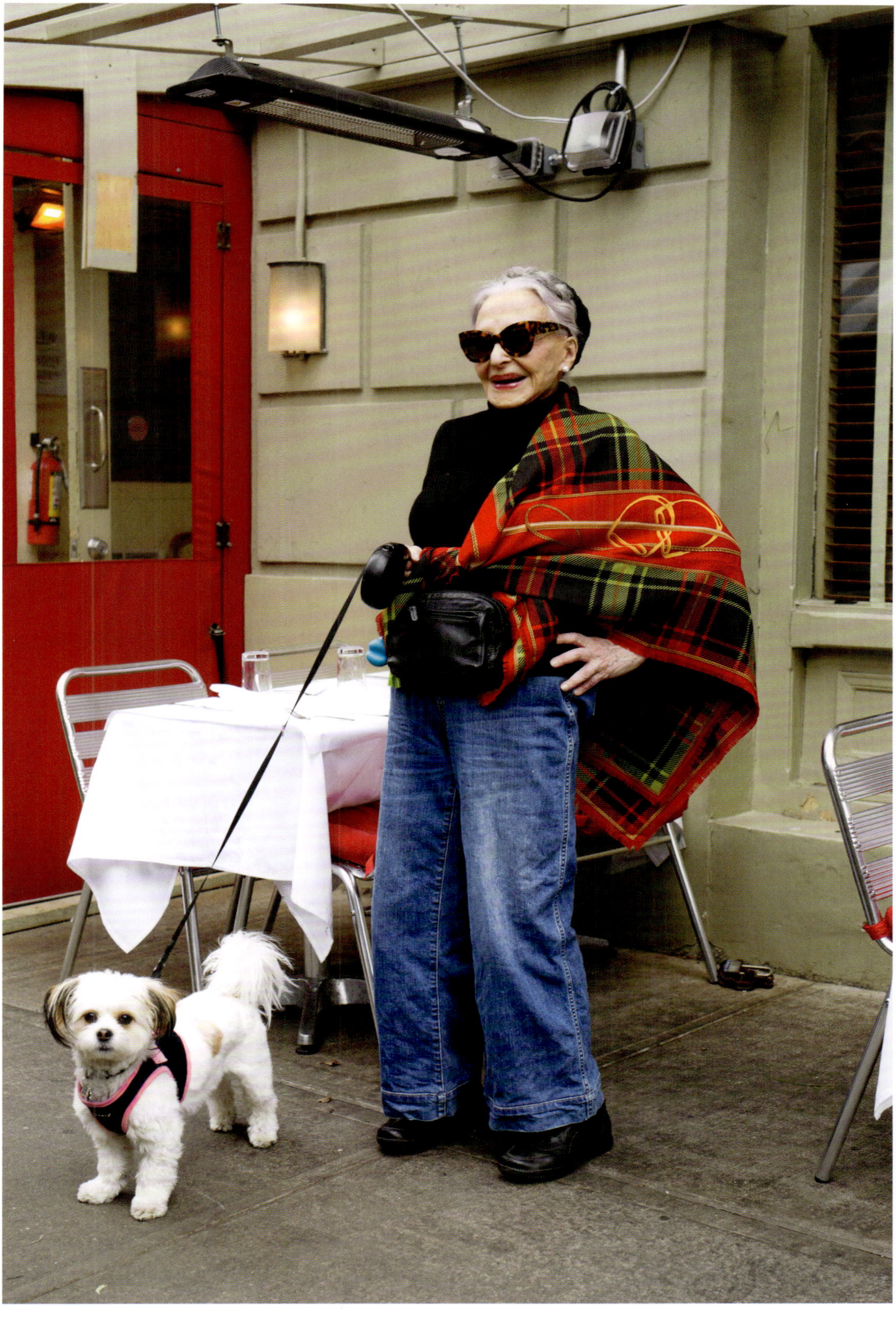

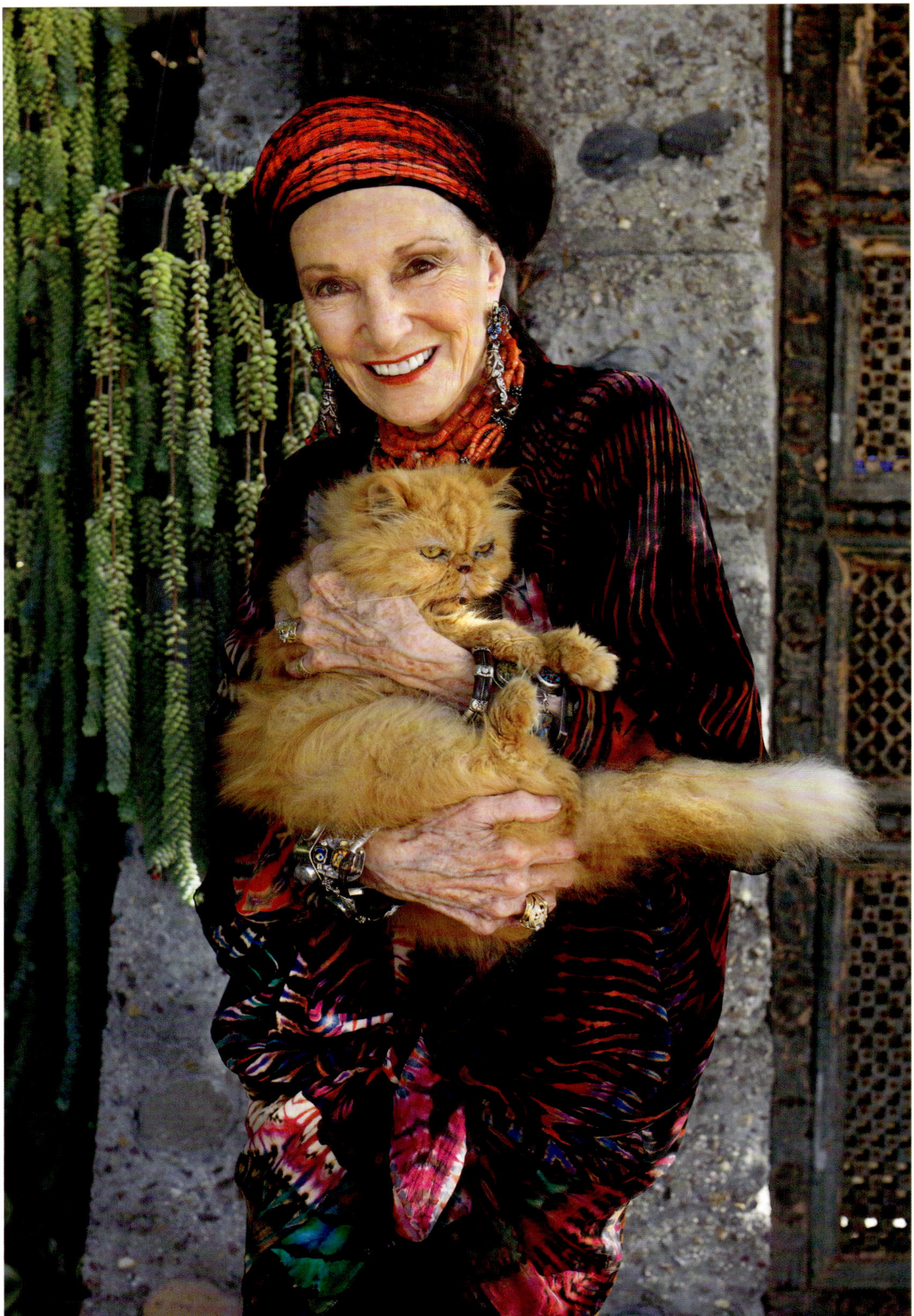

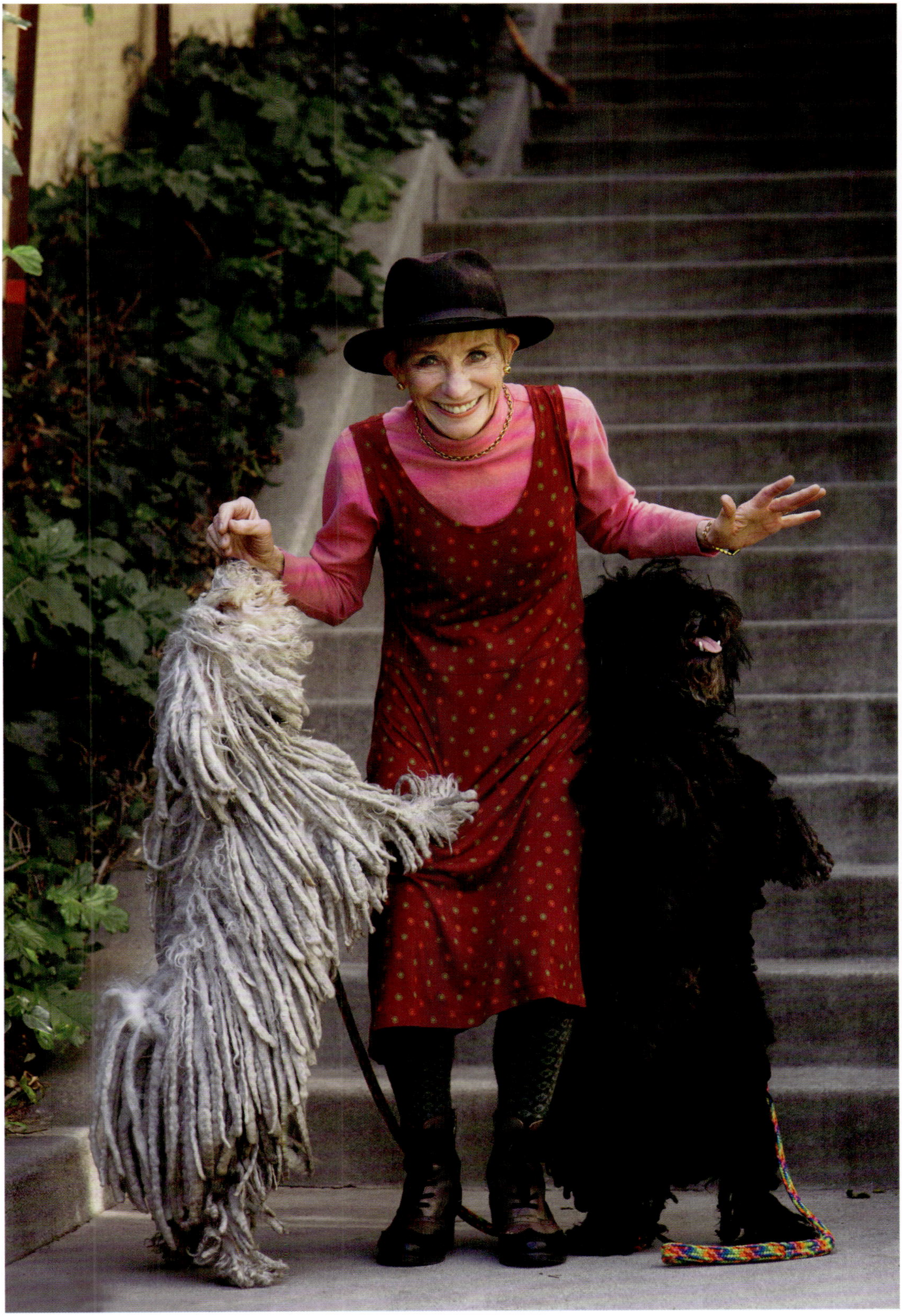

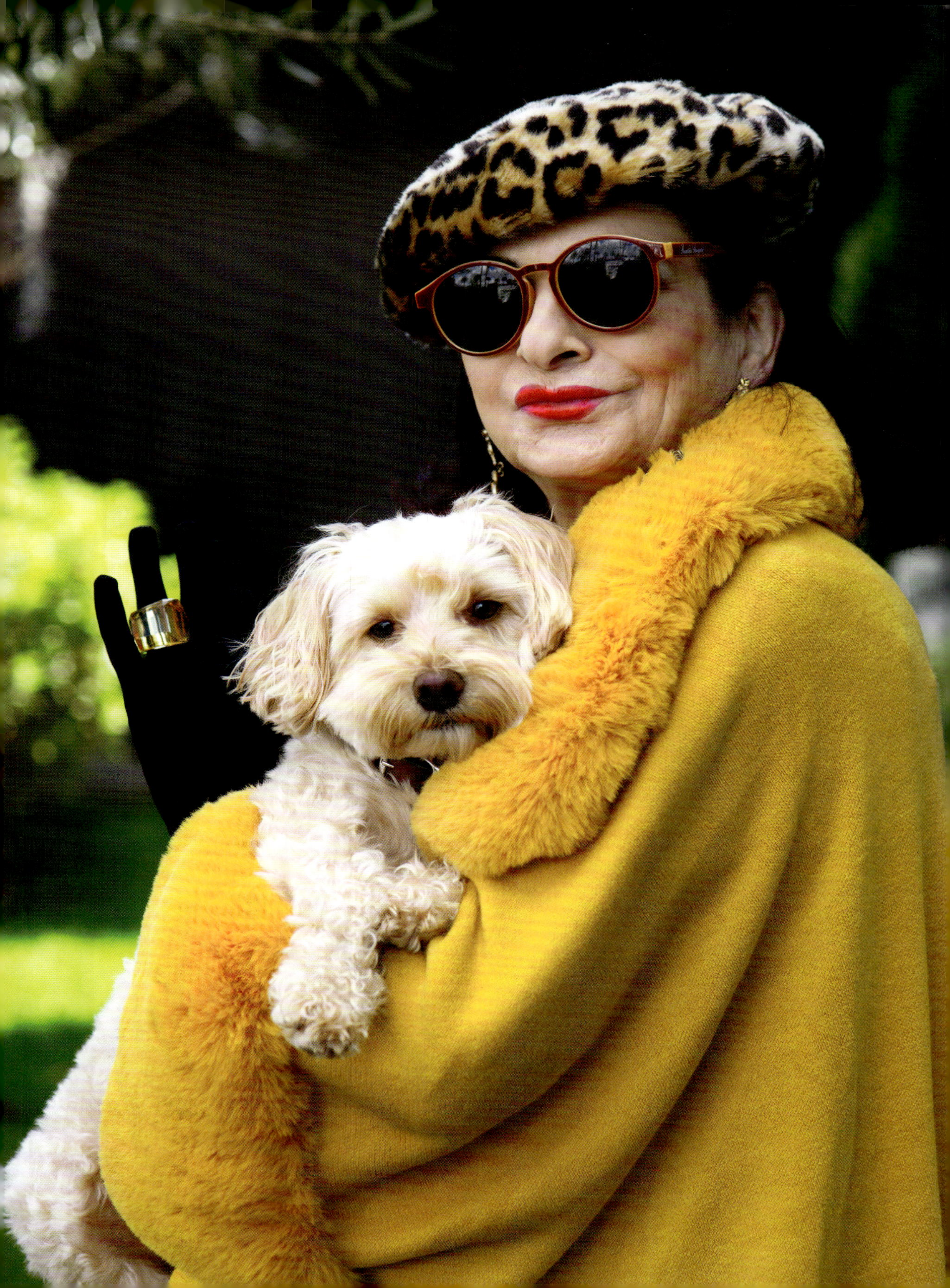

Marion, Louis, and Miles

I love to dress up to show off my dogs. They are very photogenic. We adopted Louis Vuitton from the Humane Society. He came with the name so we didn't change it. He is a full-bred Pomeranian and he just turned two. His brother Miles is also a very good boy. They get along most wonderfully, but Louis is definitely the boss.

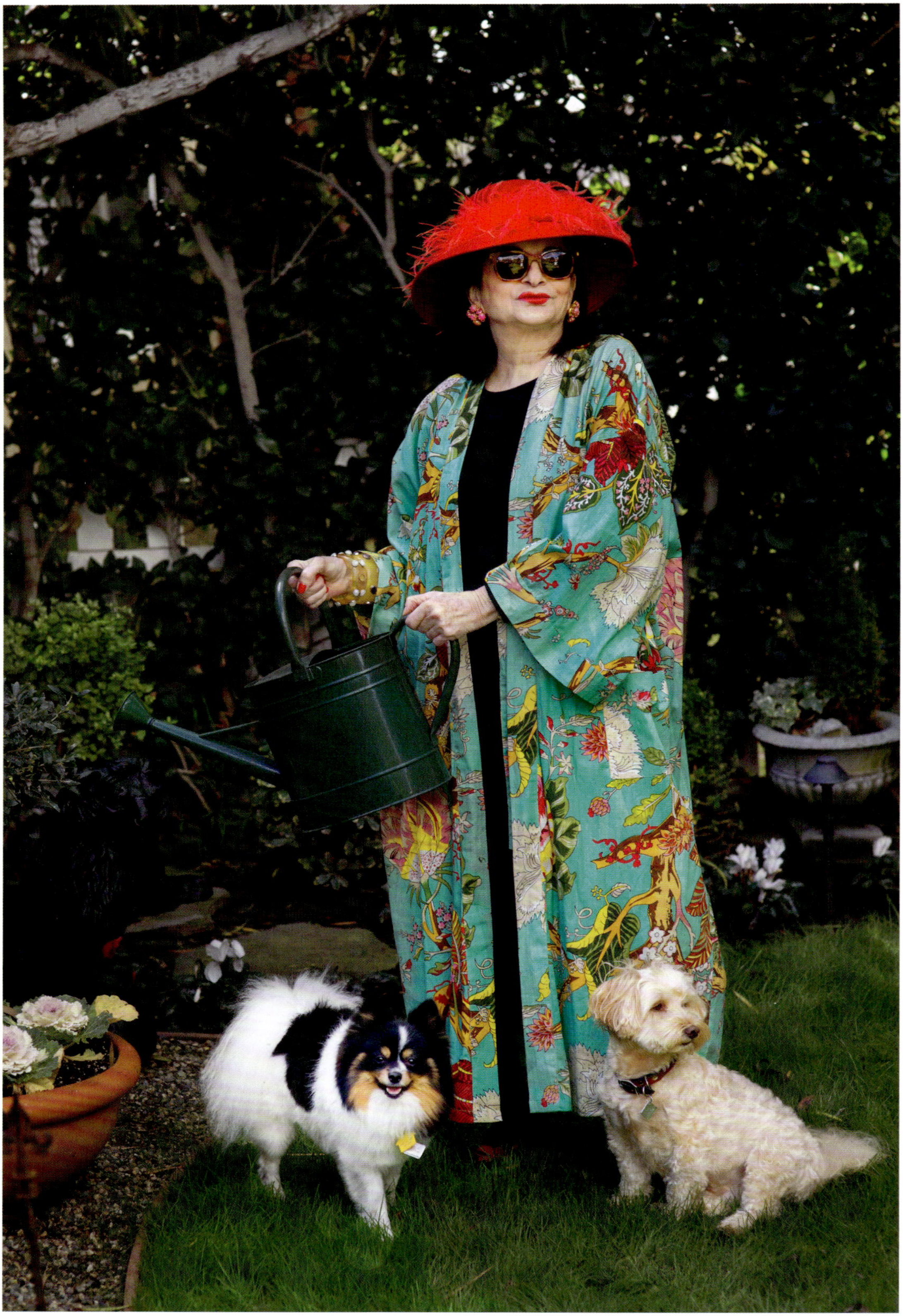

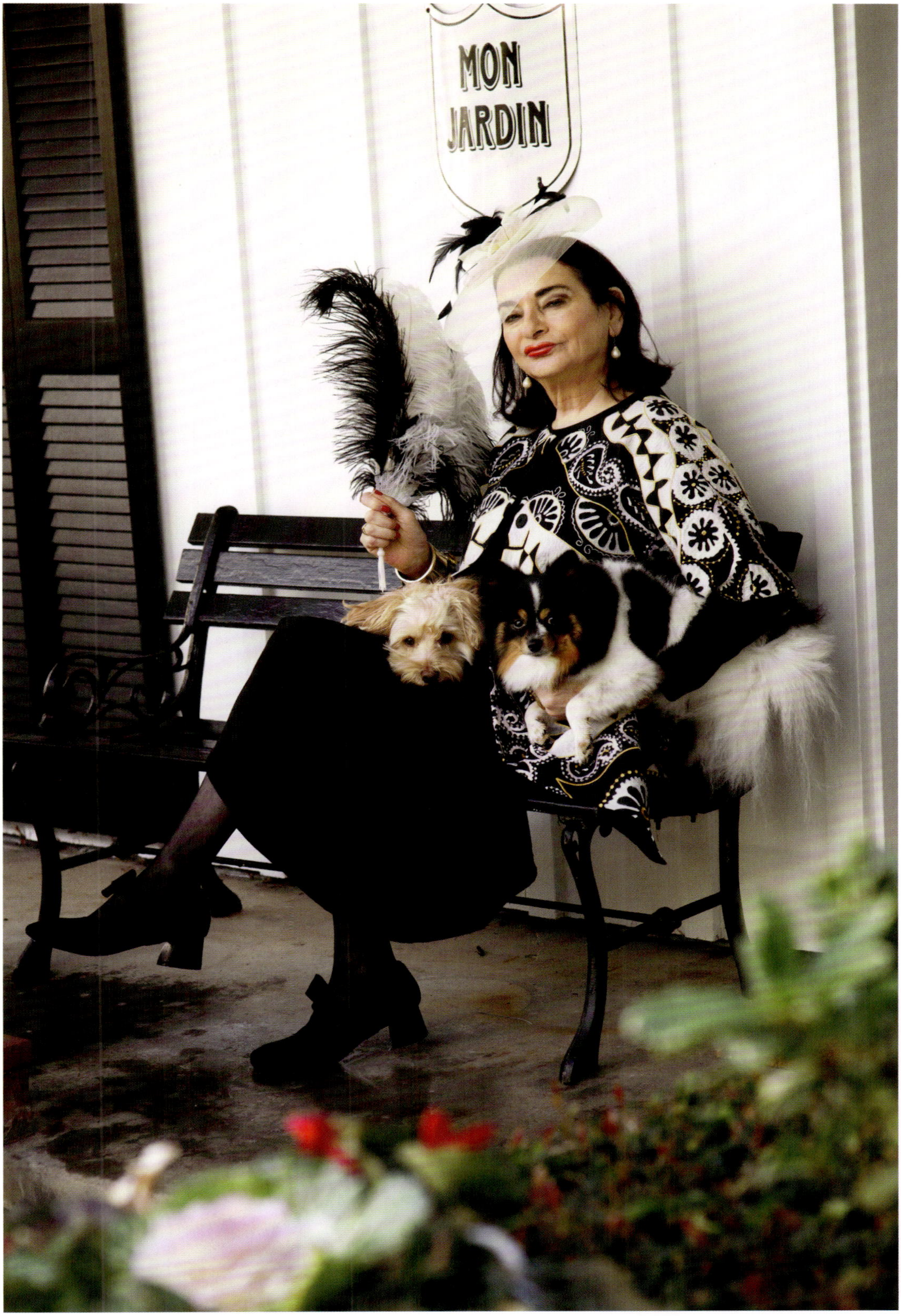
MON
JARDIN

Mara and Bruiser

Bruiser was born in a barn in Tehachapi, California. He was given to me by a friend who knew I loved Siamese cats. He can be described in two words: talkative and territorial. He is now sixteen, and I am hoping to see him live for many more years. Life would be a bit empty without my little buddy.

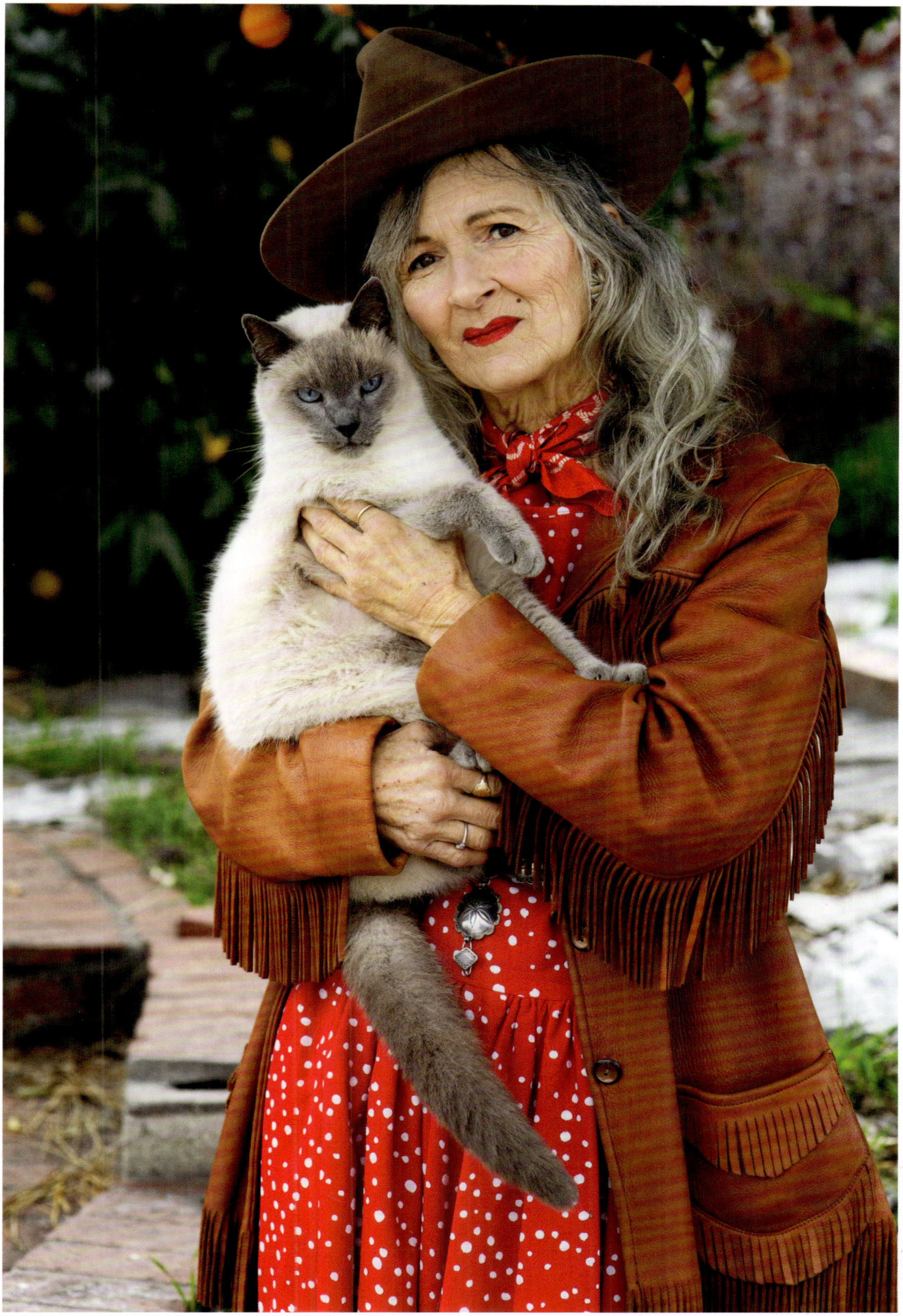

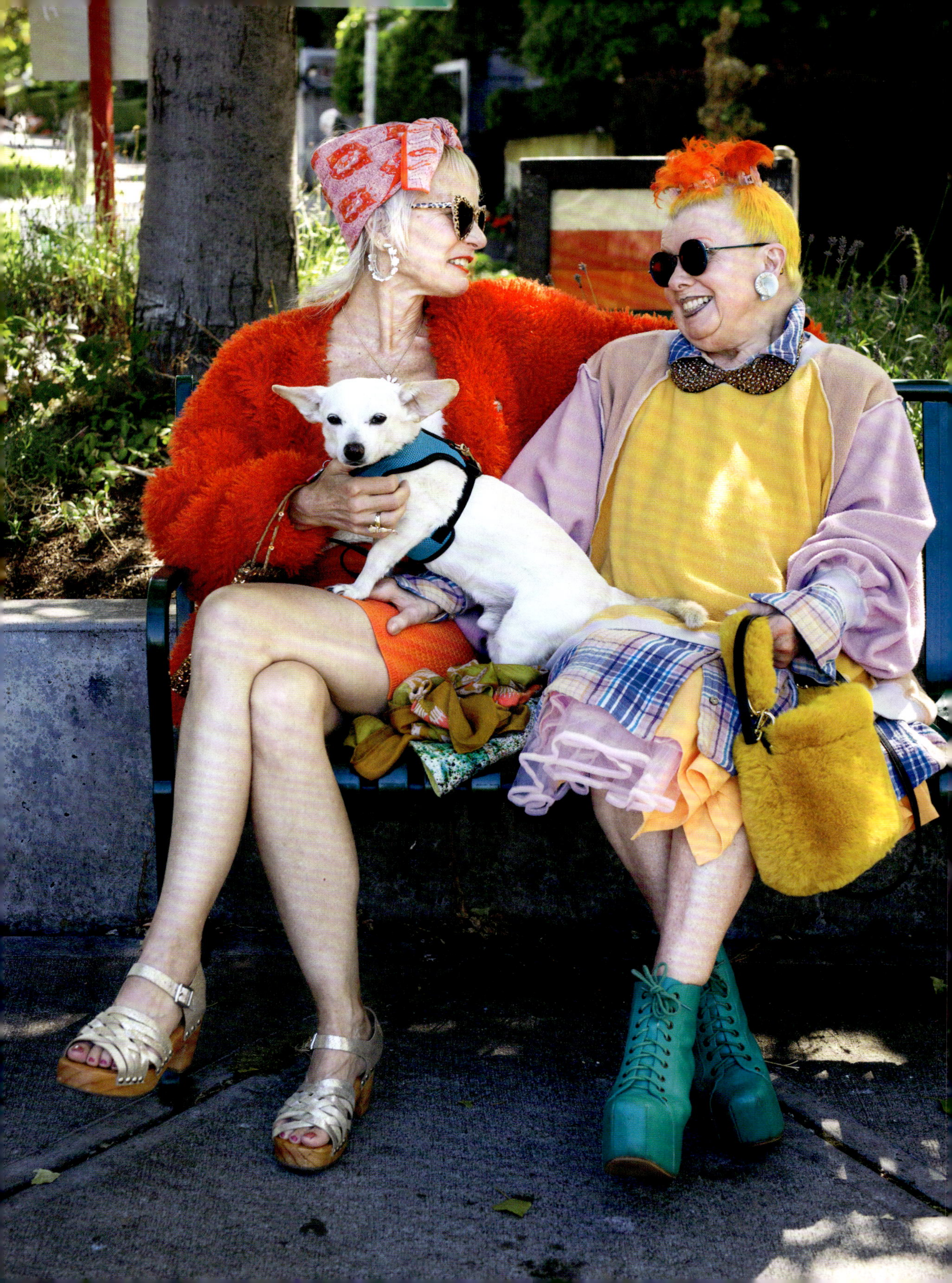

Paula and Murphy

Murphy is a fourteen-year-old Chihuahua mix. He was posted on the Old Dog Haven website as an abandoned senior dog who needed a home. He is a bundle of joy. He greets me every morning with a smile on his face, ready for another wonderful day. Dogs live in the moment and I marvel at their resilience and never-ending enthusiasm for all life has to offer. They teach us that life is a journey meant to be experienced with joy, passion, and wonder.

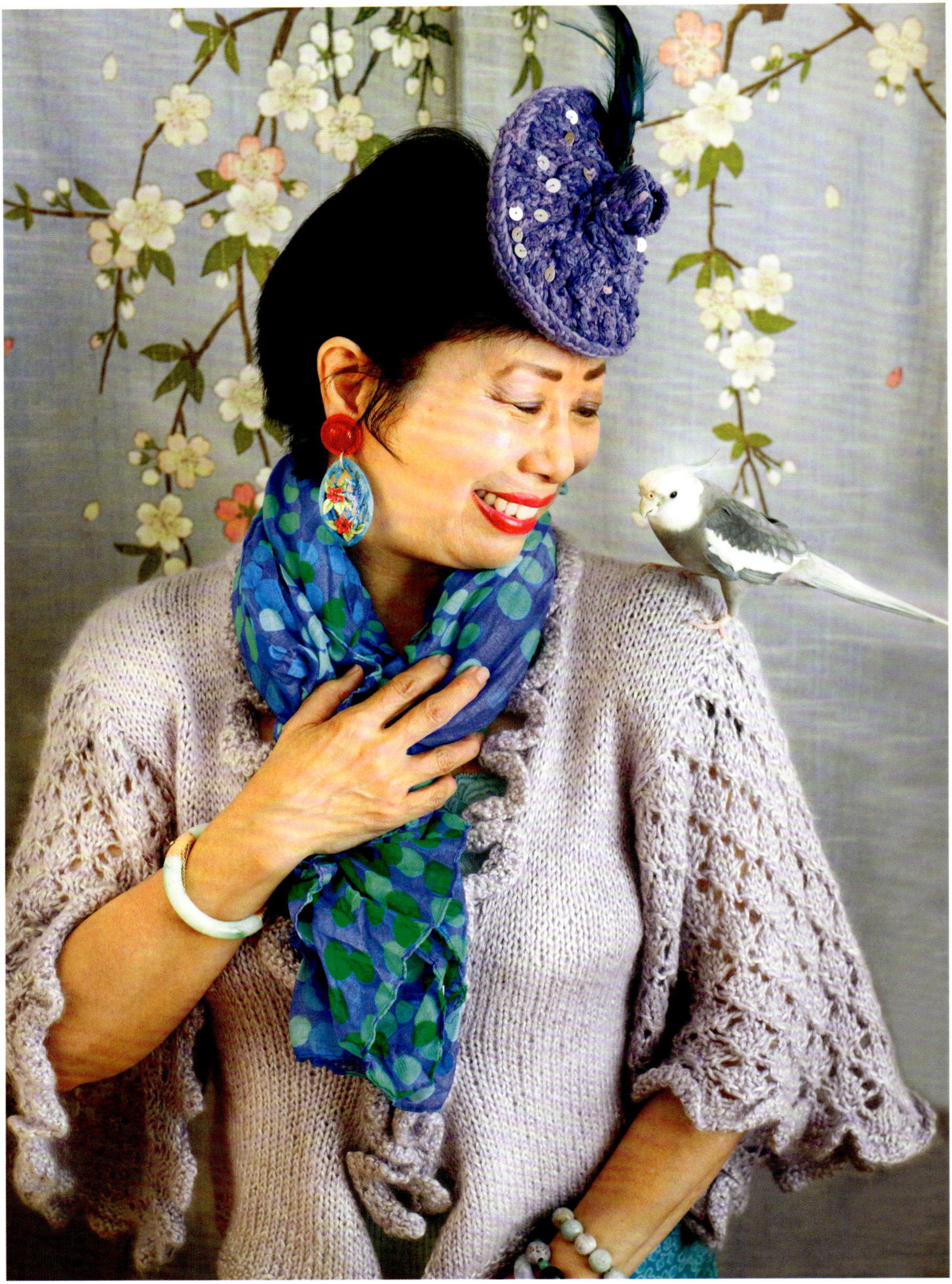

Terri and Snowball

Over the past forty-eight years I've been privileged to have the company of numerous feathered friends. My first husband gifted me my first bird, a blue male parakeet, and I found my vintage tall round cage at a garage sale. All my boy birds enjoy full, decadent lives in my colorful house filled with orchids, textiles, and music. I adopted Snowball—the grey and white cockatiel in the photo with me—from my local pet store when he was two years old. He came to me underfed and extremely shy. Within a week of being at my home, he was bulking up on proper food and whistling "If You're Happy and You Know It, Clap Your Hands." Birds fill my heart and home with joy, laughter, exquisite music, and unconditional love.

Pattie, John, Darling, and Diego

What I love about dogs is that they are not people. People can really hurt you, but you can be yourself in front of a dog. Dogs make me feel safer. They don't judge you. People ghost you, but you will never catch a dog ghosting you.

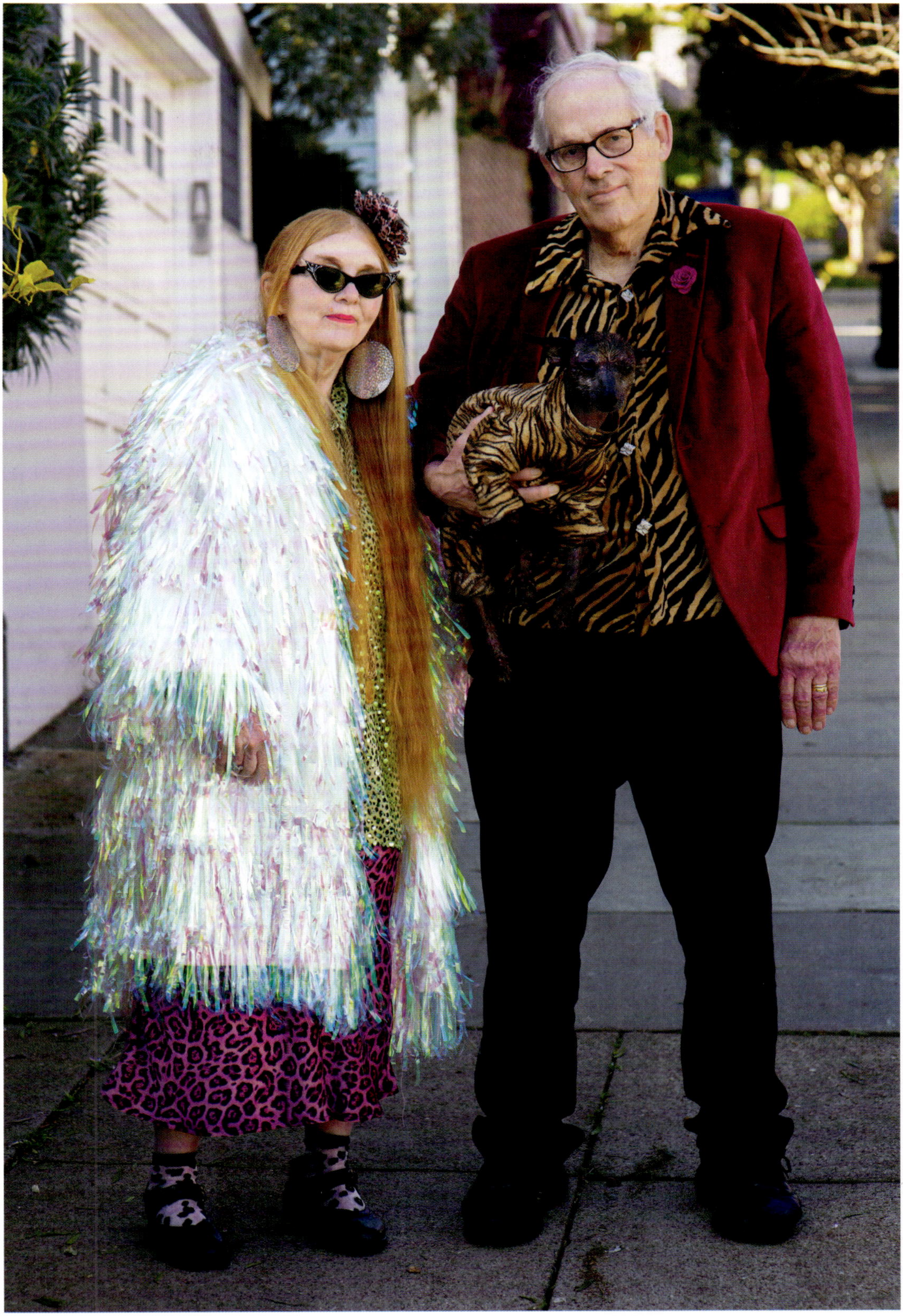

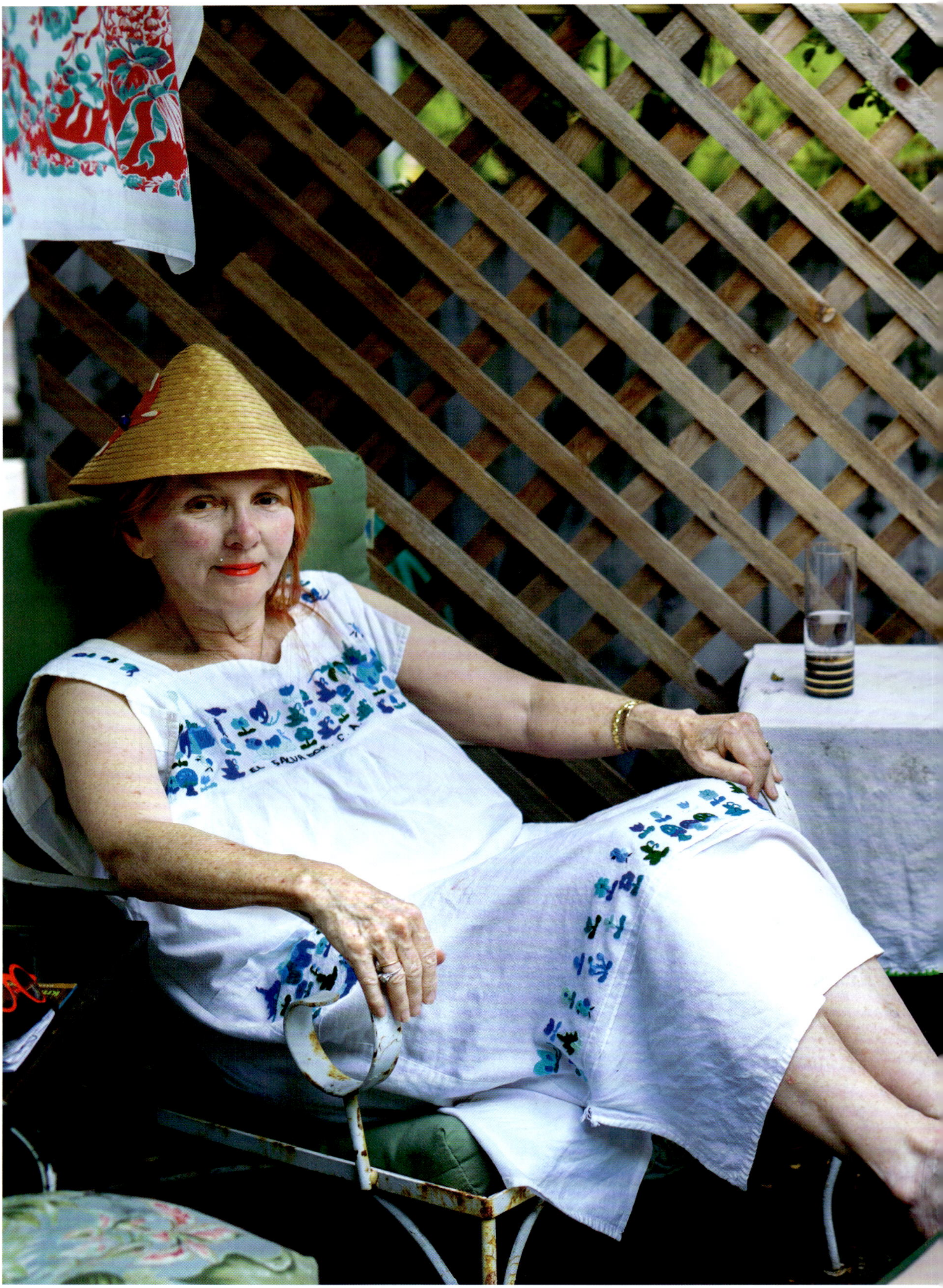
EL SALVADOR C.A

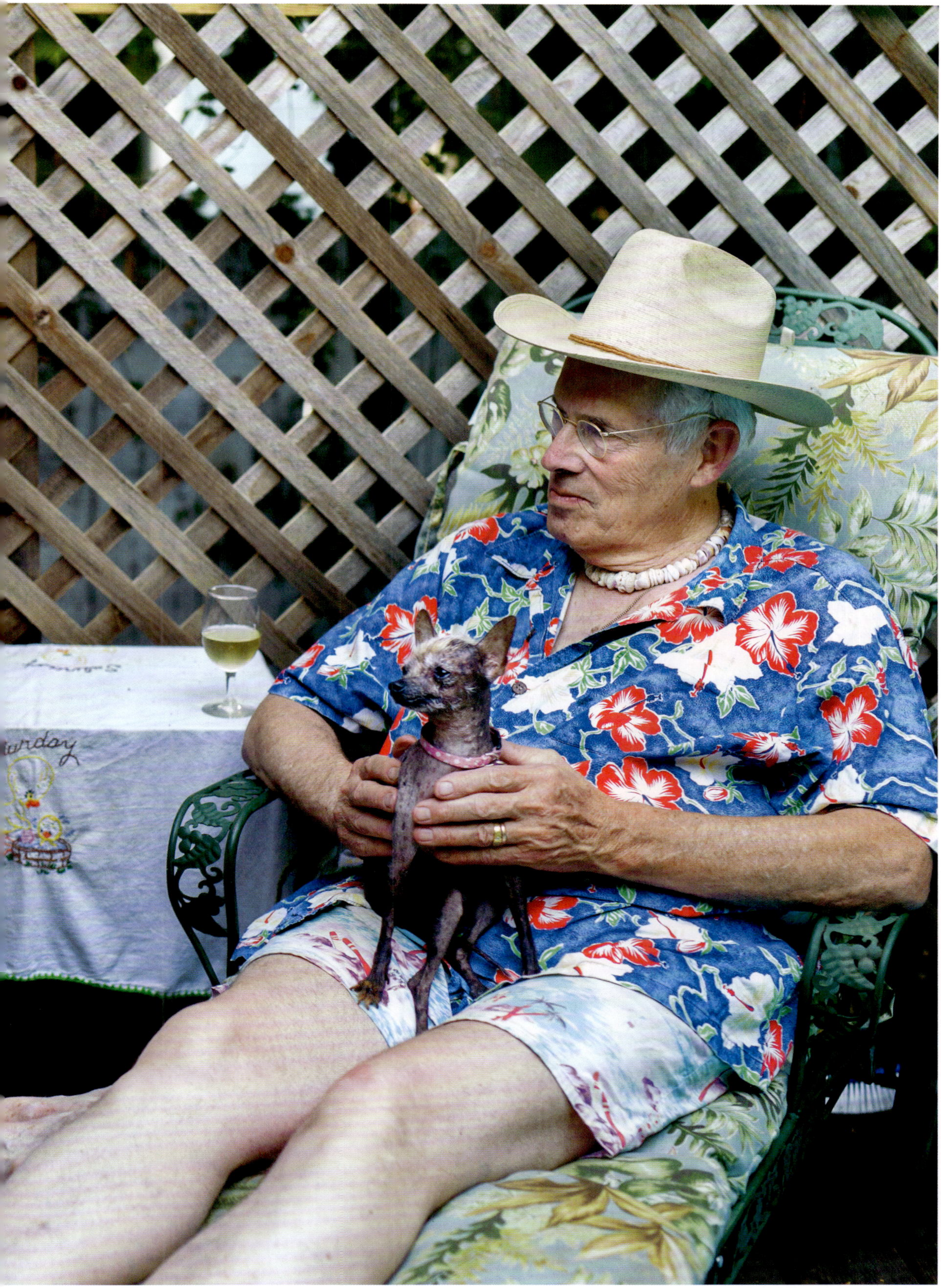

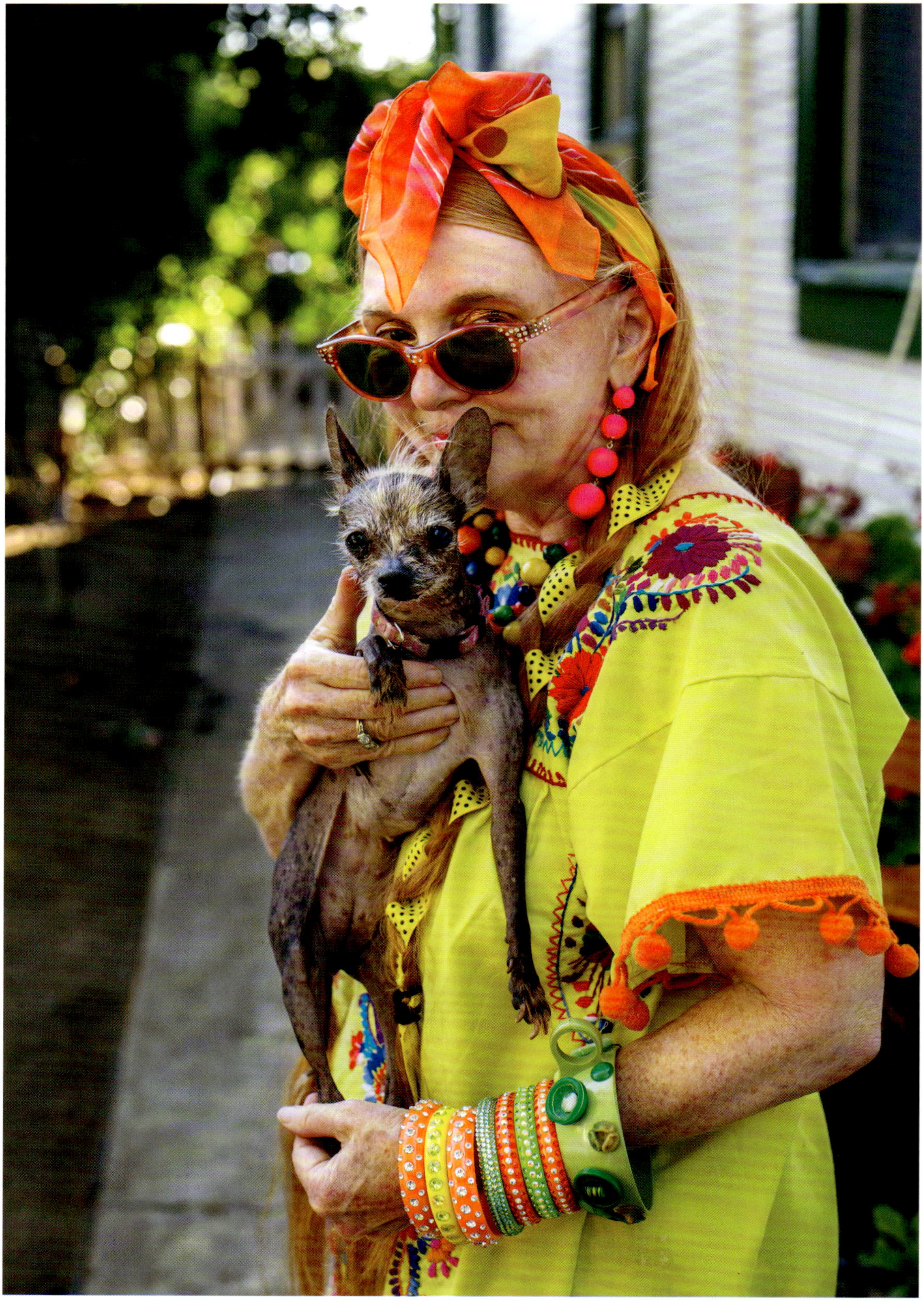

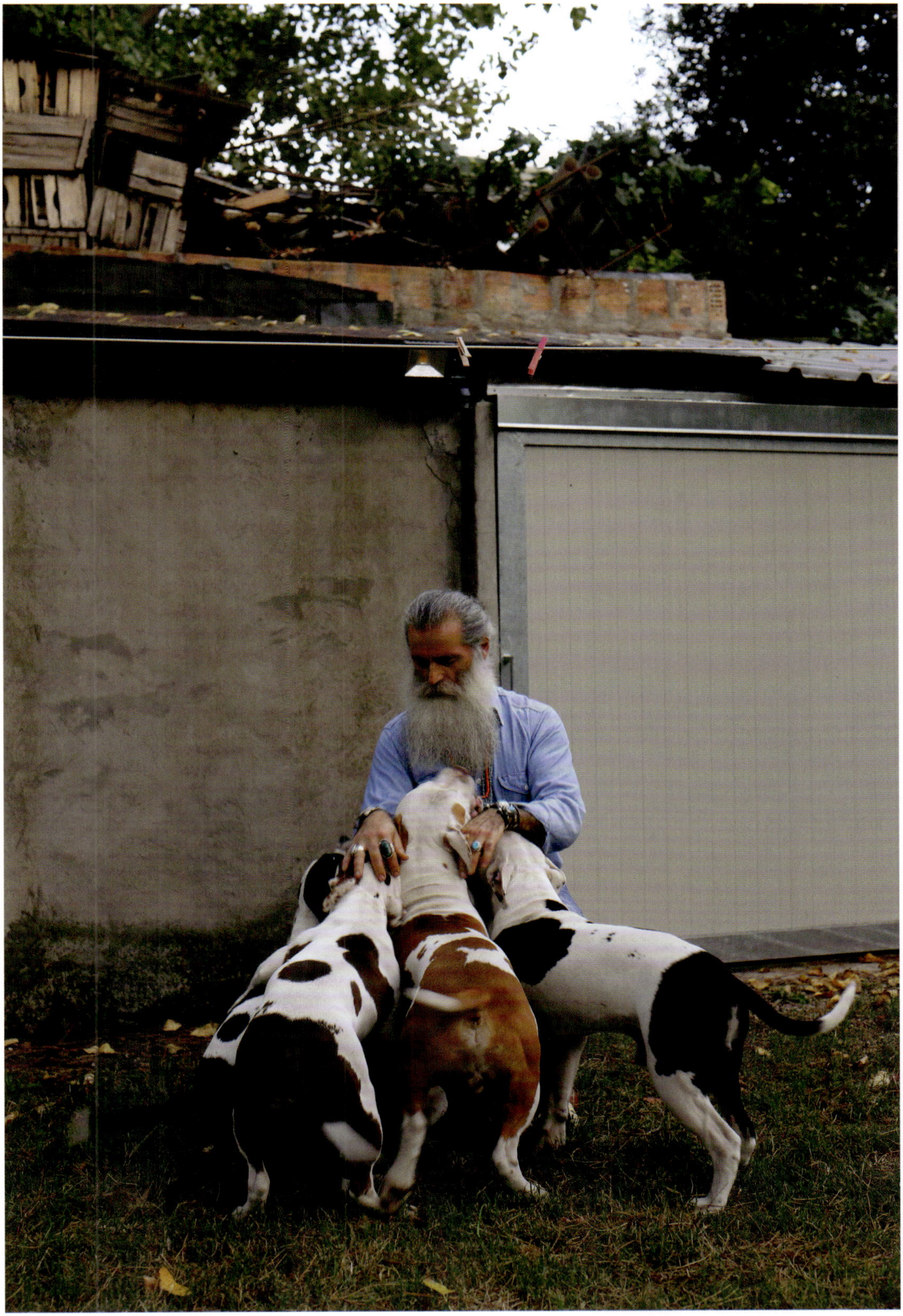

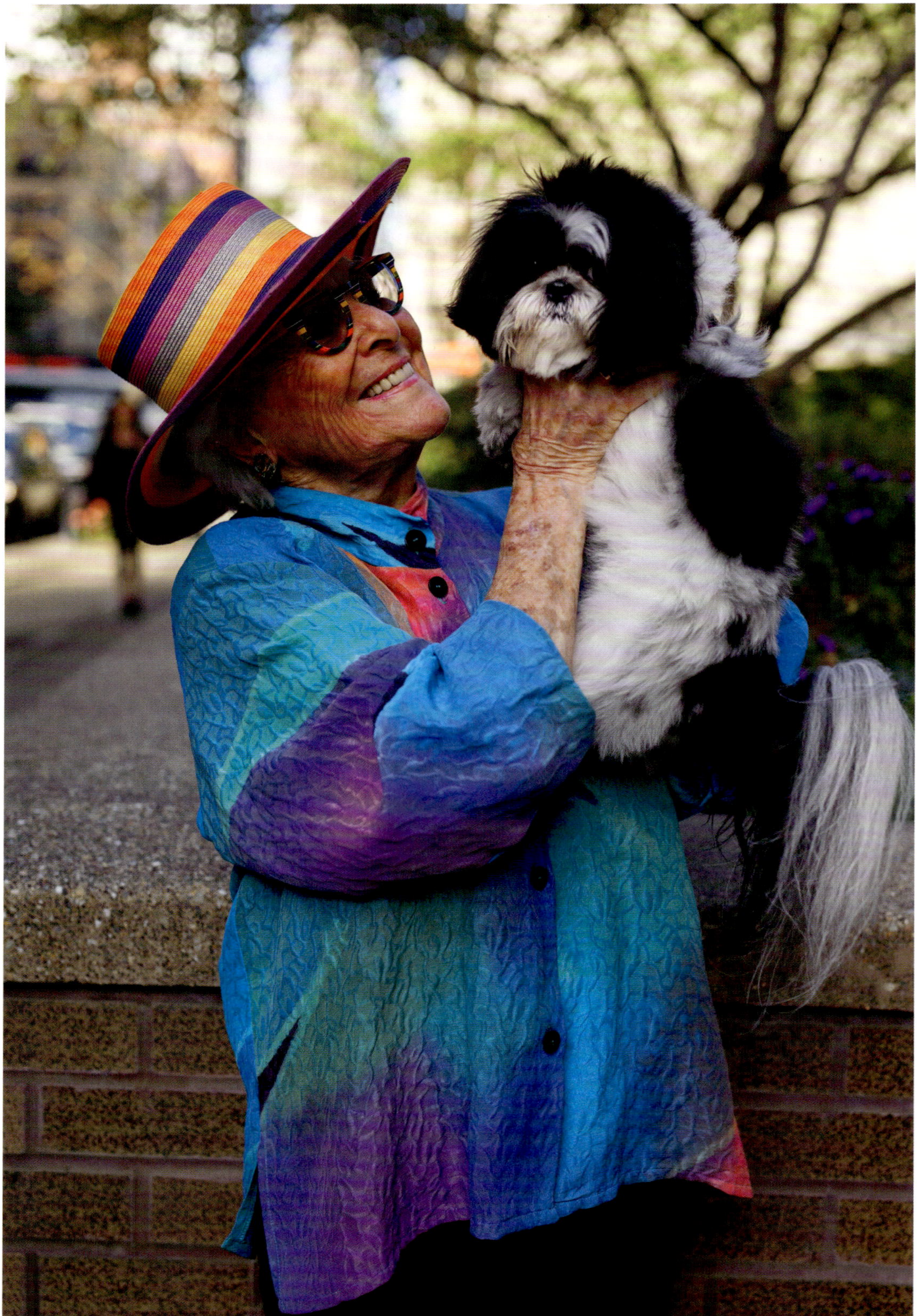

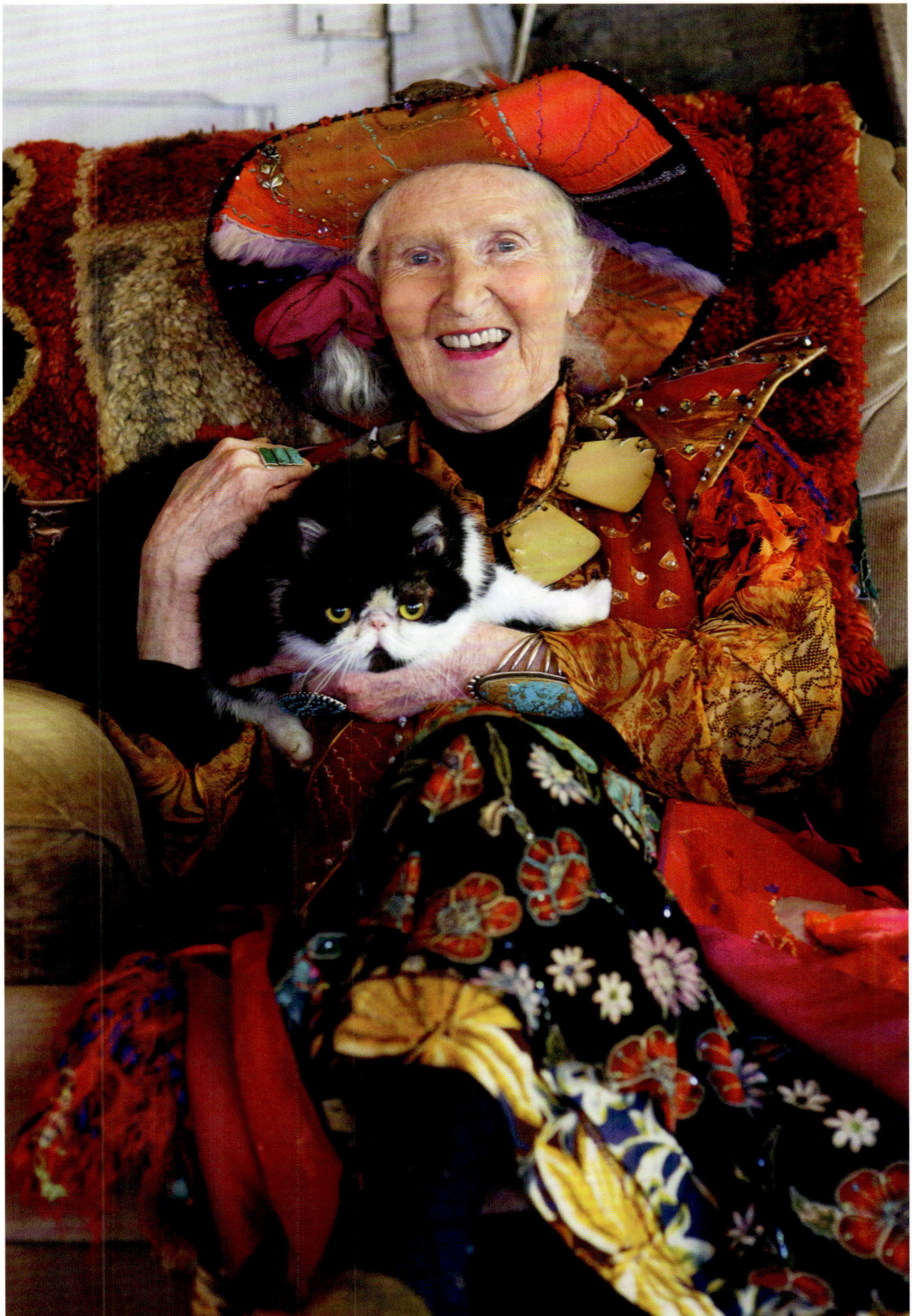

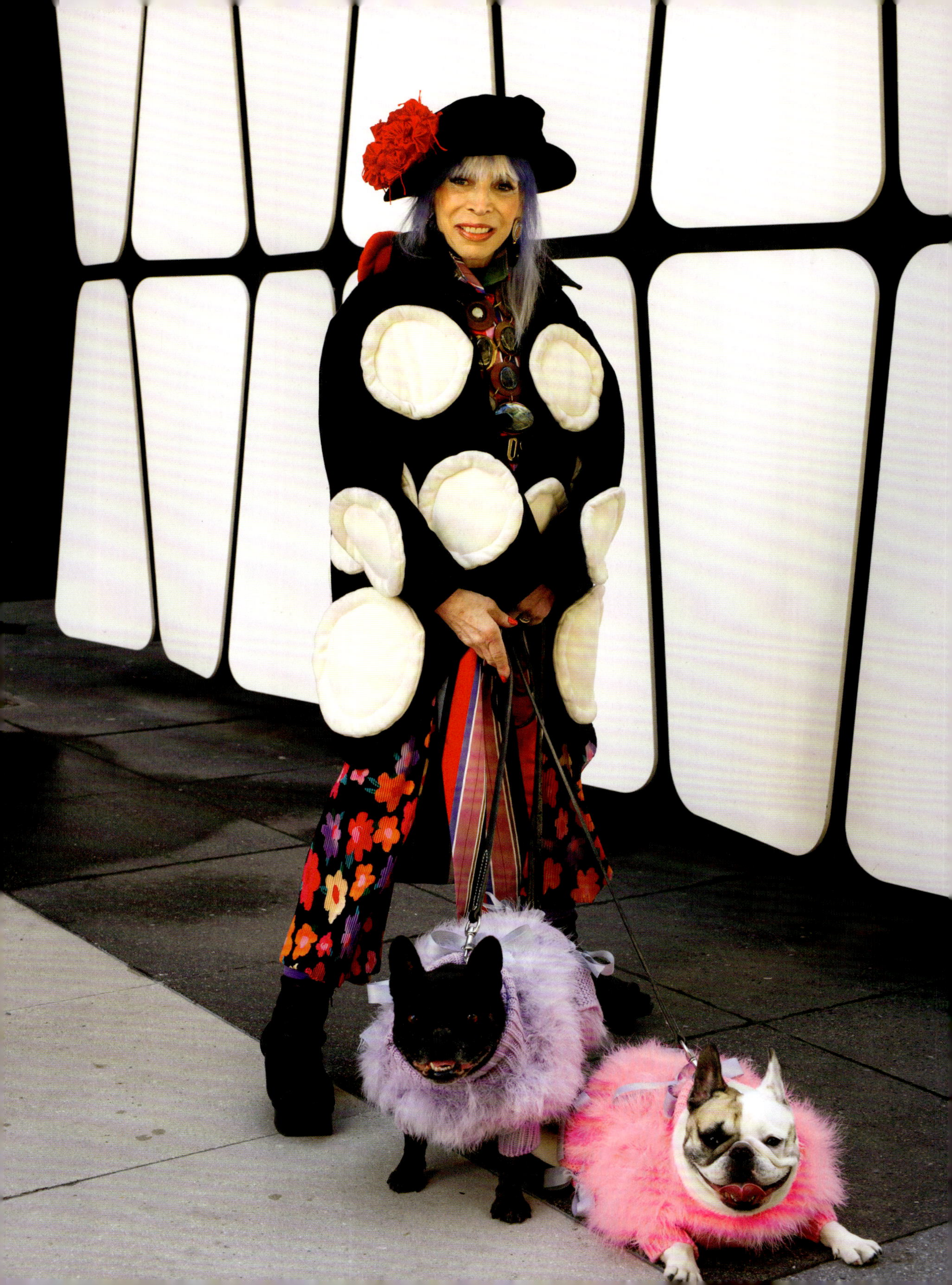

Sara, Star, and Dolce

Star is our therapy dog. She always goes along to get along. She's sweet as a bowl of sugar and great to cuddle with at night. Dolce is our clown in a dog suit, always smiling and looking to get into trouble… which is not hard to do. She is adorable and a great cuddler! We started dressing up the dogs during Covid because people would smile as they passed by. When you put a funky sweater on a dog, all of a sudden people light up.

"Rex is a friend to many and a constant companion to us. Some angels choose fur instead of wings."

Orren, Rob, and Rex

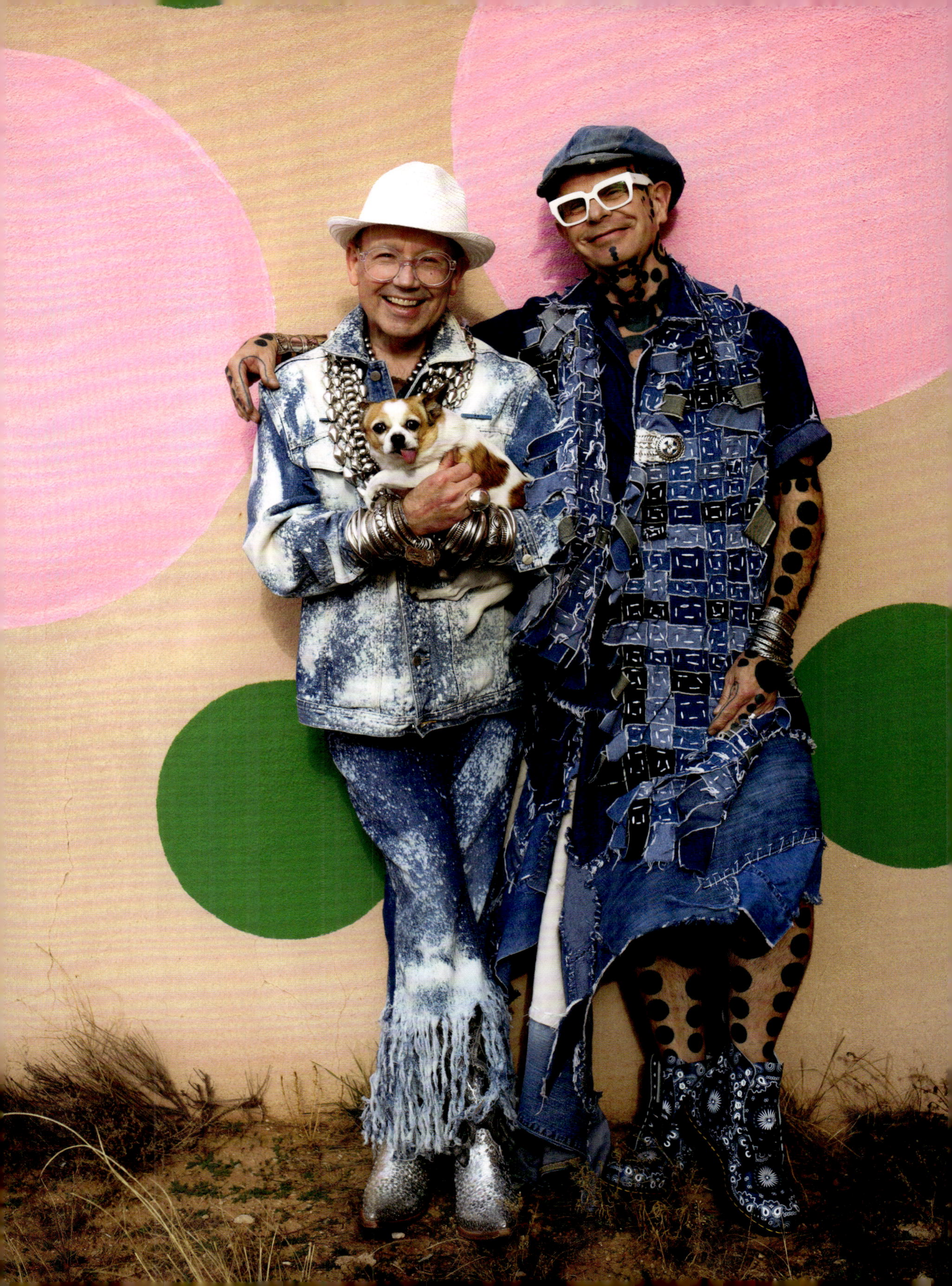

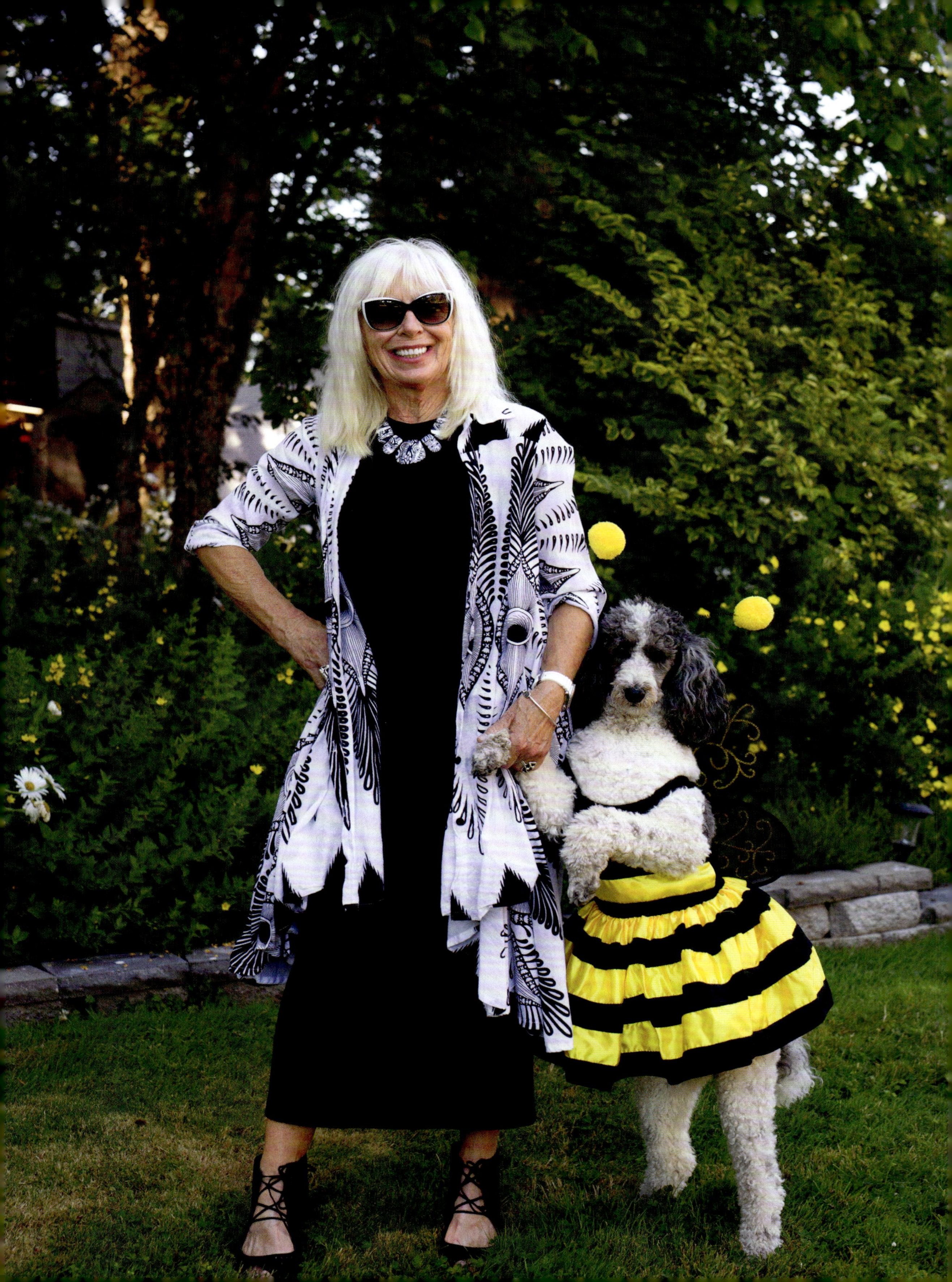

Susie and Charlotte Marie

Charlotte is our Pinocchio puppy; she wants to be a real girl. From the day we brought her home, at only eight weeks old, Charlotte began following us around the house on her hind legs. She will walk upright beside me and paw at my arm until I hold her hand. She loves music and she quickly learned to dance and spin all on her own. At dance parties, she will stand on her hind legs and make her way around the dance floor, pausing to dance and hold hands with each person. "Charlie" enjoys costumes and dressing up, which is apparently a trait shared by her poodle family. When visiting the breeder to meet Charlotte's parents on a sunny weekday afternoon, Charlie's mom and dad came out to greet us wearing black tie apparel. Mother was wearing pearls, a tiara, and a chiffon scarf. Daddy sported a tuxedo and a sequined bow tie. The breeder, Jaqueline, seemed nonplussed—I had to ask, "Are they attending an event later today?" She laughed and explained that her large family had many little nieces and nephews that visited regularly and the family saved outgrown human baby clothes so that the children could entertain themselves by playing dress-up with the puppies. Charlie's outfits aren't dog clothes—she wears a toddler size 5. She has recently mastered the cha-cha and is looking forward to our next dance party.

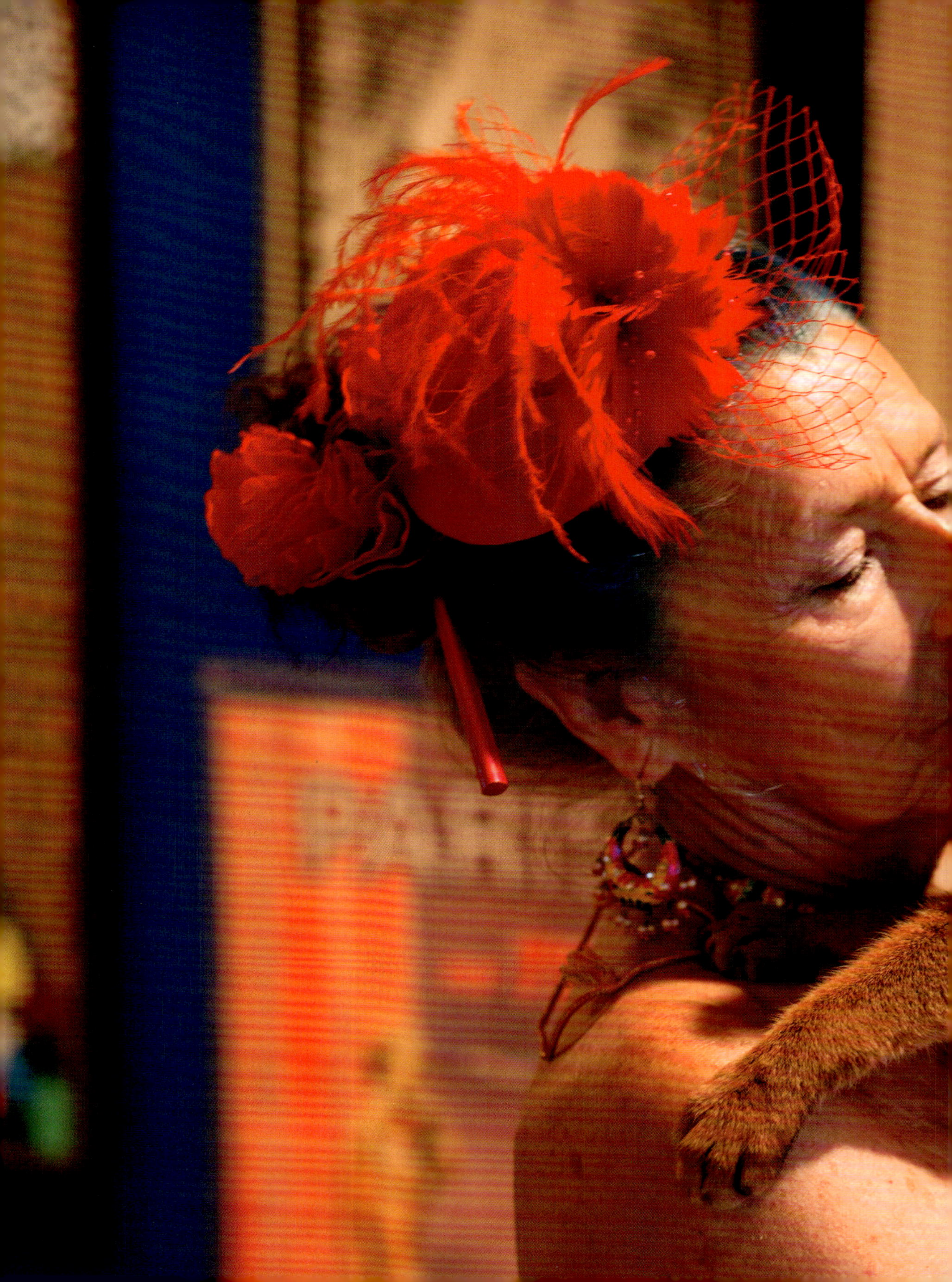

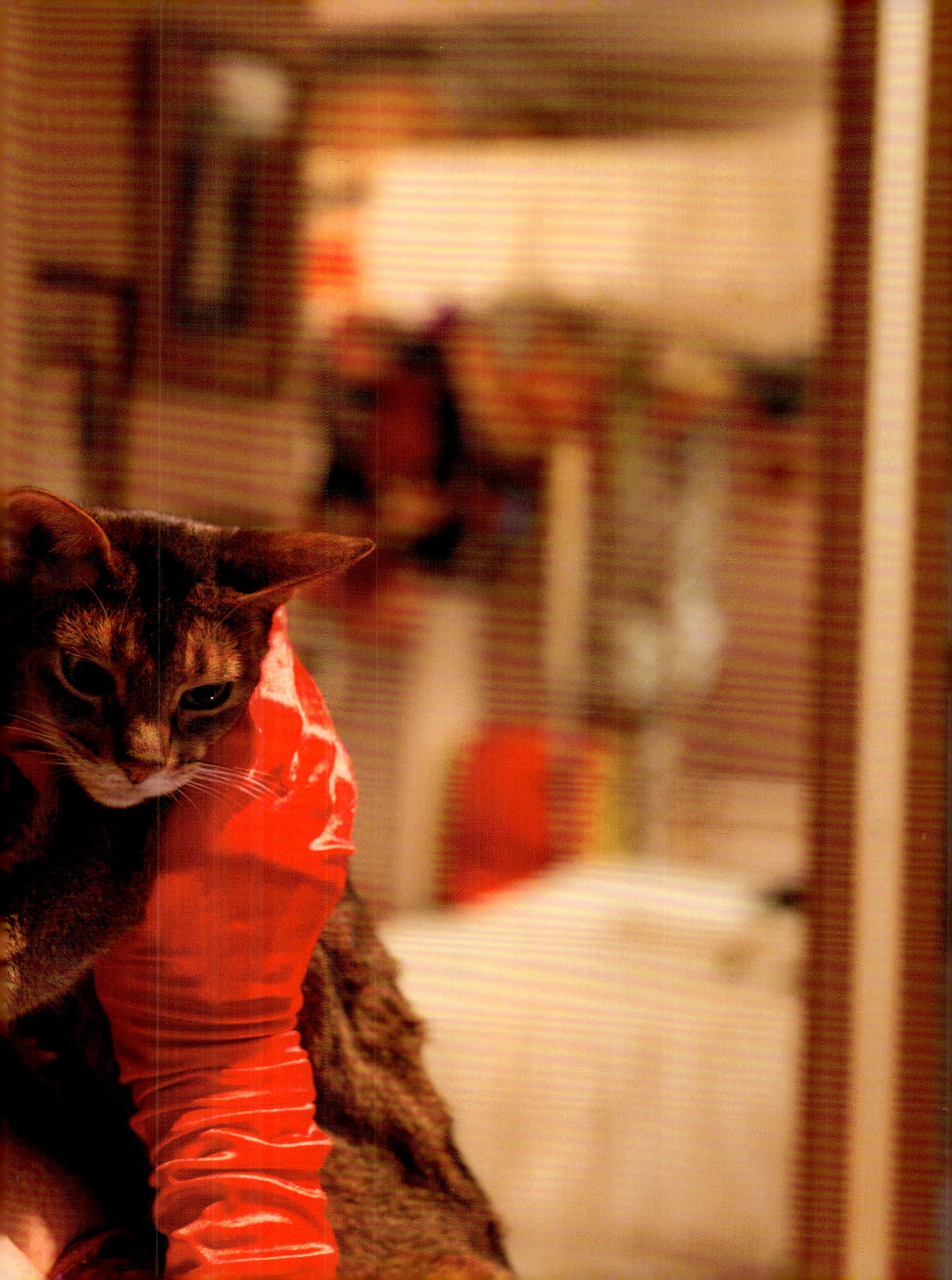

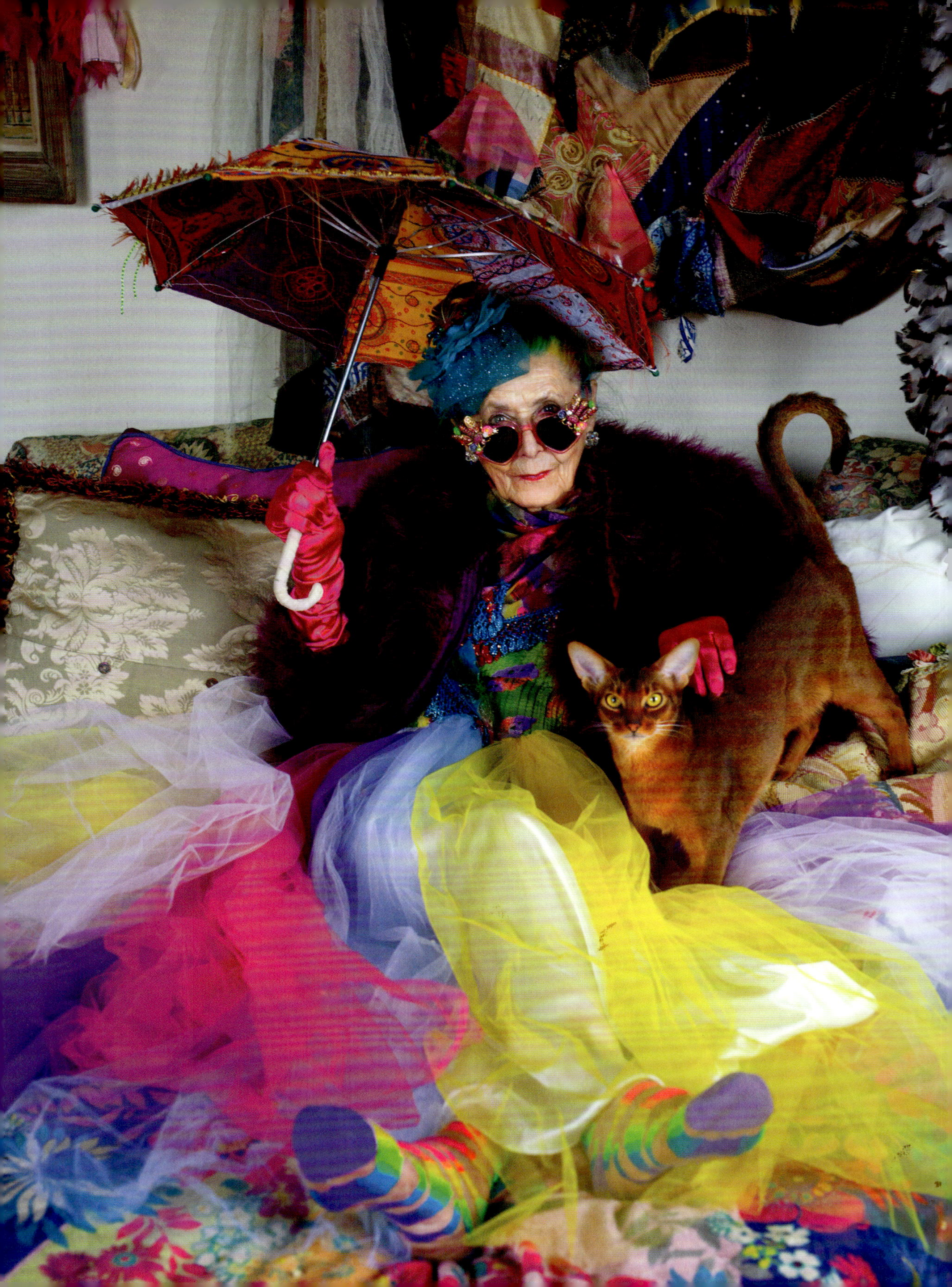

"One should never risk life without a cat or two or three or ten."

Emily and Kitties

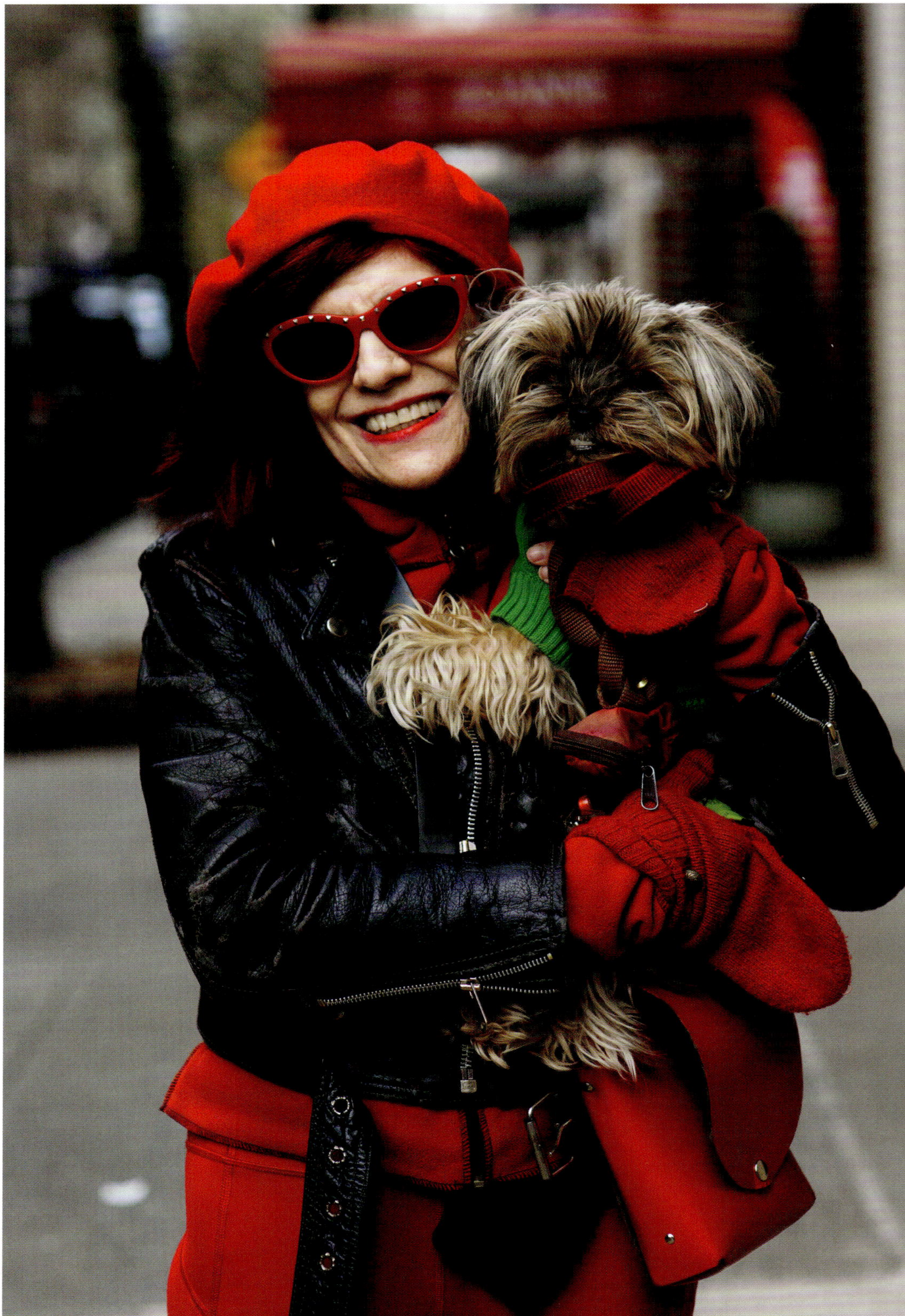

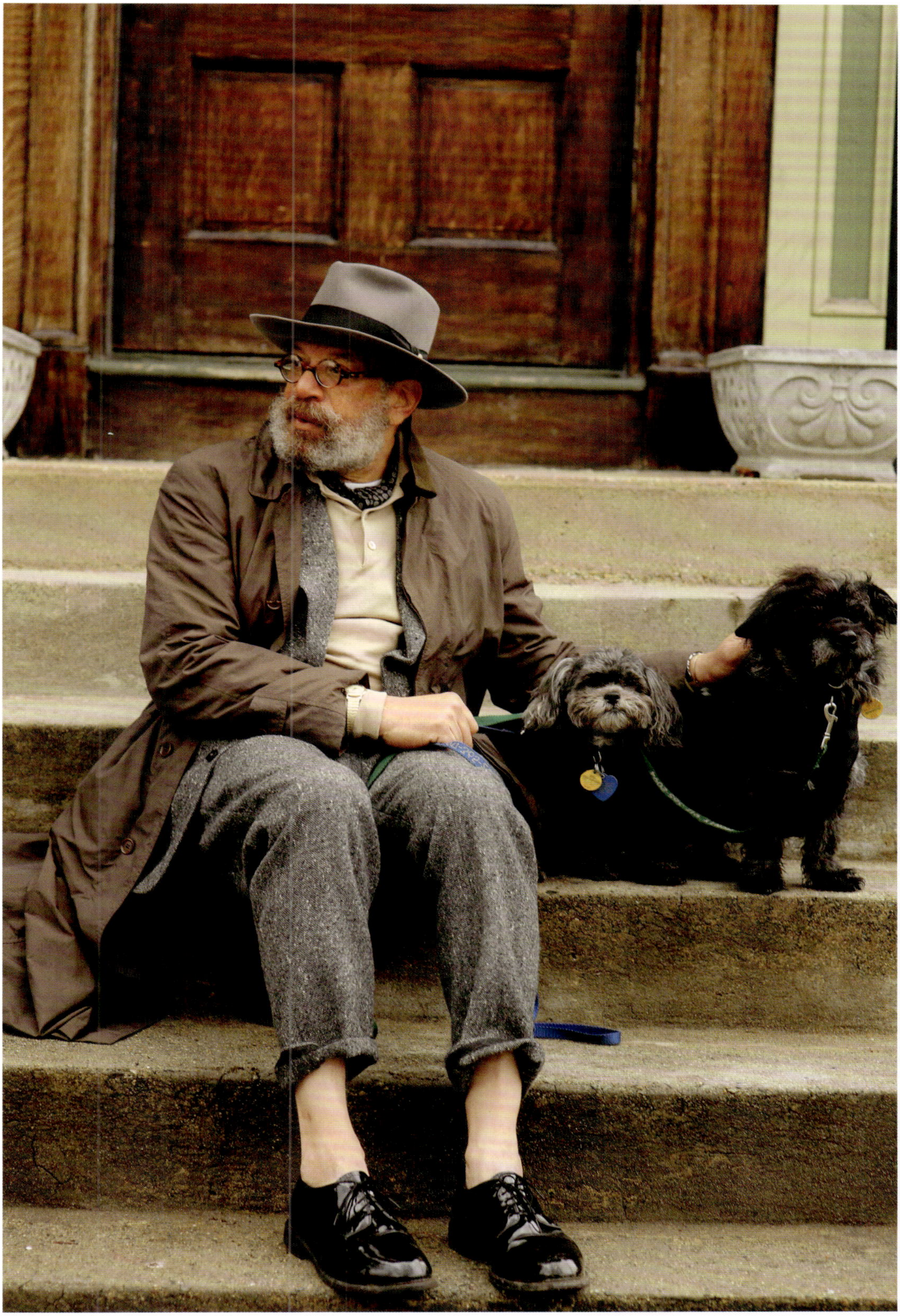

Susie, Jello, Gucci, and Bear

My three little characters are my most loyal, adoring, and sometimes aloof guardians. They guard me in bed, follow me everywhere (there is no alone time), and get particular pleasure in crowding into the bathroom to observe, what I think they think, is enormously interesting behavior. I believe I wanted three dogs because I wasn't allowed many pets as a child (ok, maybe a turtle from Woolworths), and vowed to have many in later life. Of course, having many is pretty close to a three-ring circus, and that is absolutely not an exaggeration. The snoring, sneezing, and gagging from the Frenchies means there is rarely a moment of peace. But I have come to adore it!

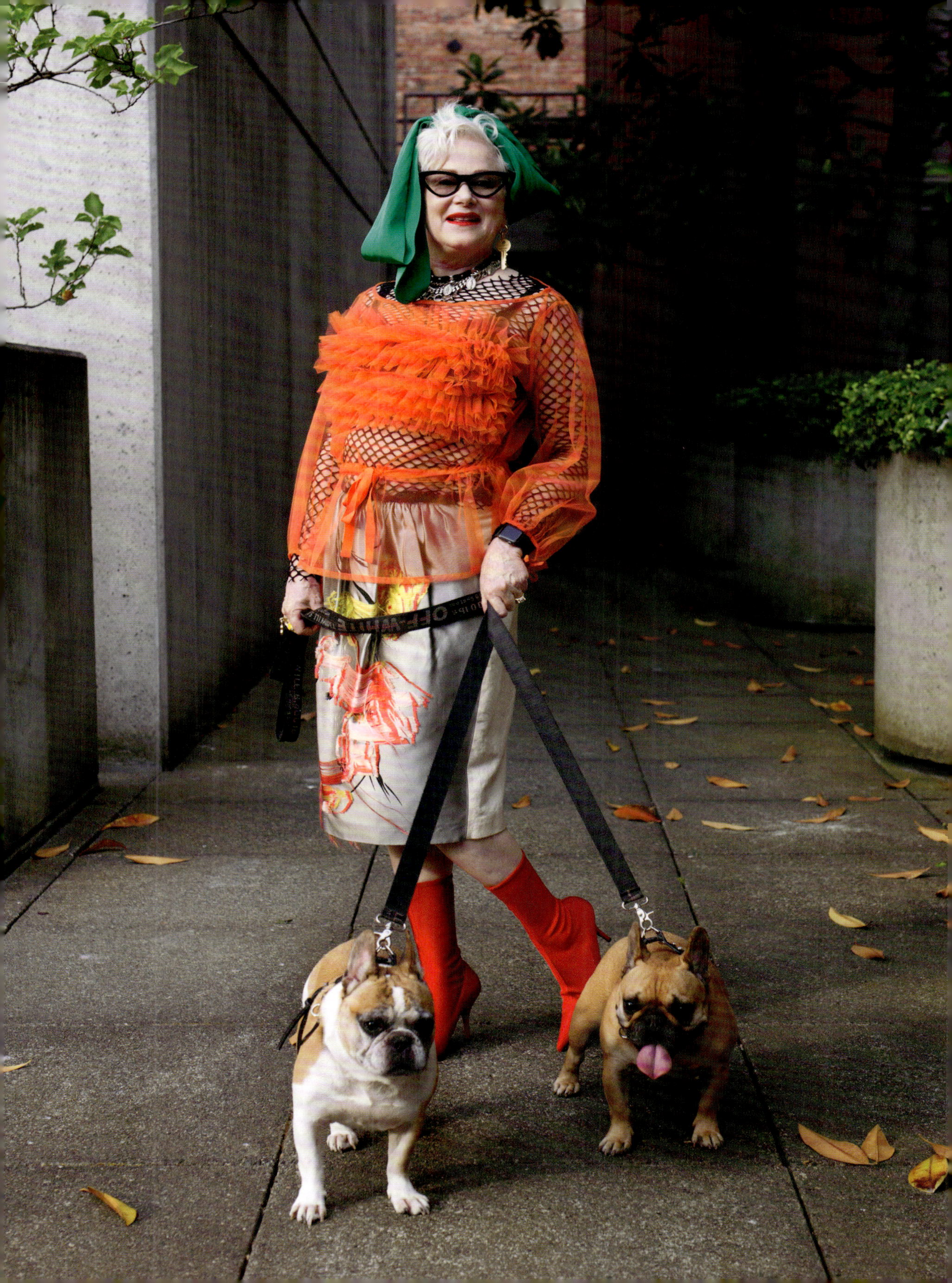

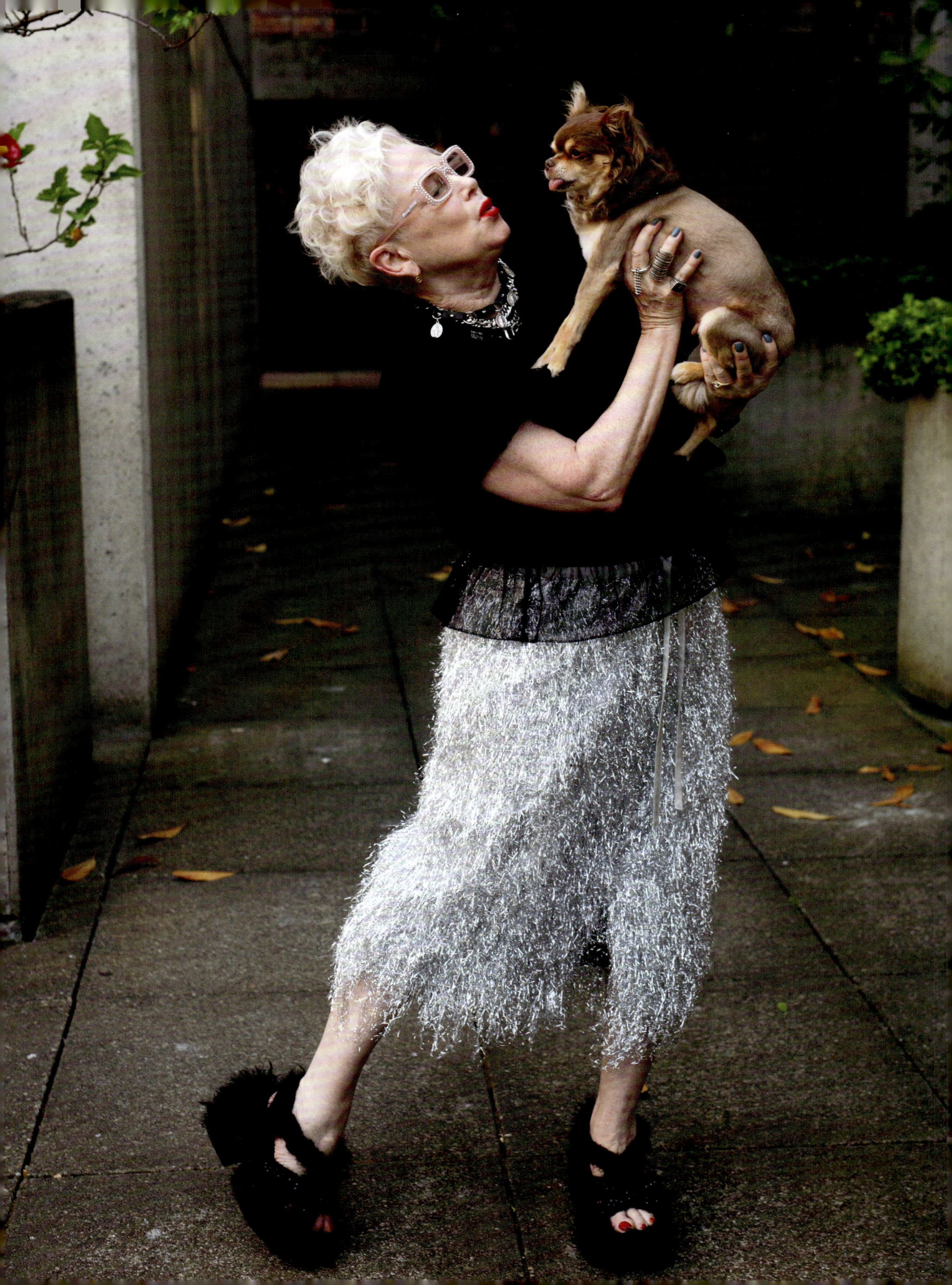

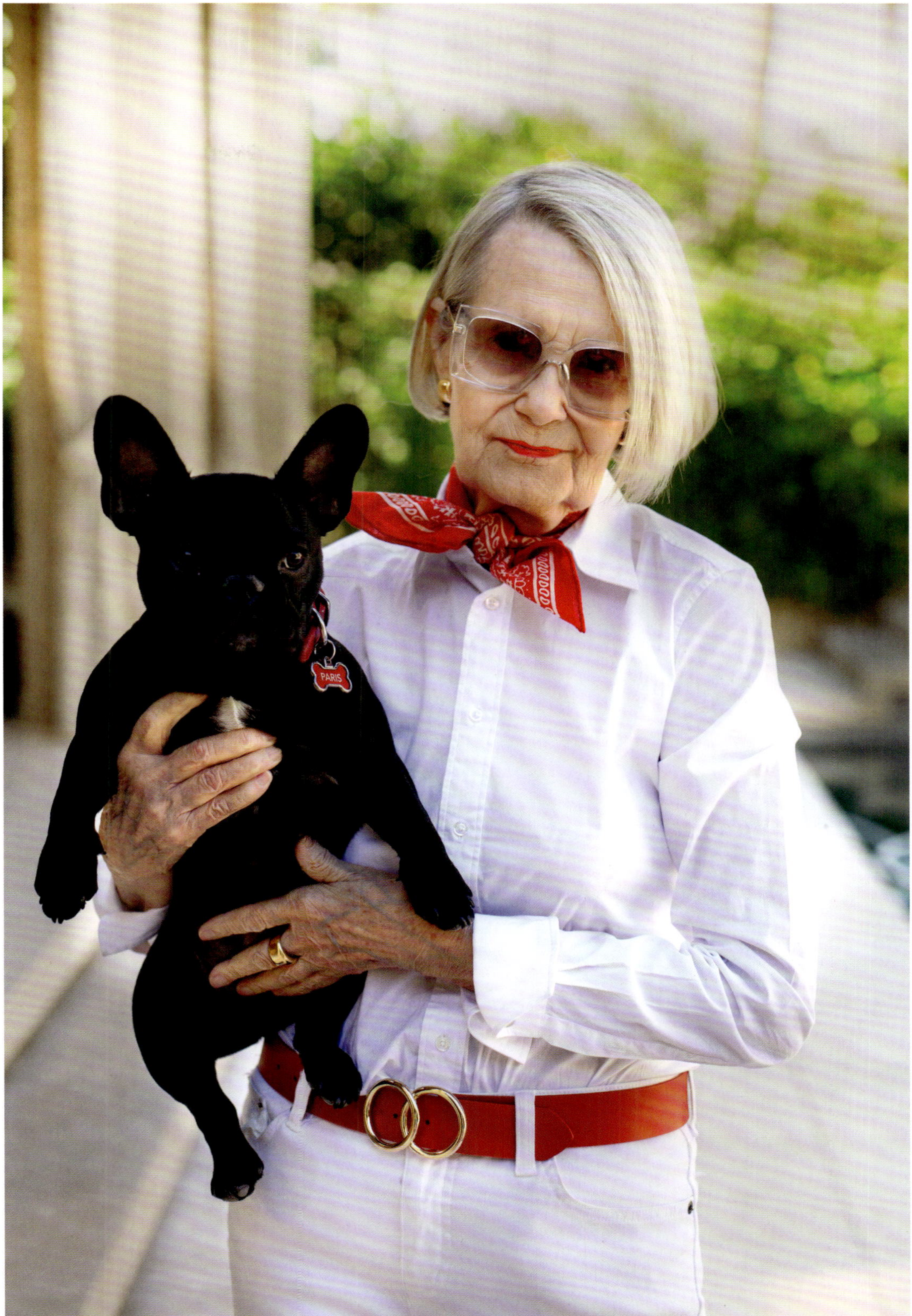
PARIS

Elliott and Lucky Frank

Lucky Frank is the most loving dog I've had the privilege of living with. We got him from the shelter when he was about six months old as a pal for our border collie Happy Betty. Lucky Frank reminds me every day to stay in the present and that life can pretty much be distilled into four achievements: a good sleep, a good meal, a good poop, and a good toy. He loves all people and has two raven friends who often fly with us on our walks!

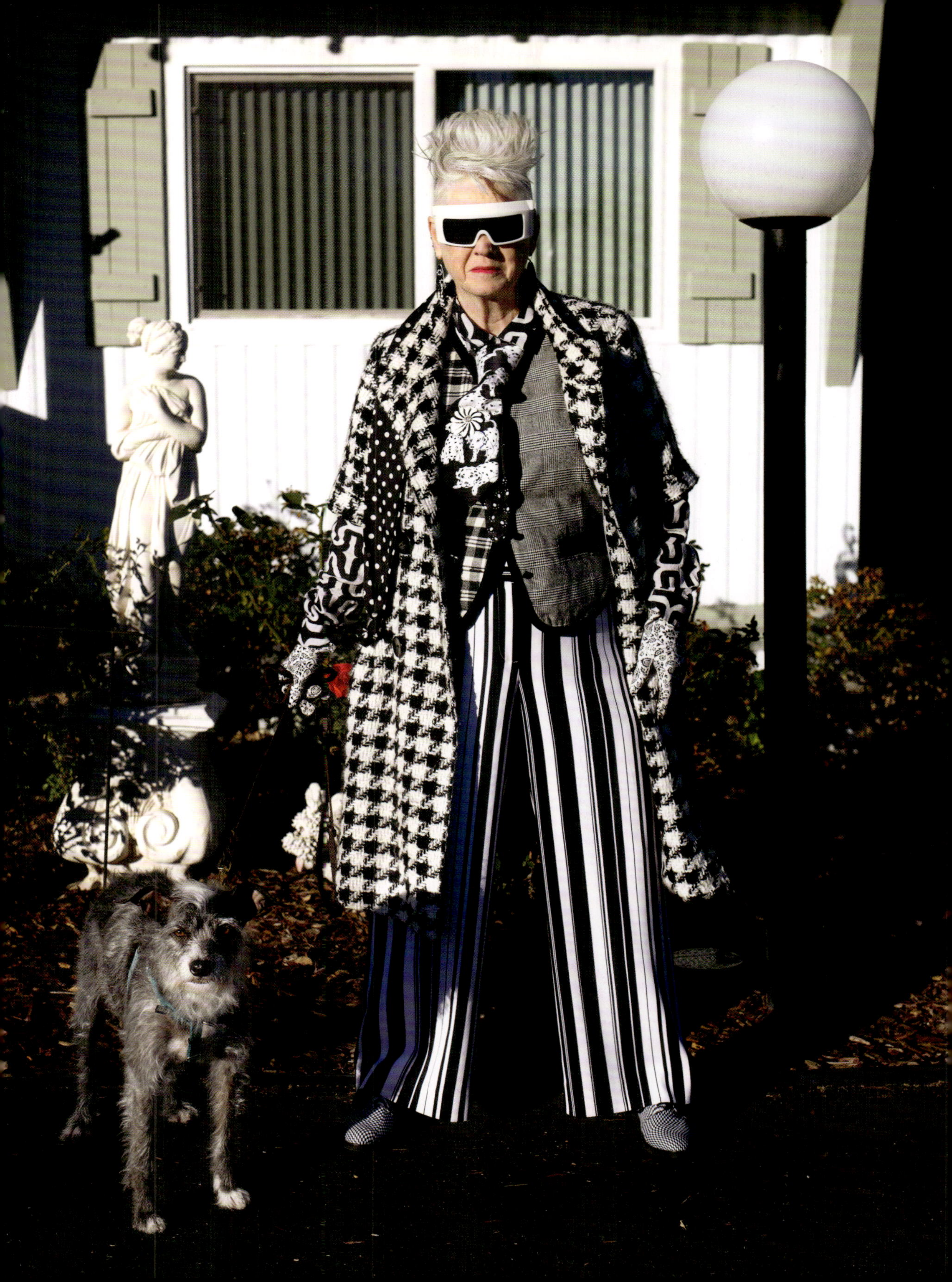

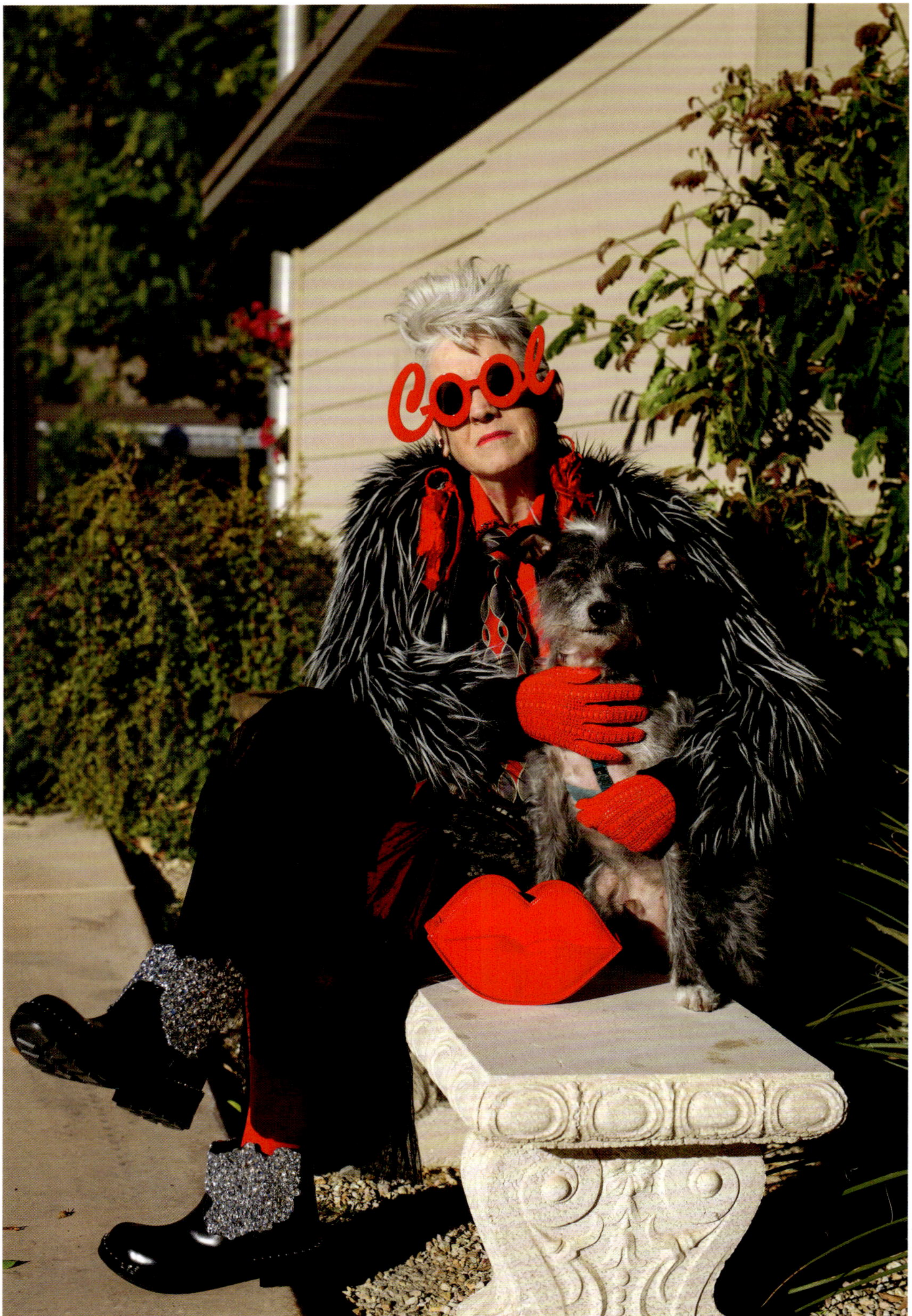
Cool

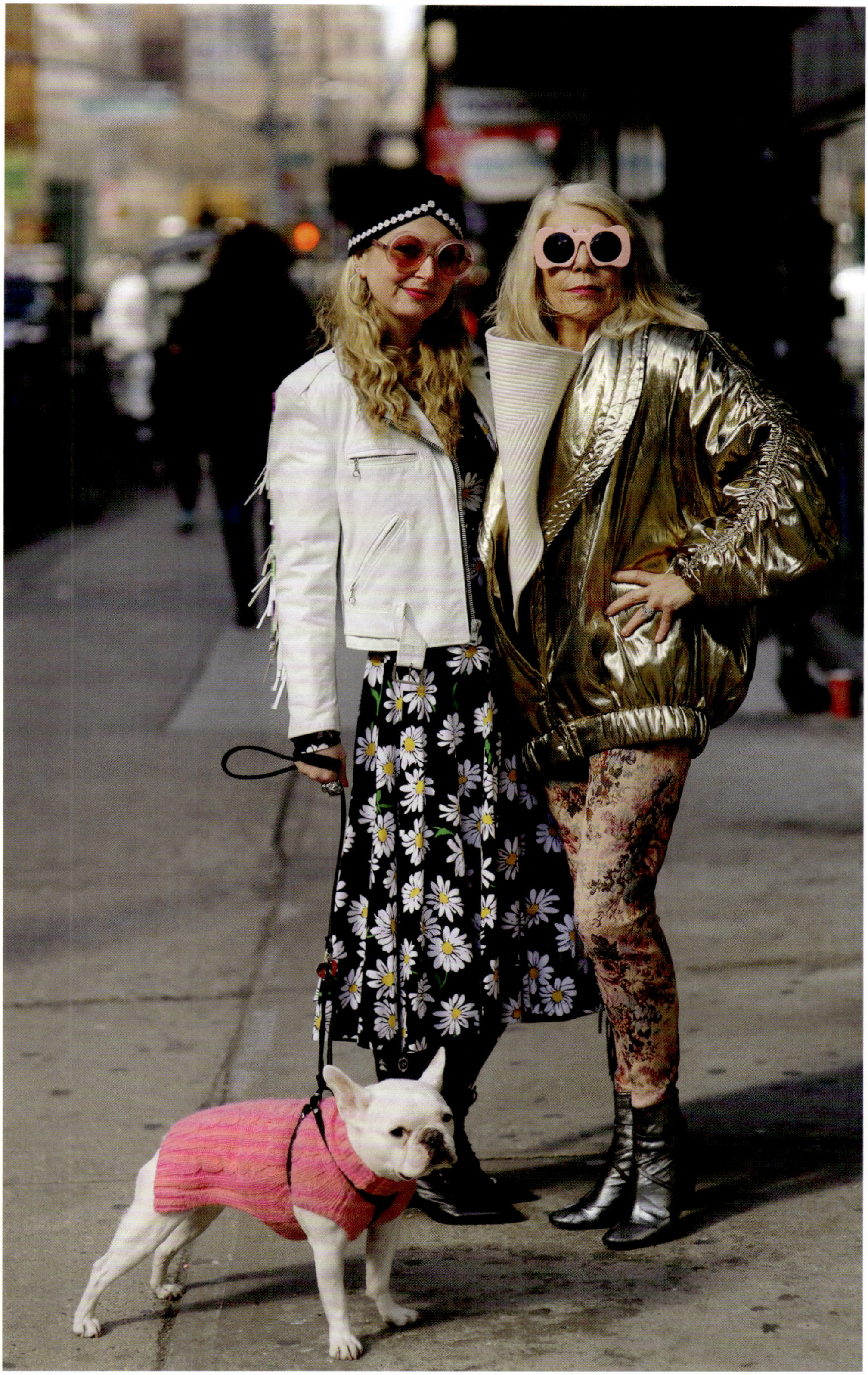

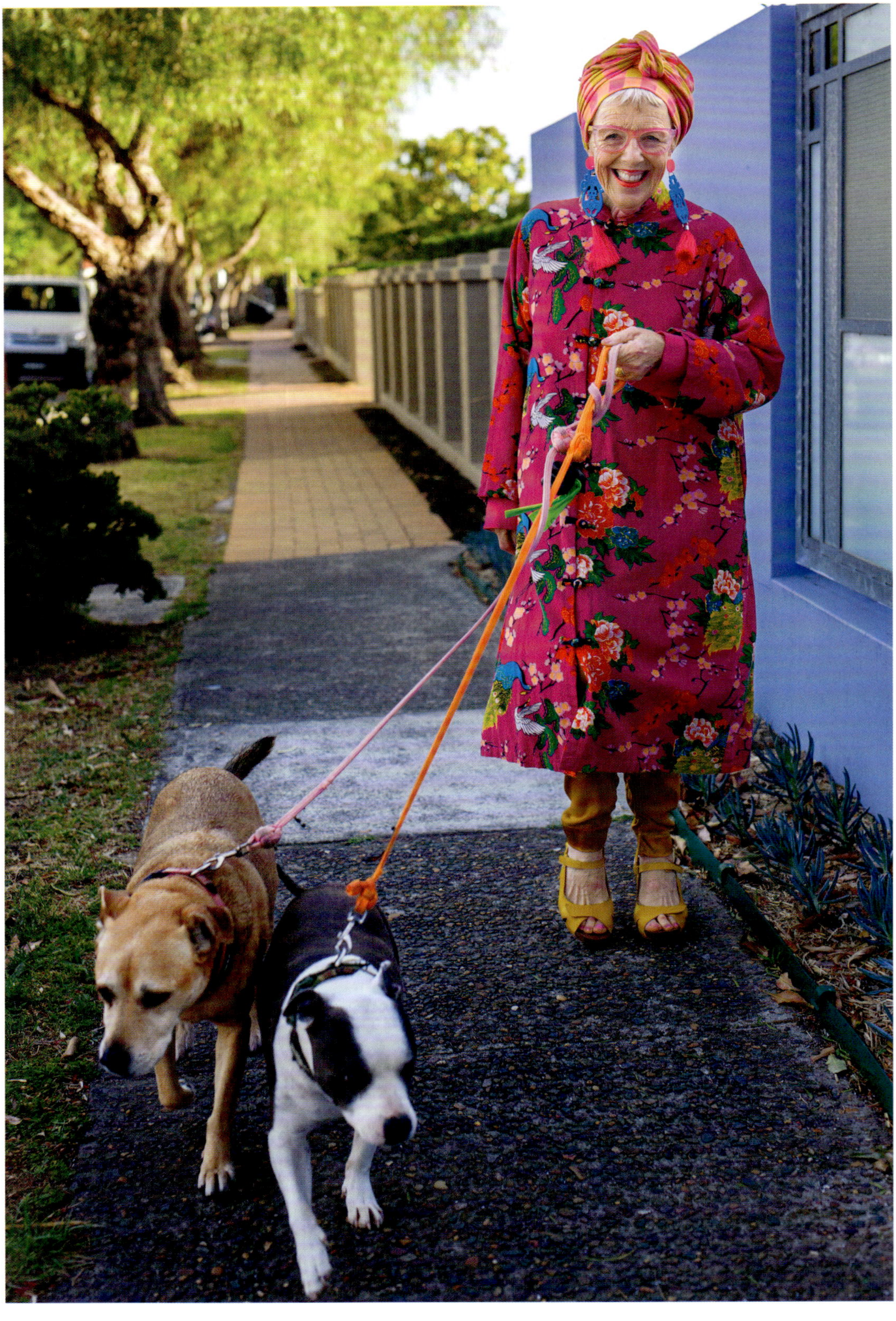

Lesley and Fred

Fred made my life better every day. From the moment I stirred he was by my side. A loyal, loving companion with a barrage of sloppy kisses, an infectious smile, endless energy, and unconditional love. I miss him terribly.

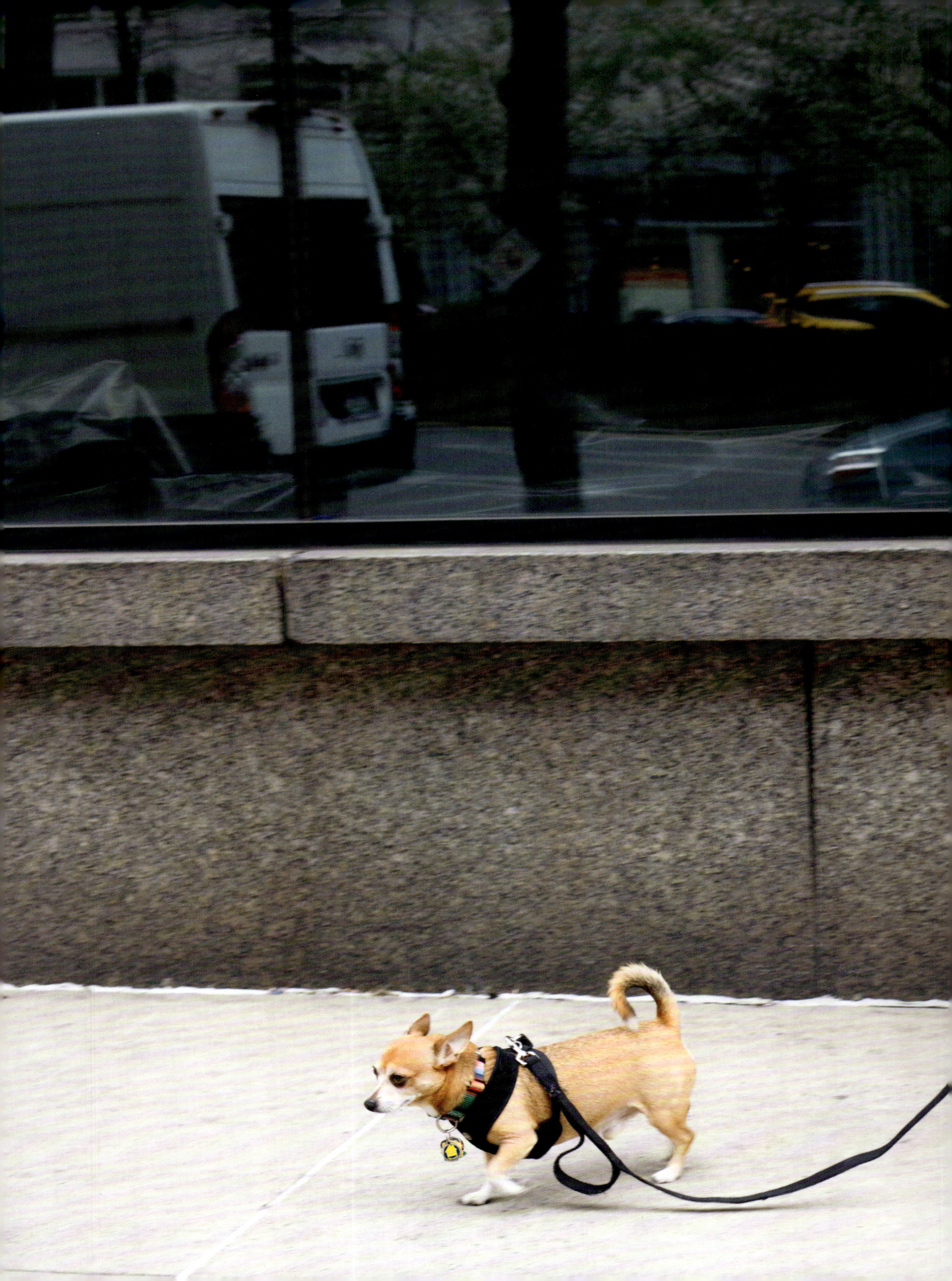

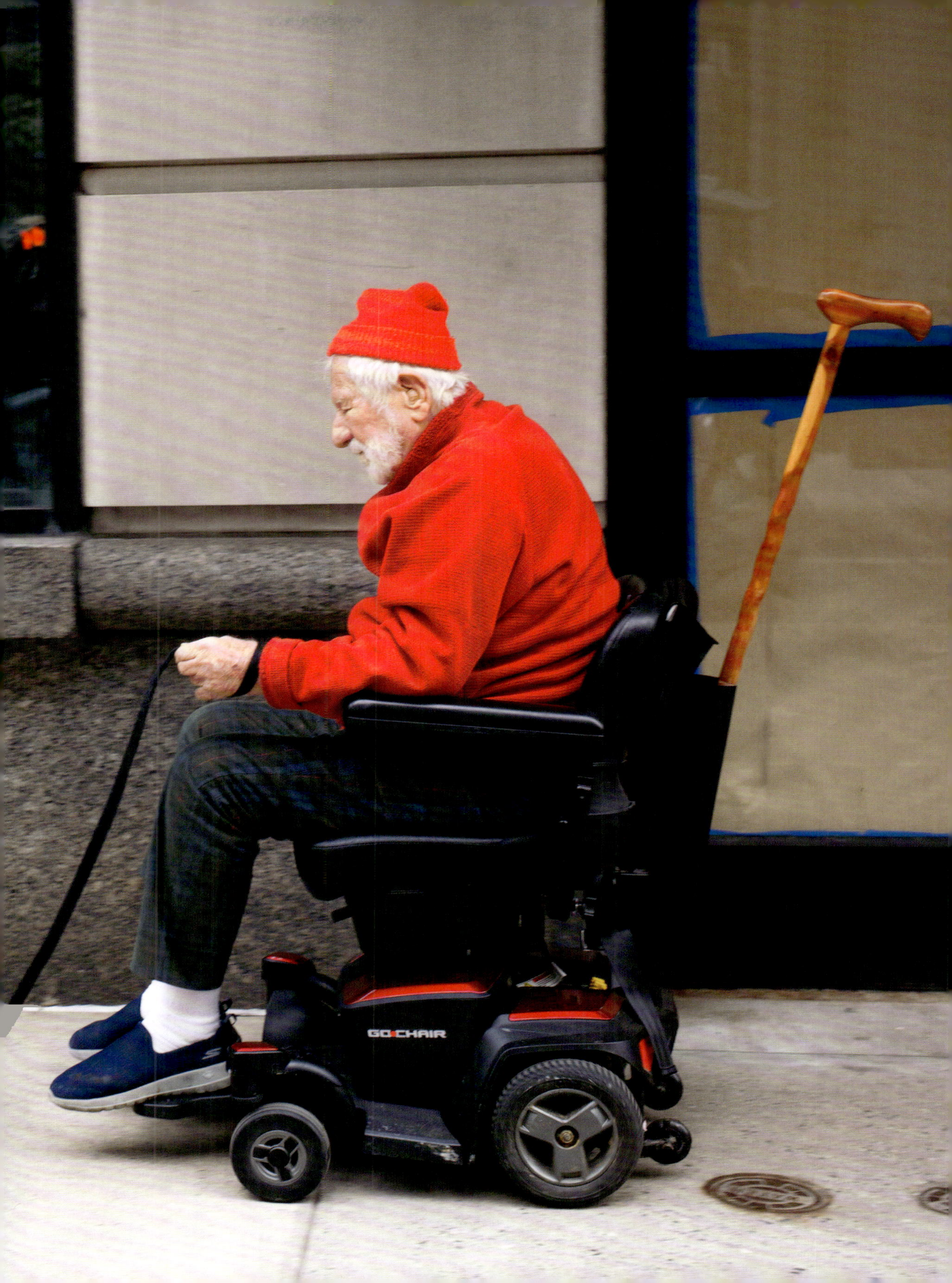
GO CHAIR

“Jack has been my best friend for sixteen years. He enjoys adventures and wants to go everywhere I go. He’s my sweet little shadow and I just love his little Westie smile.”

Linda and Jack

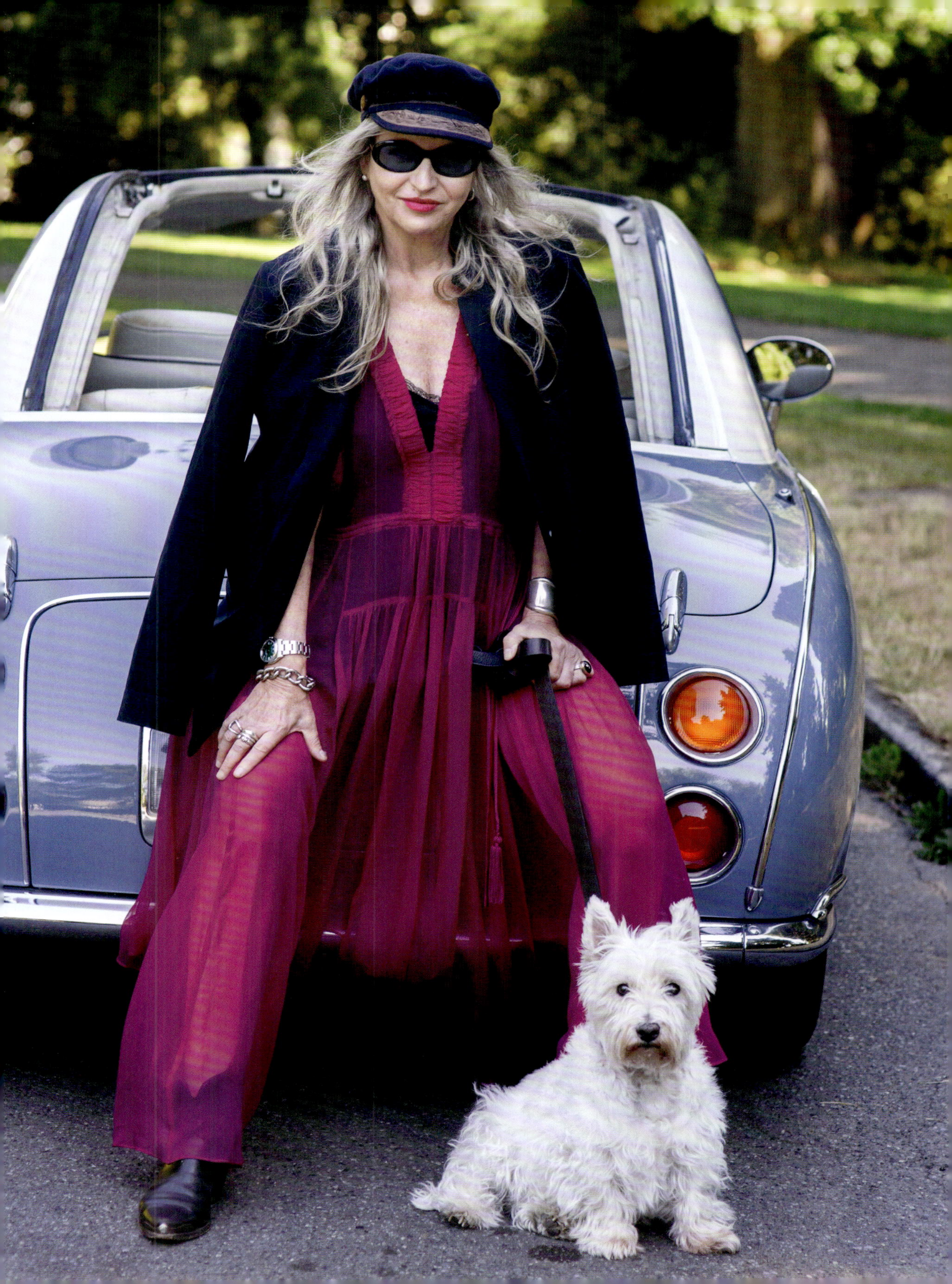

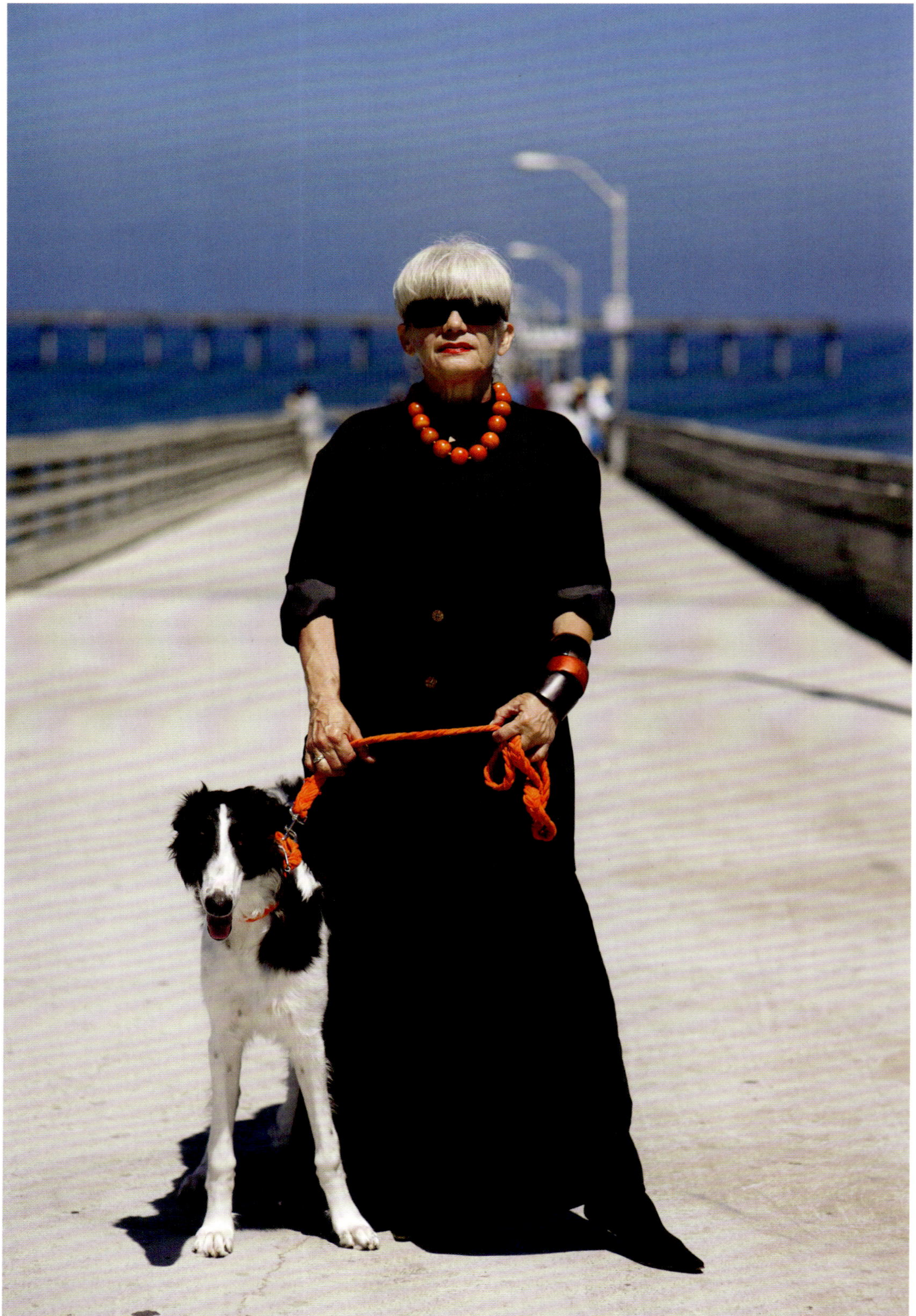

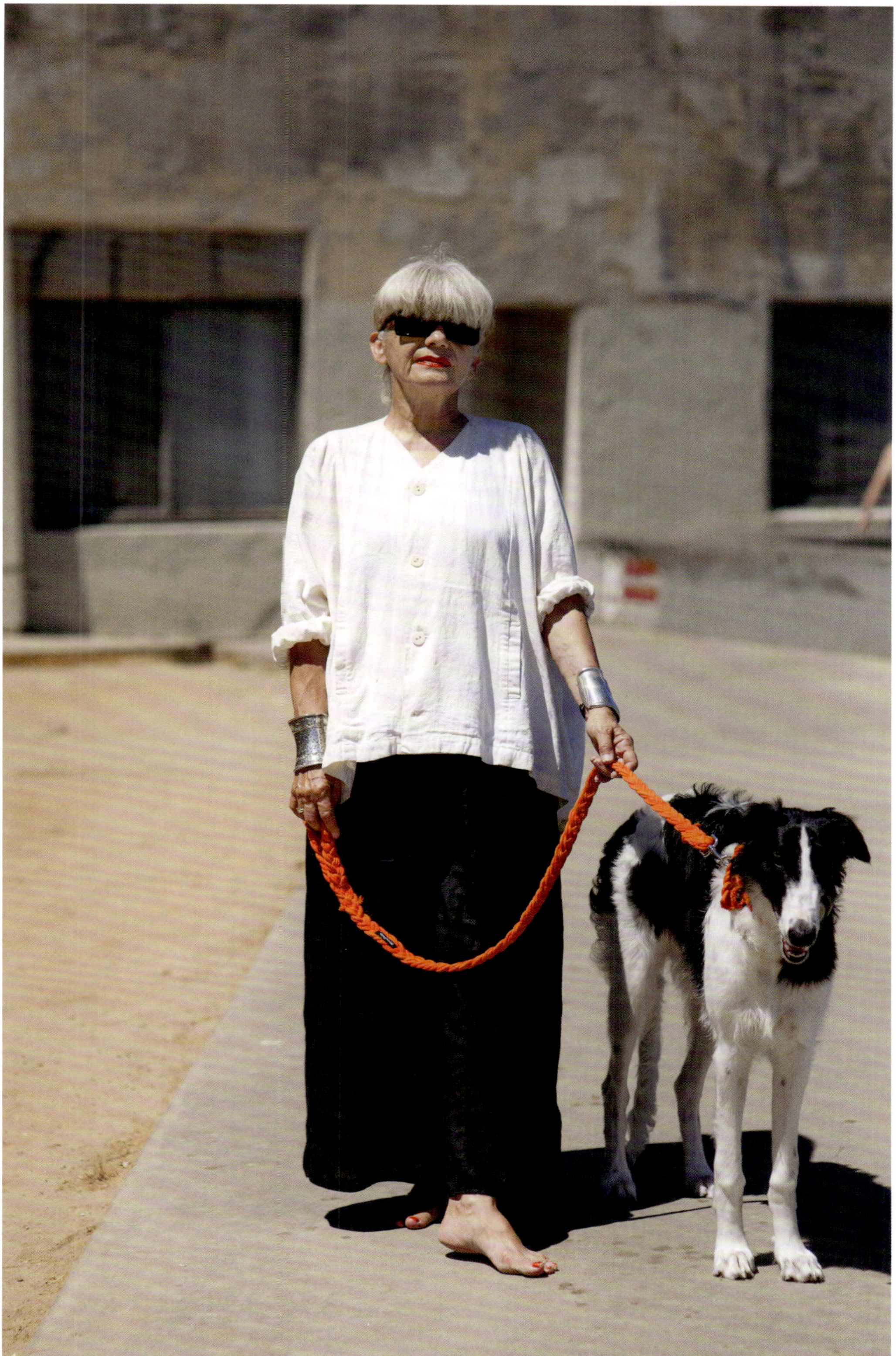

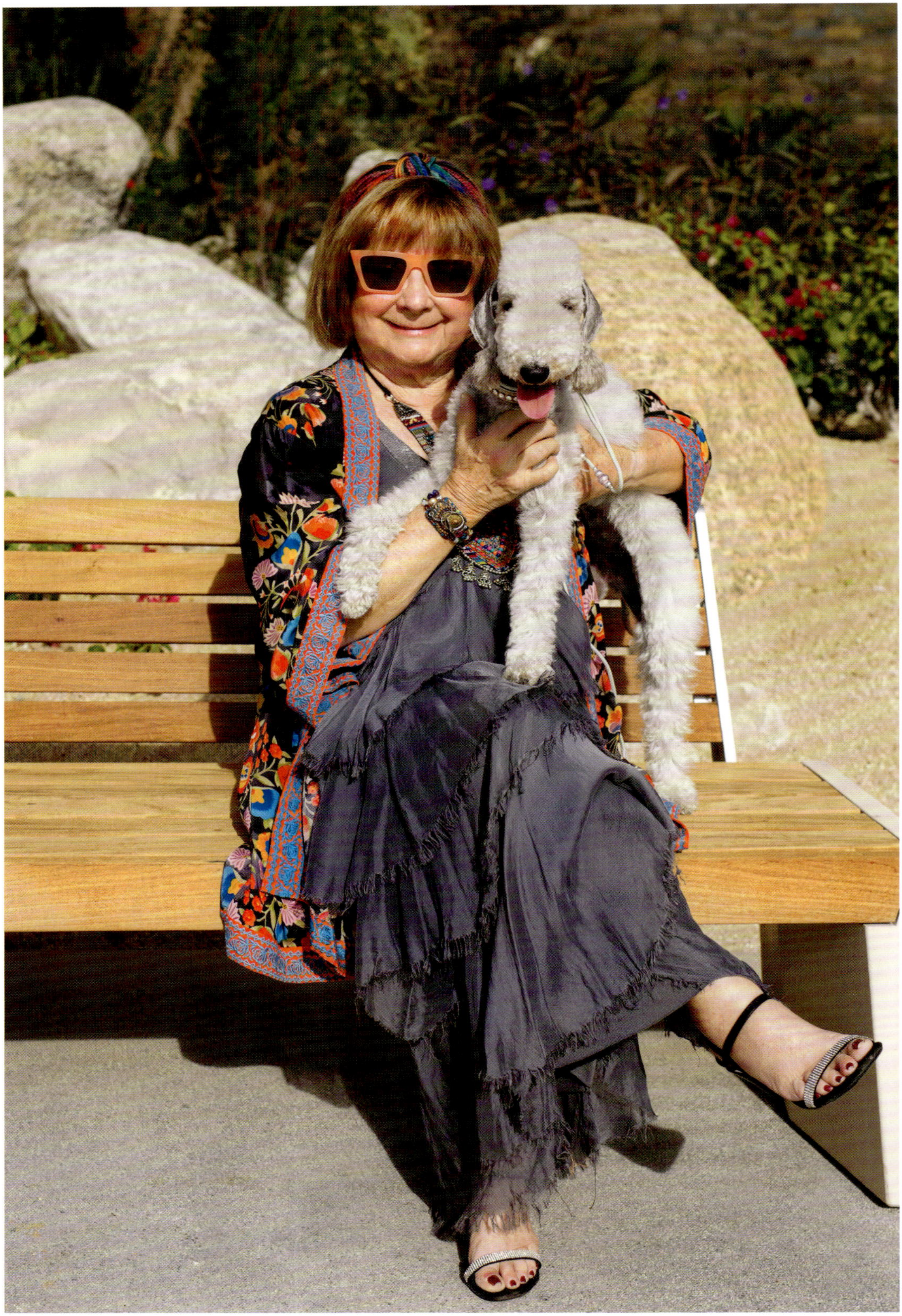

Barb and Gracie

My love affair with Bedlington terriers started when I was a young girl reading dog books. My favorite was this little white dog that looked like a lamb. Gracie is now our sixth Bedlington and the best dog we have ever had. She is a champion show dog, has her therapy dog credentials, and also runs in agility competitions. Gracie, with the heart of a lion, has been the best companion anyone could wish for.

Lady Krishna and Waffles

My neighbor found Waffles in the alley. He wrapped him in a leopard negligee and gave him to me. I had just lost my cat Jasper and he knew how sad I was. Waffles fit in my hand and I fed him from a doll's bottle. He instantly fell in love with Alma, the cat next door. They like to sleep in the fruit crate together and watch *Animal Planet*. Animals are so intuitive. They know things about you that you don't even know, and they come into your life when you need them the most. I come home to Waffles and I never feel like I live alone.

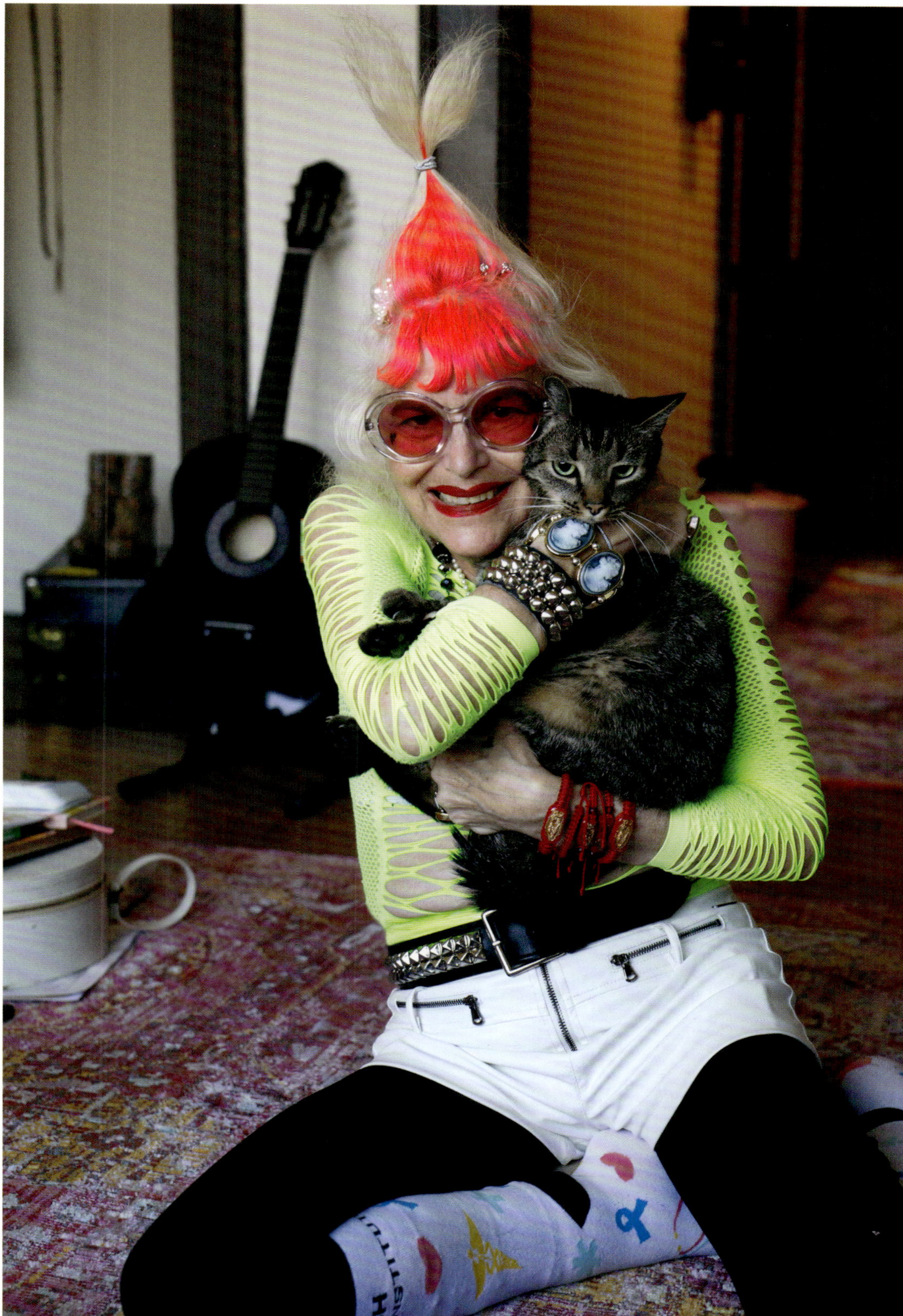

Zazzu and Titan

Mighty Titan is the smallest of the four furry friends I live with. His stature may be slight, but his personality is gigantic and, like me, he is an "Elder," —both of us in our eighties.

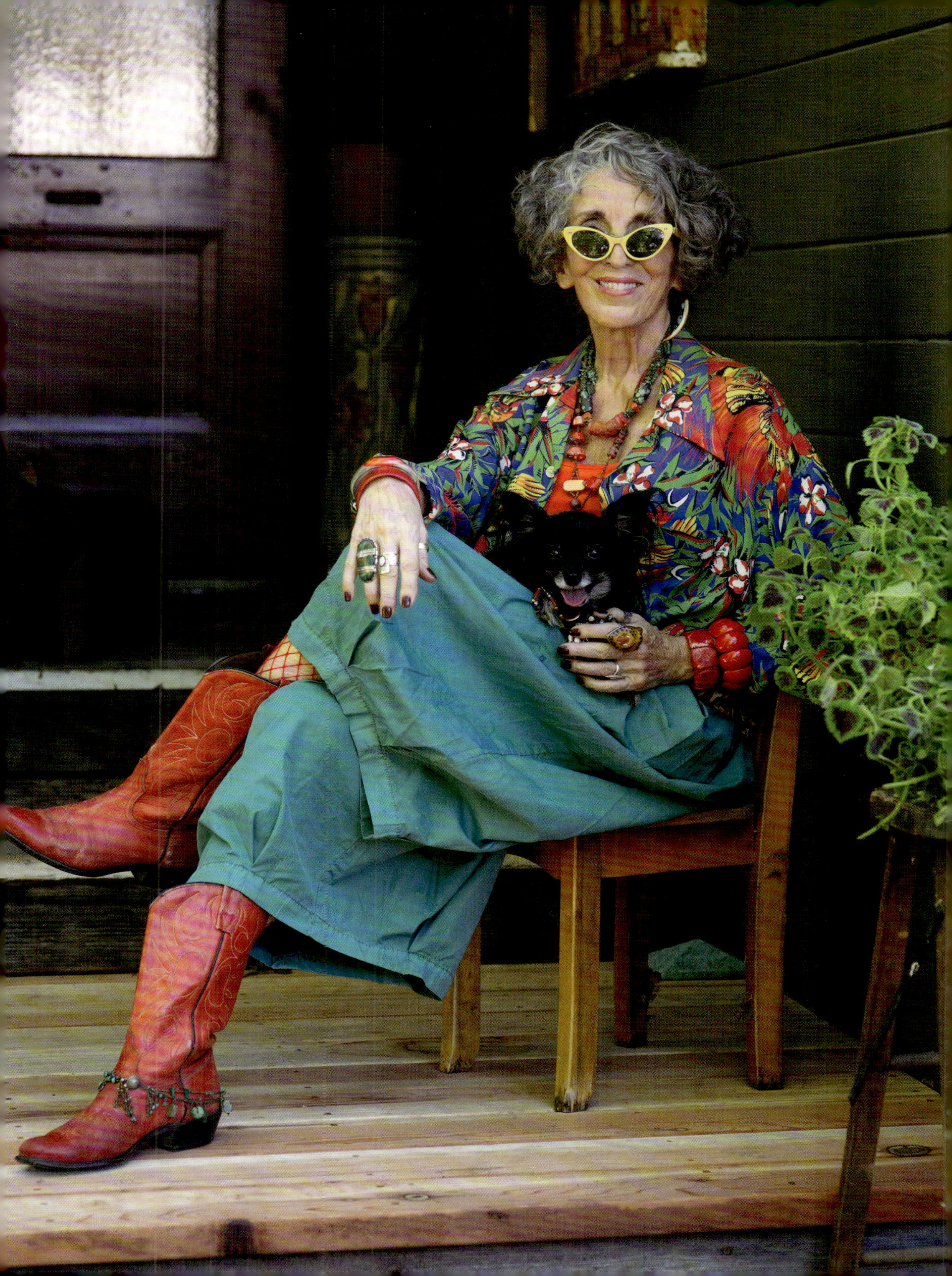

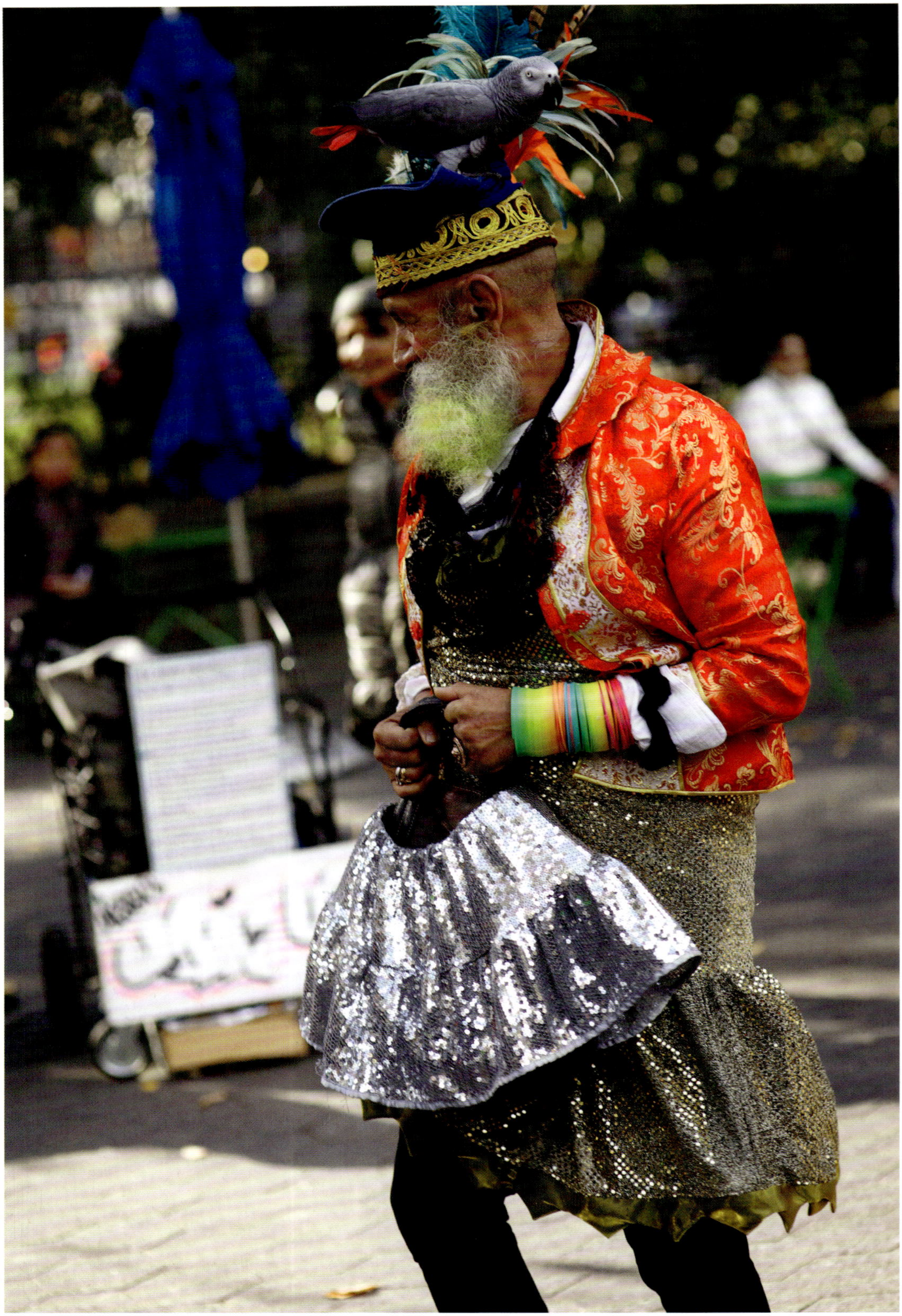

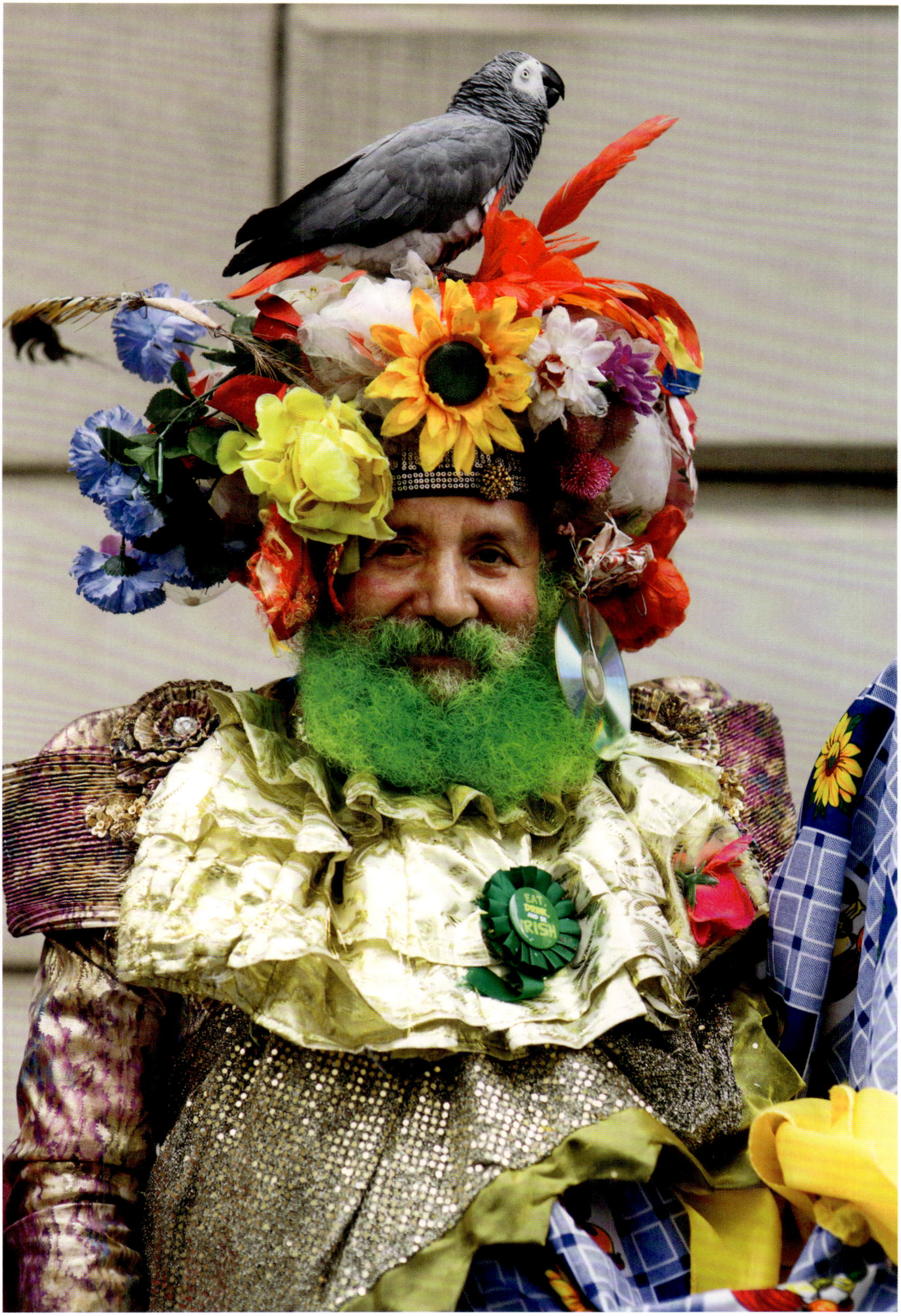
EAT
IRISH

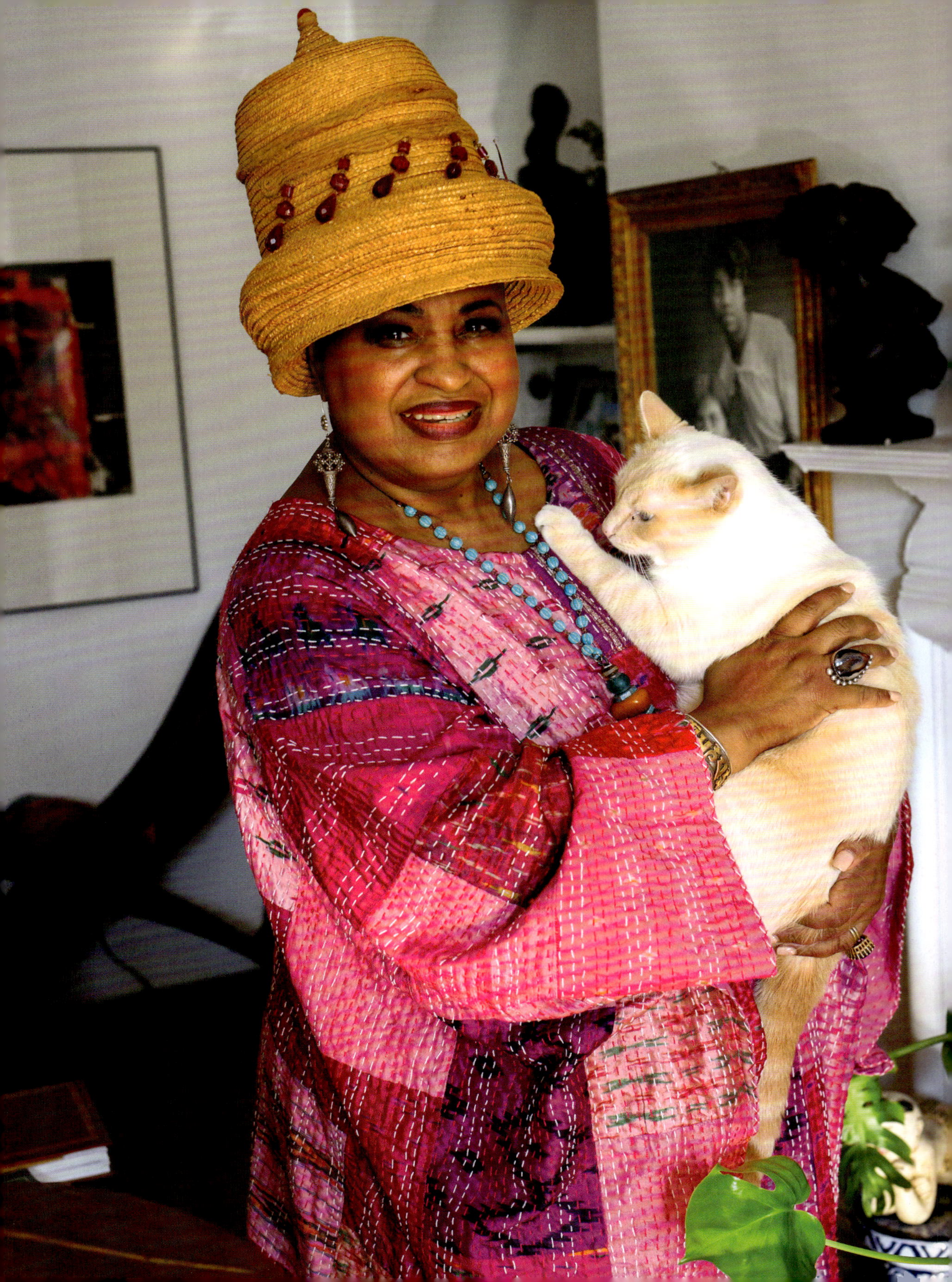

Marsha and Pinky

Pinky attends all of my online meetings, coming to sit on the arm of my chair as soon as he hears the Zoom tone—he's known internationally. He is a good cat and loves to perch in the few high places that I allow so that he can sit and look down upon us here in his world.

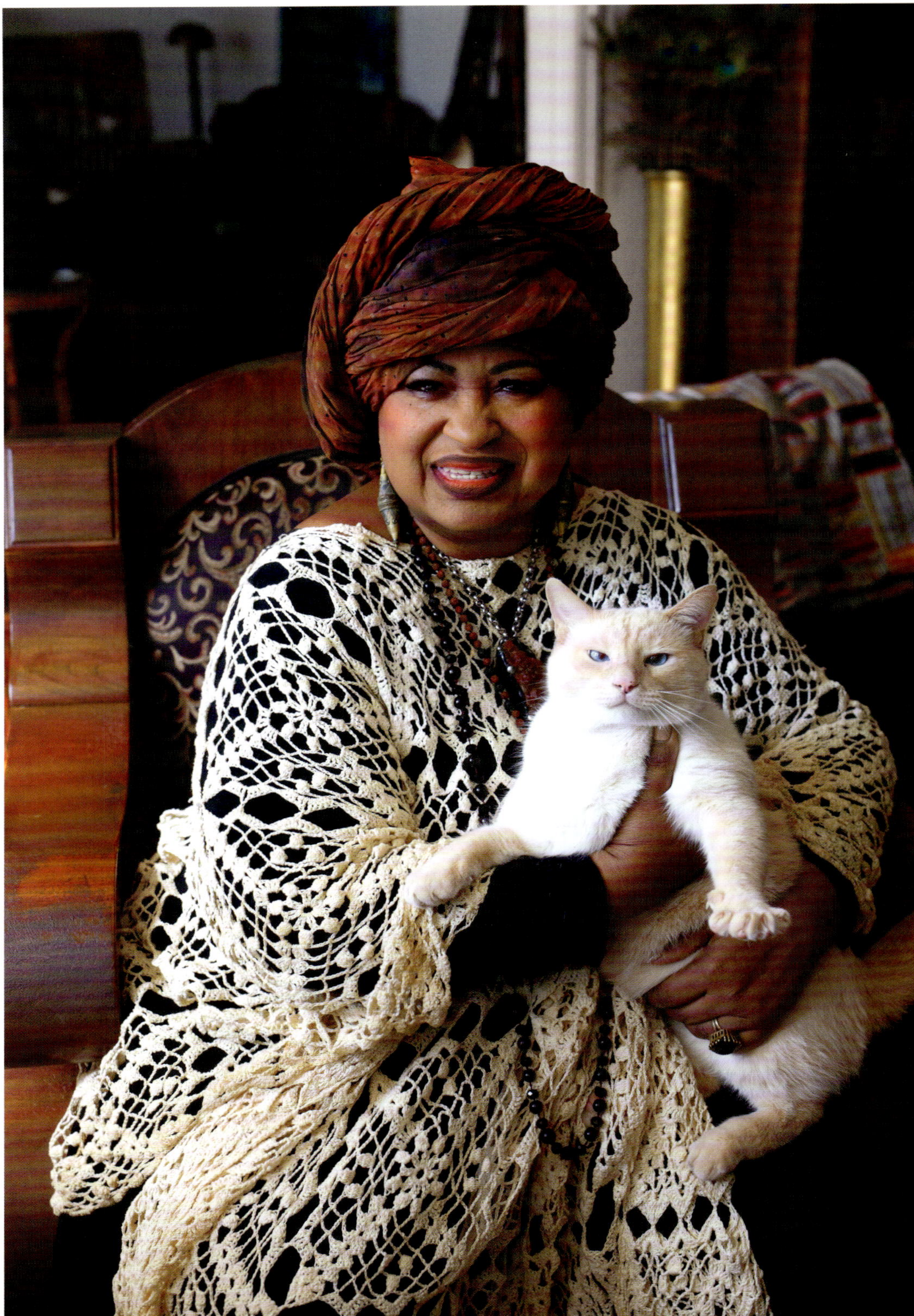

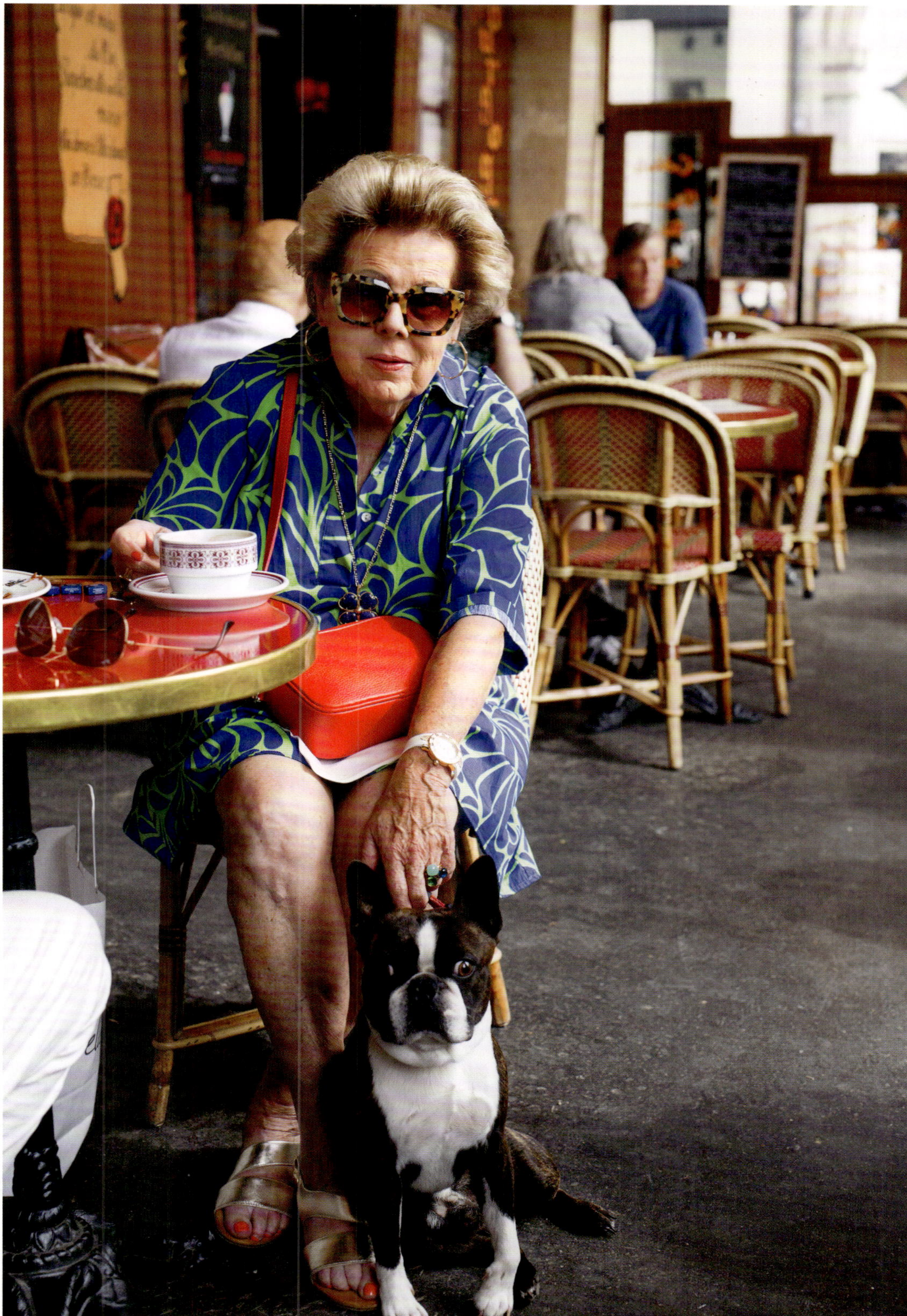

Pearl and Earl

I knew when I adopted Earl that it was gonna be me and him against the world, and that's how it's been for sixteen wonderful years. He is half Chihuahua, half Jack Russell, and is super smart! I taught him to speak, dance, sit, lie down, stay, jump through a Hula-Hoop, and behave like a gentleman. Earl is the best dang dog in the world! He really is a true gentleman!

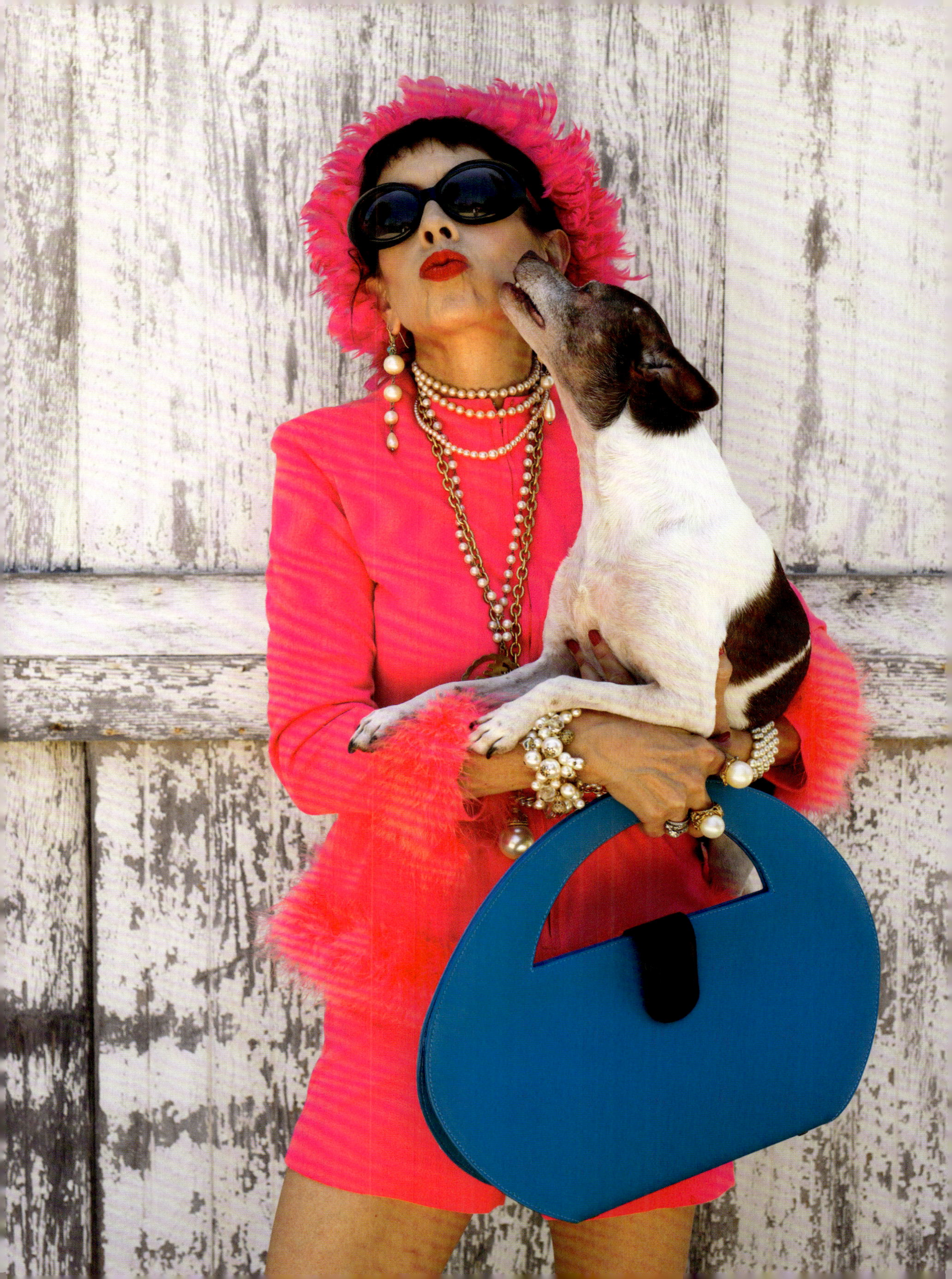

Shannon and Daisy

I've always had dogs. My previous dog got cancer at the age of five and my heart was just broken. When she passed away it was horrible. As I've gotten older, I've learned that the only thing that cures a broken heart is another dog or two or three... more love.

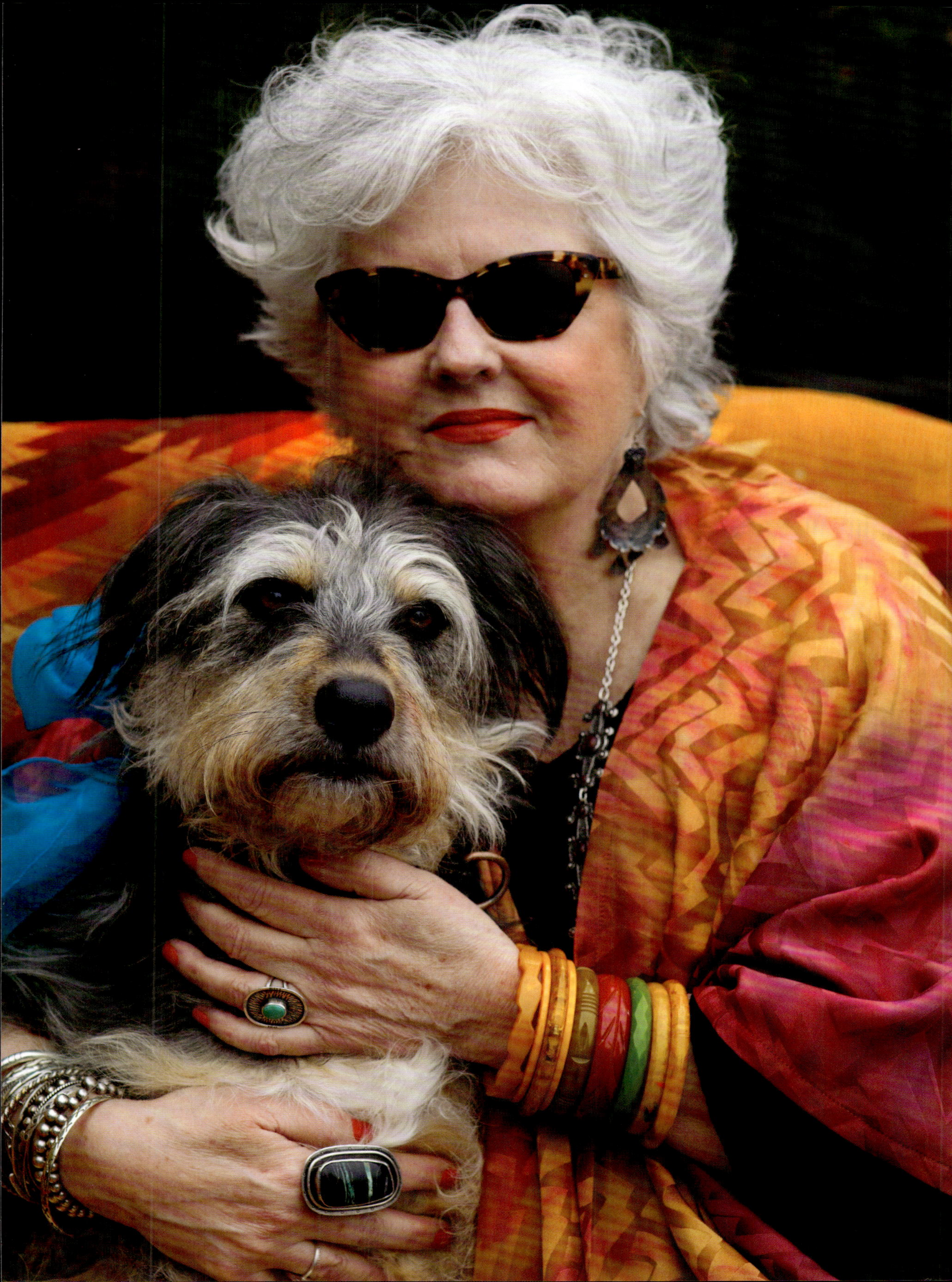

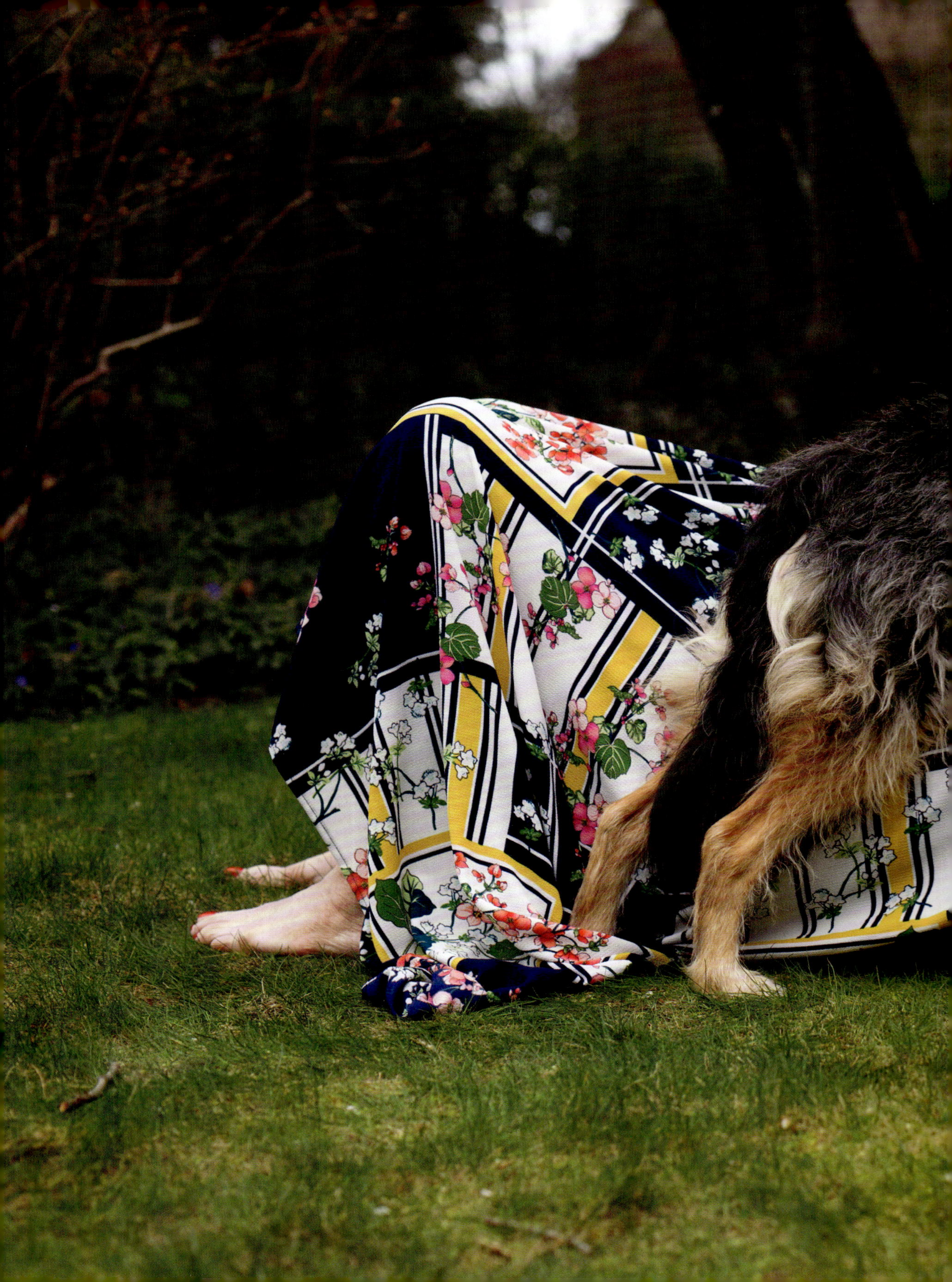

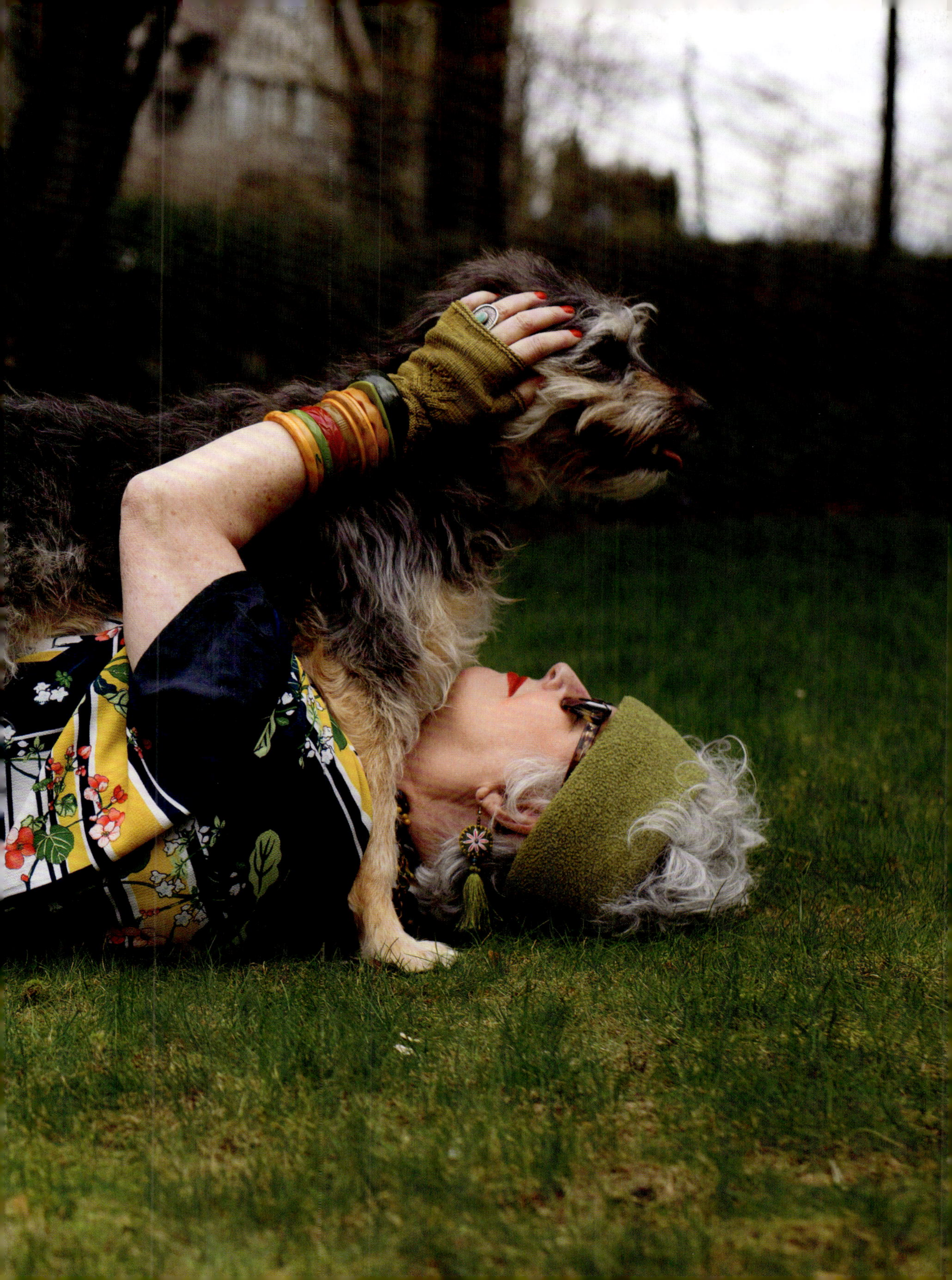

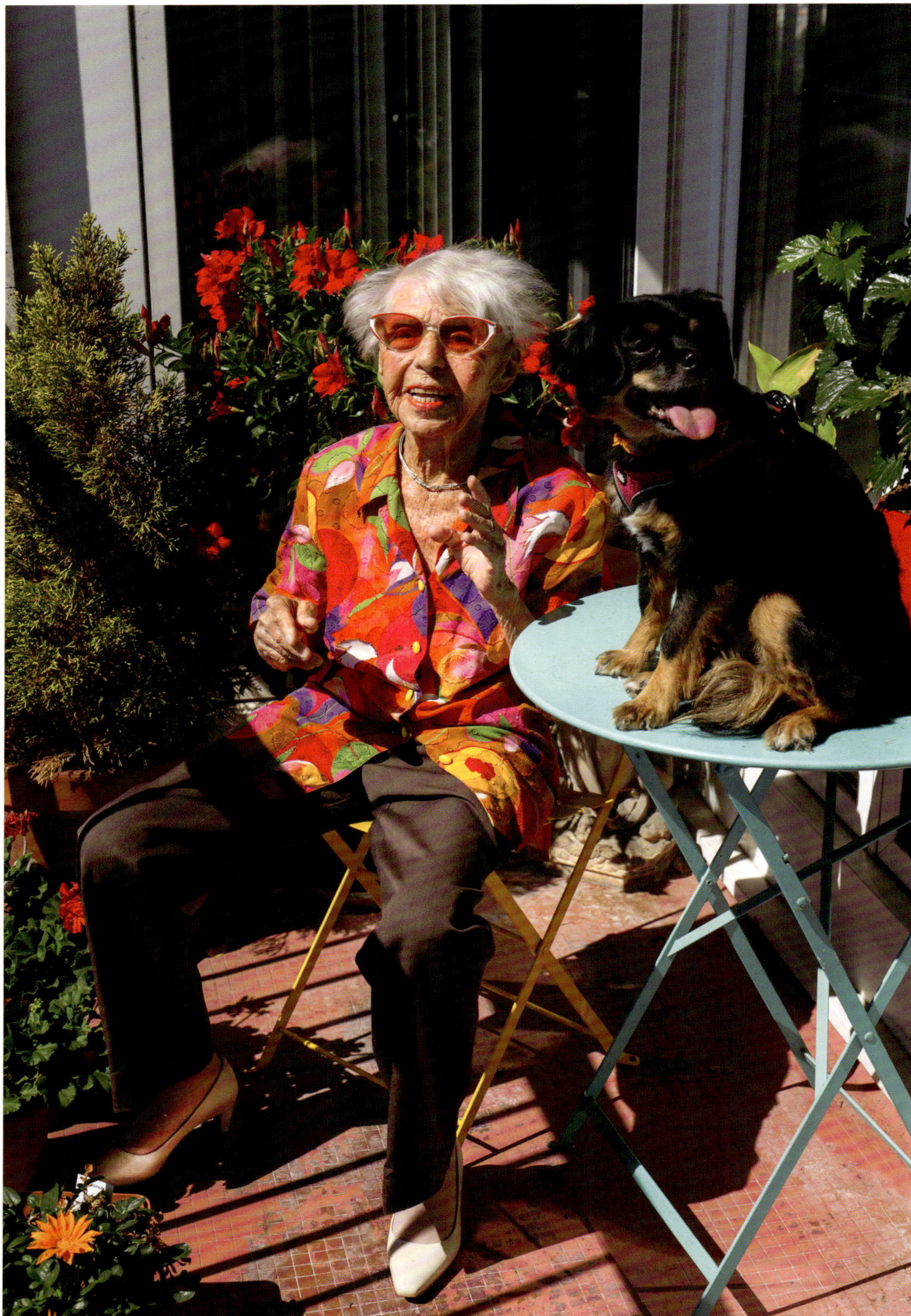

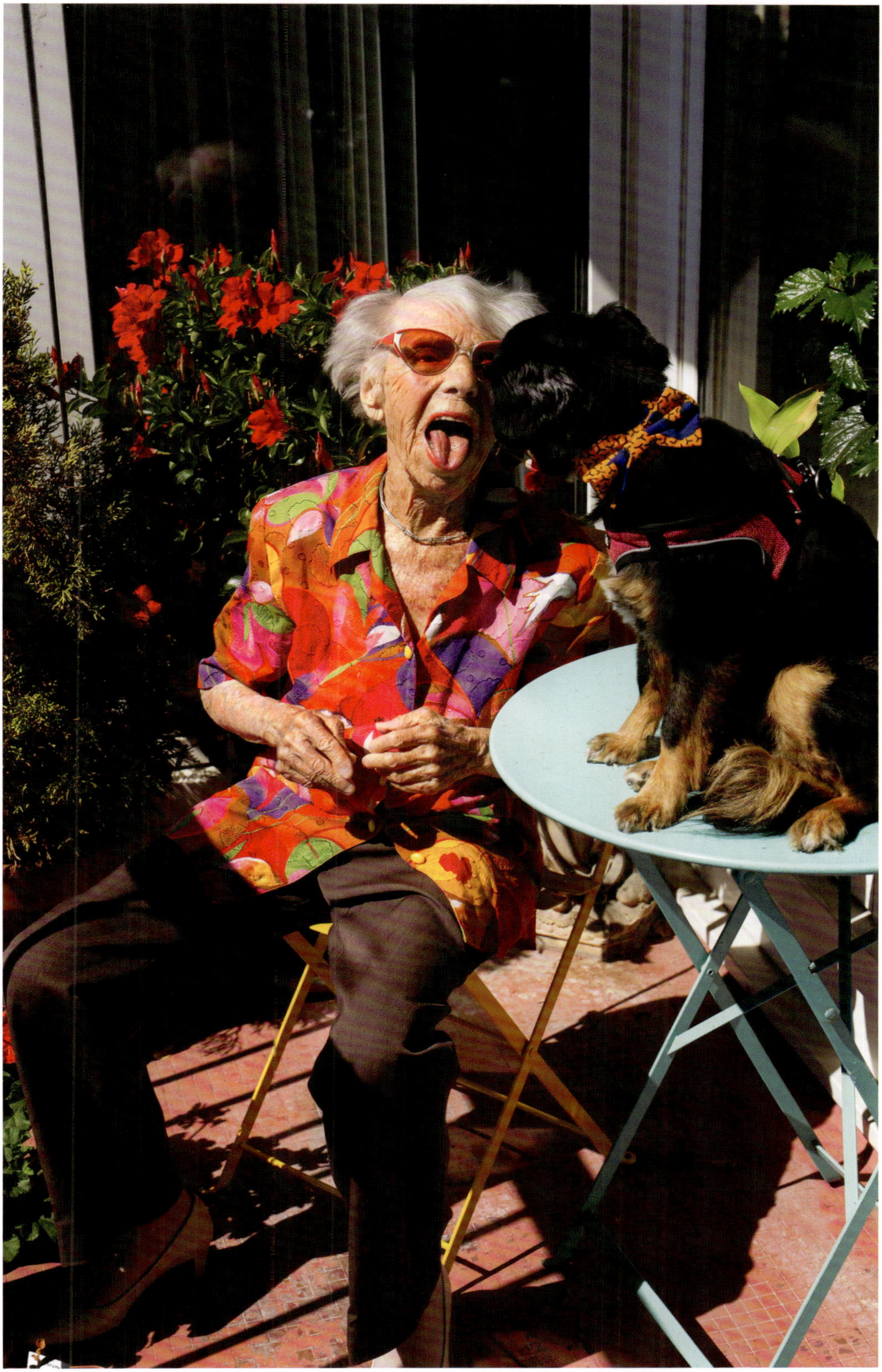

I dedicate this book to my wonderful canine-loving mama. You are the reason for my great love of animals. Thank you for introducing me to vegetarianism at a young age and helping me understand the simple truth that life with a dog, or two, or three is, the best way to live.

Thank you to all the beautiful animals and their human counterparts for allowing me to share your photos and stories. To all those that helped whistle, clap, and hold treats during shoots, I am forever grateful.

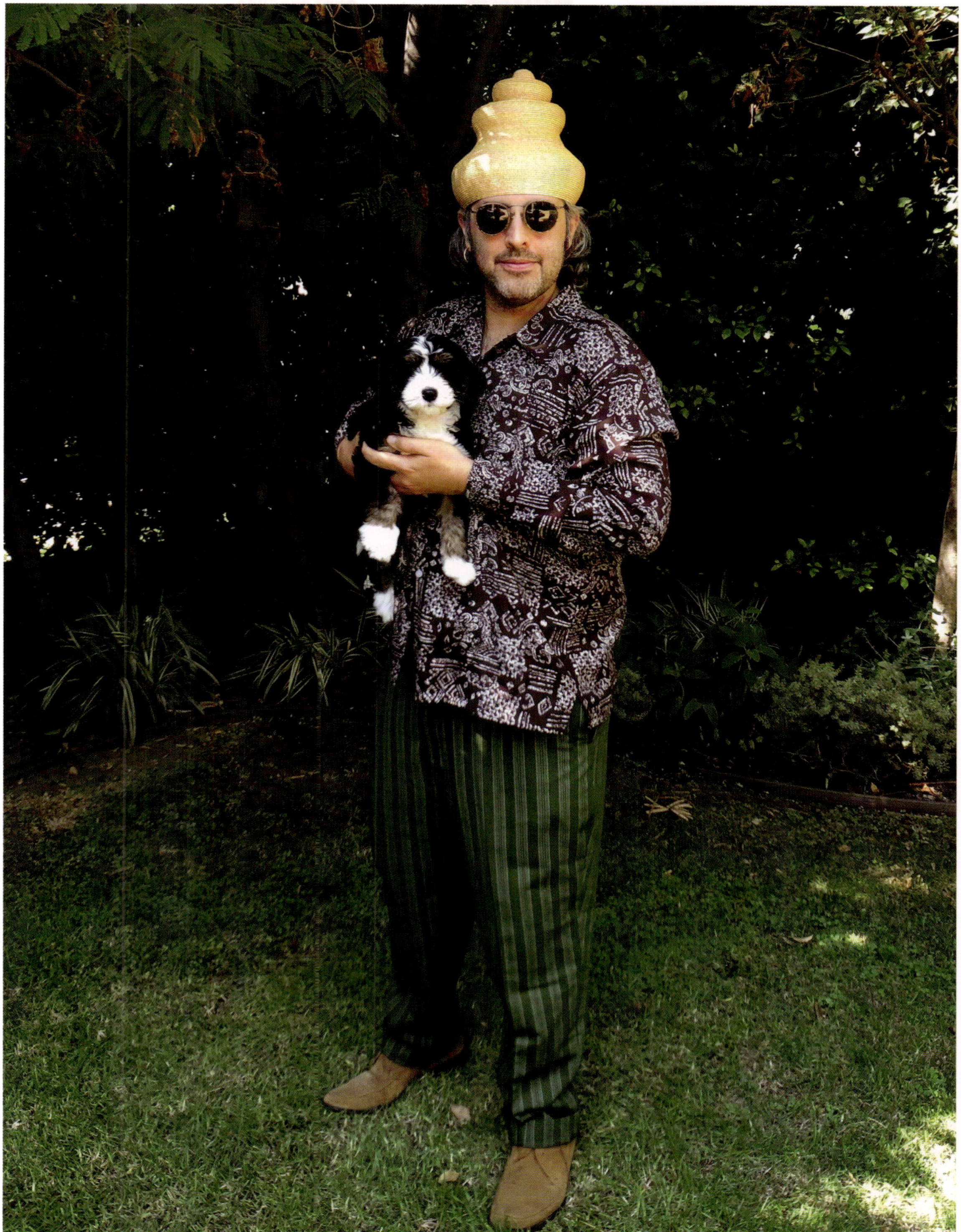

Advanced Pets

Published in the United States by powerHouse Books,
a division of powerHouse Cultural Entertainment, Inc.
32 Adams Street, Brooklyn, NY 11201-1021

www.powerHouseBooks.com

First Edition, 2024

Library of Congress Control Number: 2024936369

ISBN 978-1-64823-076-9

Designed by: Naomi Falk and Sydnie Hyams

Printed by Midas Printing in Hong Kong

10 9 8 7 6 5 4 3 2 1

Printed and bound in China